ENVIRONMENTAL RESOURCES AND TOURISM DEVELOPMENT IN THE HIMALAYA

ENVIRONMENTAL RESOURCES AND TOURISM DEVELOPMENT IN THE HIMALAYA

D.C. PANDEY
PURAN C. PANDEY

ANAMIKA PUBLISHERS & DISTRIBUTORS (P) LTD.
4697/3, 21A, Ansari Road, Daryaganj
New Delhi 110002
Phone: 23281655

First Published 2003

ISBN 81-7975-054-X

(Photographs taken from Dr. P.C. Pandey and Kumaon Mandal Vikas Nigam)

PRINTED IN INDIA

Published by Anamika Publishers & Distributors (P) Ltd., 4697/3, 21A, Ansari Road, Daryaganj, New Delhi 110002. Typeset by VGA, MU-61D, Pitampura, Delhi 110088 and Printed at Nagri Printers, Delhi.

Contents

Preface

Environment is defined as a life supporting mechanism spread around living organism. Living beings feed, thrive and grow on the resources, the quality and quantum of which decide the quality of life. Environment as a resource constitutes an important part in the economic development of a country/region. In the recent era, the biosphere hangs in a delicate balance between the technological advancement of human beings and environmental destruction. Thus a compromising scientific approach for making a balance between human progress and least environmental degradation is almost acceptable to all the environmentalists in the globe. Environmental problems are now a global issue and none is unaware of the current human worry round the globe and thickening frustration about a probable environmental catastrophe which is likely to eliminate the life systems on the earth.

The Himalayan mountains have a unique place in the spheres of natural environment and ecology, socio-economic and cultural environs, political alertness and awakening, and are also the panoramic sources of many other everlasting things—visible and non-visible, concrete and abstract; and animate and inanimate. Remote from the din and turmoil of the wider busy world, the Himalaya, as land of holy shrines and divine habitat has long been a source of inspiration of saints, sages, poets, philosophers and artists since an aeon. The gorgeous snow-capped lofty peaks, lush green forests and other plentiful natural grandeur on one hand, and abundant cultural heritage, historical and archaeological monuments, religious shrines and other splendour resources always attracted the attention of tourists, adventurers all round the globe. Beside being rich in splendour resources, the Himalaya is endowed with the wealth of valuable natural resources such as minerals, timber, medicinal plants, hydro-electric potentials, etc. The unscientific, indiscriminate and ruthless exploitation of naturo-physical environment and resources have created and posed an acute crises to the Himalayan ecosystem. The bounty of nature by promoting tourist practices have contributed a large share of valuable foreign exchange to the income of the regional economy. The side effects of infiltration in the region have led to the problem of land erosion and land slides caused by stretching roads and ropeways, problems of garbage management in resort towns, extra load of vehicles, promoting smokes, dust and turmoils, hygienic problems, boosting up the social evils and inter-region antagonism among people, etc. These can by no means be neglected by the policy-makers. Though extension of development activities by expansion of transport linkages helped in stimulating vibrant tourism in the Himalaya, yet, it is feared that not unoften, the ecological interests of the region have been violated. A potential danger has now been posed to preservation of this splendour. In the existing and emerging state of new challenges, it has become increasingly difficult for policy-makers to sustain the heavenly beauty of the great Himalaya for a long span of time ahead.

The role of tourism in Indian economy as well as in cultural, social and educational field is well-recognized and it is the mainstay of the economies of many countries of the globe. Tourism promotes national integration, international understanding, brotherhood and peace. Though the multiplier effect of tourism in an underdeveloped economy is extremely slow and meagre, unless the initial jerk is too large to mobilize all levers involved, yet the income so generated by tourism activates the entire urban economy of Himalaya in the proximity of tourist sites. The development of tourism in underdeveloped countries is a marked feature of change in recent times. Some very tiny and poor countries of the world have abundant opportunities to develop tourism potential for promoting their foreign exchange earnings. In spite of considerable international cooperation the developing economies have to face a few formidable obstacles like policies of foreign governments and airlines, which operate detrimentally to the growth of this industry in these small countries. Transport and tourism are interrelated phenomena. An efficient transportation network is not only the base of tourism development but it is also a key note of regional developmental arch. Thus transport and tourism may be considered as a 'means' as well as an 'end'. Though tourism has been stimulated by transportation network, the truth behind the vice versa cannot be underrated. Transportation network is decisively the sole factor in the development of tourism round the globe. The global unification of cultures is resulting from global movement of people in a very large scale. In the modern context, it is well-nigh impossible to imagine of a developed mind and vibrant humanism without undertaking tours and extensive travels. Constantly expanding transport linkages have reduced the distances and eliminated the isolation of so far unknown parts of the globe. Tourism has woven all fragmented areas in a single web of contacts and interactions.

The Geography of Recreation, Leisure and Tourism which has been recognized as a separate branch of Geography very recently, has vast scope in applied sciences. The fundamental objective of this work is to present the developmental account of Geography of Splendour Resources with one of its most essential responsible ingredients i.e., transport linkage in the context of the Himalayan region of Uttaranchal. The human knowledge about the beauty resources of the great Himalayan tracts, specially Uttaranchal, is not that recent and fresh. The region has long been famous for the beauty world, solitude, and strange tribal concentration on the one side; and highly sophisticated cultural centres on the other. The people of the Himalaya have ever lived with low aspirations and in philosophy of hypocritic austerity. They could never comprehend the idea of using the beauty resources of great mountainous tract for economic prosperity and a participative tourist industry. The transport networks woven recently laid the basic infrastructure. Thus the dimension of management of splendour resources needs upkeep, preservation, development and exploitation for the regional, national and international well-being. Its forests, rivers, beauty spots, scenery, wild life and above all, the environment need management skills of experts for a sustained growth. The management plan is executed in bits and parts under a monitoring authority of tourism management. The annual plans and phased programmes in multi-dimensional spheres make the monitoring strategy.

This treatise, summarily, presents before the readers, the results of in-depth empirical surveys, study tours and prolonged discussions with policy, plan formulators and experts of tourism management in the region. The present study has been organized in nine chapters with maps and diagrams.

Chapter 1 deals with the concept of environmental resources and their conservation. Chapter 2 analyses the physical and cultural milieu of Uttaranchal Himalayan region. Having discussed the various spatial zones of the Himalaya, the drainage systems and patterns, climatic regions, geology, mineral resources and soils etc. have been discussed in the first part of this chapter, while in the second part, the demographic analysis, migration, agricultural development and size of holdings, transport and communication gaps; and development strategy in the Uttaranchal Himalaya have been discussed at length.

The theoretical aspect and conceptual framework of this study found sufficient coverage in Chapter 3. It introduces the readers with the basic concepts of Tourism and Transport Geography.

The prolonged analysis of the impact and role of transport and linkages in the various spheres of human life, regional development and cultural built-up have been incorporated in Chapter 4. Tourism is an angle of life-approach and adds tremendously to development of human personality.

Chapter 5 is devoted to the study of tourism from the chronological angle of approach. The significance of tourism in the globe as well as in India has found a well all round coverage here.

Chapter 6 devotes itself to an assessment of the tourism tendencies as an effective tool for generating employment and injecting income flows in this region. How far the income, so generated, multiplies itself in every new transaction done with it, is the actual assessment of the income-multiplier. The impact of tourism in the social, economic, cultural and ecological development has already been marked. This part of analysis provides the clue to understand how development of tourism promotes human development as well as the development of resource together with growth of income, employment and efficiencies.

The structural design of transportation network with the help of topological measures has been incorporated in Chapter 7. Movement of traffic flow, traffic management, road development and revenues, etc., have a unique character in this mountainous tract. Transport as the most essential and basic infrastructure of tourism needs more advancement in its mode and quality especially in this Himalayan tract.

Chapter 8 aims at analysing and comprehending the morphological studies of tourist attraction sites and pilgrimage centres of Kumaun and Garhwal regions of the Himalaya. A detailed picture of natural grandeur of various beauty spots and places have been fully exposed in the background of their historical (past) and present perspectives.

The last chapter (i.e. Chapter 9) presents the overall integration of various problems and potentialities of tourism in view of transportation network development and finally suggests a few measures of splendour resource management and its monitoring in the Himalaya.

This treatise shall go a long way to work as a primary text for all the students, researchers and the policy makers in the sphere of management of tourism and development of resources of Uttaranchal. As the saying goes 'the wearer knows where the shoes bites', the learned readers can best assess the extent of success of this endeavour.

Nainital
6th June 2003

D.C. Pandey
P.C. Pandey

1

Resource Conservation and Environment

Optimism of Humanity

The essence of all 'resources' lies in human resource. The focus of all development lies in boosting up quality of man. Health and creativity of man needs all encouragement. The shrinking space and time and disappearing of the national borders under globalisation have the sole purpose of human welfare, which can be realised by conservation and optimal utilisation of global resources. The resource endowments of nations are mitigated by trade exchange worth 1.5 trillion US dollars every year. New markets, new actors like WTO, NGO, UNO, etc., new norms of welfare of humanity, new global solidarity behind protecting resources of world, etc., mark the current trends. The emphasis on new ethics of humanism, equity, avoidance against marginalisation of backward, emphasis on sustainability and general war against poverty and deprivation indicate the new approach.

Suffocating Gases

'Green House Gases' and their threatening for climatic disorders resulted in hurried discussions and global agreements under Kyoto Protocol (1997). Release of arsenic and infra-red radiations, tend to trap solar heat in atmosphere. CO_2, CH_4, CFC, NO_2 releases are as deadly. Fossil fuel burning and auto-emissions cause CO_2 and can be treated by water bodies and forest wealth preservation. Chemical scavenging can save against CH_4, CFC caused by propellants, foams, refrigerators, etc., can be treated by statospheric photo disassociation in reaction with O_2. The preservation measures for forests and greenery round the globe can help against these dangers. USA and USSR (now Russia) release 25.5 and 12.4 GHG in the air which is 41.94 and 18.03 tonnes per capita respectively. China, Japan, India and Germany release 8.3, 4.1, 3.9, 3.8 per cent of GHG in the air every year, as reported by Shastri and Panth (1999). India has hardly 1.4 per cent share in global gross income while US has 28.2, Japan has 16.6 and Germany has 7.7 per cent share in global income. China releases 8.3 per cent GHG and its income share is only 2.1 per cent. China has 21.9 per cent of population and India has 16.4 per cent population. Toronto conference (1988) founded International Panel for climatic change by GHG release (IPCC) and targeted 20 per cent reduction by 2005. Earth Summit at Rio de Janereiro (1992) charter was signed by 160 nations for climatic protection. US has behaved in untamed manner and it imposes the burden of afforestation on developing countries.

Role of Resources

Any region depends on its combination of national capital and human resources to eke-out its total annual product. The economic lot of the people is largely dependent on the development of natural resources available in the habitat. The resource potential is the major limit to the level of development which a region can attain. Initially there is neither large-scale trade nor developed form of transport available to utilize resources obtained from outside the region. Therefore, in the initial phase of development the locally available manpower exploits the locally available resources like – land, water, climate, forests, minerals, animals, marine wealth, rocks, sand and other things to generate enough to consume and surplus to reinvest in capital resources so as to expedite the pace of the exploitation of local resources. It is the surplus output which is promoter of exports to other regions or outside the country. Exports yield the capacity to import the rare resources and animate the pace of growth of capital equipment. Experts like Arthur Lewis (1952) and Fisher (1964, 32) emphasize the role of local resources in the initial stages of economic progress of regions. How the resources are recognised and their usefulness for economic progress is understood? The recognition and identification of resources by population depends much on human resources, their skill, inquisitiveness, and active search for things which promote the result of the effort to create greater output, better output and at lesser cost of time, energy and management. There are several gifts of nature. It is the human being who gives them the meaning of resource. Sharp edged arrow like strips of rocks were the first to be used as a capital asset by human being to kill the wild animals for meat. The bows and arrows were drawn from forest products. Wild life, fishery, birds, etc., became resources when human being recognised their use for maintenance. Some resources are quite simple to recognise like seeds of plant life, stretches of land for cropping, water streams, rainfall, etc. In the initial stages of human civilisation, these were recognised and utilized by human being but, later, the rock pieces worked as bricks to erect houses as replacement of the natural caves. The advanced experimentation and trial-error system led human being to recognise use of glass-sand, monazite sand, coal, iron, fire resources, use of downward dashing streams for water-mill, etc. Experimentation led human being to recognise the mineral oil and its usefulness for human civilisation. Animals tamed and trained led to draught-power resource for cultivation and invention of wheel led to development of bullock-cart.

The invention of the uses of things depends on human knowledge and day-to-day experimentations for searching alternative uses of the things provided by the nature. A 'resource' may be a thing, commodity, service, situation, location, combination, interrelationship between things, knowledge, understanding, art of doing, possibility of help, means of support, etc. In a particular reference or context a thing may be a resource and not otherwise. To be a resource or to act as resource is the trail of commodity service or situation. It may not be a resource otherwise. Thus, resource is a use-specific traitor attribute. The concept of 'resources' is used in context of possibilities of better economic lot for inhabitants. In this sense human resource is primary to all resources because it is the human being which uses a situation or commodity to his purpose. Unless utilized resource has no meaning. Therefore, there may be very well-endowed areas bearing abundant natural resources where the human beings have not utilized them well. Consequently such populations invariably keep poor. Unless the inhabitants react to the situations and surroundings in a manner of using them to the utmost good of human being, the soundings do not act as a resource. A natural situation may be a barrier in human progress like the vast oceans check human mobility unless these are crossed by ships and boats. Oceans become good situations for transport if the shipping arts are developed. Favourable climate with good rainfall, fertile soil, good drainage, etc., help human being in leading a prosperous life provided human being makes the use of these situations in his favour. The role of resources is generally, passive in economic progress and the role of human resource is active which assigns the value to the natural resources. A situation, combination, application, thing commodity or service, device may act as a resource till its whole or partial replacement by its substitute, and in this sense the attribute of being a resource for production in some form is not a permanent feature. It may change with time. The technological advancement, scientific knowledge of interrelationships, relative availabilities of substitutes, and the relative cost of installing or using alternate devices may determine whether a thing could act as a resource in specific context of production process.

True Connotation of Resources

Resources are often defined as those things present in the physical environment of man which afford or have the capacity to afford sustenance and support towards satisfaction of human wants. If we take a broader view of the ecology, we find, everything in the physical environment supports the sustenance and survival of other biota. Things assume the role of resources for each other. The resources may be undiscovered, hidden below surface, intangible like magnetism, gravitation effect, electricity or radioactivity. These phenomena are utilized by human ingenuity towards human interests. Water, air, warmth of the sun and surface of the earth are the basic resources. Coal, petroleum, gas, uranium, etc., are resources because their use has been discovered by man and his devices to use them towards human interests. Human reaction to the natural surroundings led to the discovery of things which could act as resources for the human being. The plant life, forests, biodiversity of nature, animals, fishery, insects and worms, etc., assumed the role of resources for maintenance and support of mankind and for realisation of his dreams on earth. Human awareness about the resources is limited by knowledge and understanding about the earth, its phenomena and contents. Greater the knowledge new vistas shall open and new resources shall be devised.

The age-old geographers were aware of the limited resources like land, climate, minerals, plant life, marine life, situation, rivers and oceans. The economists of those ages treated economic progress restricted by the quantum of resources. Now, of course, the trend has changed in view of the dynamic concept of resources. The technology has amply proved that the resource substitution is possible, therefore, economic progress can continue even after the exhaustion of one particular resource. Generally, the natural resources known to mankind were more or less fixed, therefore, it was felt that an exhaustion point would reach, after which scarcity of resources would check the further growth. In fact, the law of diminishing returns was based on the scarcity factor. The more recent thinking on the future of human civilisation favours the pessimism of the darker side because of the alarming rate of the pollutions of various kinds in human environment and consequent risks of accumulating disaster. The ozone destruction process is an example. It is emphasised earlier that the economic growth in initial stages in developing world has to depend on the natural resources like land, water, forests, minerals, etc., and there are only few possibilities to cover-up the resources gap by imports, therefore, resources determine the prospects of progress to a large measure while in Japan, for instance, the import of valuable natural minerals can also afford very high level of industrialisation at competitive costs. High grade human resources and capital resources permit enough surpluses to cover-up the dearth of natural resources by imports. For major shortages of surplus capital resources, technology and entrepreneurial skills the economically lagging countries have to depend heavily on the natural resources for economic progress. Fertile soil and rivers were the first eminent centres of human civilisation in history. The industrial growth also prospered in river-basins. The rivers and oceans offered prospects of navigation and trade. Irrigation on fertile river basins and valleys generated great agricultural surplus available for reinvestment. The hydro-electric generation technology has added to the significance of water resources. The water and fertile soil obviously offer great prospects for highly productive forests supplying industrial timber, panel products, furniture and wood-based raw materials, by-products, animals and wild life, besides the environmental strength. Bamboo, cane, grasses, industrial leaves, lac, resin medicinal juices, gums of great variety, honey, hides, dyes, oils, tanning materials, etc., are obtained from forest resources. The forests have a number of indirect advantages in precipitation, humidity, check on extreme variation is seasons and climate, check on floods, regulation of water flows in streams, springs, reservoirs, and in upkeep of the bio-diversity and ecological balance. The wild life supplies hunting objects, meat, fats, hides and skin, silk, and so on. The rivers, ponds, lakes, seas, oceans are the sources of food in various forms, i.e. fish offering highly proteinic diet for mankind.

Fear of Exhaustion

The resources are often classified as the non-renewable resources and the renewable resources. The former include the minerals, the quantity of which only limited in view of the time taken by the nature in their replenishment. Formation of coal and radium, etc., take millions of years. The stock of these exhaustible minerals is fast eliminating. Nature has the capacity to regenerate the renewable resources over time, of course, within limits. Water is the most plentiful resource in the globe but the supply of potable and usable water is not plentiful. Gradually the world is moving in the direction of shortage of potable water. Even the rainfall is adversely affected by environmental and forest damages. The underground water is getting scarce in some identified areas by disturbed ecology. The surface water bodies are polluted due to lack of care. The recycling of polluted water has been serving the purpose of air conditioning in some industrial installations. Growing pressure on land

and demand for agricultural area have led to large-scale deforestations everywhere. The land and soil resources everywhere are at serious danger due to erosion and lack of conservation. Sheet, sill and gully erosion has devastated several areas of fine alluvial soil. Unscientific methods of cultivation and also the overgrazing and tilling in slopy lands have led to erosion of soil at a fast rate. The animal wealth is a resource but as it grows, the grasslands are overgrazed and bio-diverstiy starts eliminating. Heavy pressure on fish has reduced the replenishment rate of oceans of produce more fish. Thus resources are at serious stress. This is mostly due to lack of proper management and lack of proper planning.

Excesses by Humanity

Resources of all kinds are facing the problem of excesses done by human race. It is well-ascertained fact that the private interest of the individuals is limited to their gain in their generation or own life period. Individuals tend to maximize gain in shortest period of time. The community interest or social interest extends over a prolonged span of time. There arises the obvious conflict between individual interest and the social interest. The social interest is represented by the state, therefore, conservation of strategic resources becomes the responsibility of the state. Each state is further represented by the government and the government also represents the groups, communities and individuals as voters. At times government for earliest reaping of gains disregarding the future needs of generations yet to come. The forest and mineral wealth of various countries has been depleting at an alarming rate. Zaire, Zambia, Kuwait, UAE, Nigeria, Venezuela, Saudi Arabia, Iran, Iraq, Libya, etc., live on the exploitation of globally short resources of oil. The human consumption of petroleum and its products is expanding at very alarming rate.

Environmental Resource and Human Values

Environment is the most primary resource which makes the survival of life on earth possible. All that surrounds us is environment. Be it earth's surface, topography, contents of earth, air, water, moisture, gas, sunlight, rivers, mountains, rocks, minerals, biotic life, herbal life, peace and calmness, beauty all around in the form of flowers, grasses, forests, fauna-flora, snows, valleys, elevations, or the wild life of very large variety and so on. The variety of natural wealth and its multiplication and thriving systems altogether weave the atmosphere where human being takes birth, learns and adjusts to make his living possible. The changes that take place in the resource-frame around man directly affect the human survival. John (1996) rightly claims that "... environmental values are economic values. It is in principle just as important in the interest of economic efficiency and therefore, economic welfare, to consume our limited natural resources to make wise and sparing use of scarce clean air, water, living space, peace and calm surrounding, as it is to economic use of labour and capital...." When efforts are laid to restore environmental variety and diversity and to preserve this valuable resource to keep the earth livable it adds to human welfare as much as any other important branch of economic production.

The development of human civilisation and the environmental preservation are deeply interrelated. In fact, the aesthetic values grow and develop in human being by the influence and impact of beauty of nature. The more we devote to appreciate it the greater aesthetic enjoyment we receive. Environment constitutes the foremost resource for human development. The preservation of vitality of wider landscape, fauna-flora, life-diversity, beauty-knit work of nature, life-resources like water, soil, air, surroundings of peace and calm, forest wealth, snow-capped peaks, extended beaches, flow of rivers and beauty surrounds of waterfalls and water bodies, etc., is preservation of the eco-sphere which is the habitat shared by all forms of life.

The scarcity of environment has been caused and continues to be caused by the heavy industrialisation based on modern experimental science and newly-evolved technologies. There was not much talk of environmental resources in earlier centuries, except in epics and Vedas propounded by ancient philosophers, because the supply was greater than the demand and natural replenishment covered the gap. The quality of environmental resources started deteriorating in the nineteenth century. Affluence made people more alert and aware for quality of environment while effluence was caused by heavy demand on this rare resource. The unprecedented population growth, enhanced consumption, urbanisation, industrialisation, intensive agriculture based on fertilizers and herbicides, insecticides, etc., gradual exhaustion of minerals, etc., have raised great alarm. Greater than the pace of consumption, there is the matter of mismanagement of natural resources leading to avoidable wastes and avoidable panic of degradation of quality of forests, quality of soil, quality of air, quality of oceanic water, quality of rivers and other water bodies. The mismanagement has led to great chaos and the extended soil, dust, water, chemical, sound, ultra-violet rays, types of pollutions. The human concern over environmental quality has been gradually growing after noticing the ozone depletion in large scale. Green House effect and climatic changes have drawn attention of human beings to the catastrophe waiting for them.

Resource Management

Good management reduces the major part of the risks ahead. World is more united and organised now. Common agreement round the globe on limits of experimentation, arrangement of food, fuel, shelter, clothing, fodder, energy, etc., for all, and evolving models of sustainable growth, is possible. This can avoid the wastes as well. The earth's beauty resources can be well-preserved by common agreement. Appropriate technologies can reduce the strain on resources. The anti-pollution campaign round the globe has raised the alertness of mankind for preserving the 'beauty centres' of the earth so as to protect sensitivity for aesthetic values in human being. The pace of exploitation of resources from the earth's reserves has taken enormous scale. Nearly 100 billion tonnes of coal, 80 billion tonnes of natural oil, 50 trillion cubic metres of natural gas, and 28 billion tonnes of iron has been extracted during 1975-2000. The demand is ever-growing. The less developed are yet to make their dreams of industrialisation a reality. How the earth's surface and oceans, rivers and air is going to bear such a big lot of pollution by effluents, smoke, sound, dust, gases, and so on. The self-replenishing cycle of nature is now threatened. The animals and humans have assumed very great unmanageable numbers. The carrying capacity of earth is exhausting. A very large number of geographic changes are occurring in the earth. The polar-ice is melting and polar-drifting ice is hitting the coastal areas of oceans. Disruption in oxygen balance has caused another alarm. Similarly the ultra-violet rays are finding straight access to earth due to ozone depletion. The earth's life protection system is at danger of elimination. The radioactive pollutants from reactors and nuclear wastes together with the dangerous weapons, like chemical weapons, have threatened human survival. Thus, the environmental resources have to be saved at the first priority.

Managing Splendour Resources

The splendour resources of the earth are the aesthetic reserves of nature which inspire the living beings with the sense of beauty, appreciation of the supreme values and dress humanity with the unique sense of divinity and oneness of the creation. The inanimate virtues are promoted by diversified beauty of nature in every part of the earth. It is indeed an everlasting joy and the feel of being one with the creator. The calm and sweet rhythm of the dense forests, fast-flowing mountain rivers, thundering waves and tides of oceans, greenery of the gorgeous mountains, plentiful grandeur of snows, the silent but ever active play of the fauna, the blue transparent pure water bodies of uplands, delightful gaze on the dainty flower-ridden meadows, the abundant herbal wealth of isolated mountains, and so on, captivate the living creatures and humans and for a while steal their fatigue of working in din and turmoil of busy world. The splendour resources are the heaven on the surface of the earth.

The 'Beauty of Nature' is the rarest of the resources known to the sensitised being. The aesthetic pleasure is the supreme pleasure which human being can ever derive from the gifts of nature itself. Bread alone is not the need of man. Economic betterment leads to life comforts but the 'beauty' inherent in nature and its appreciation gives meaning to human existence. The satiety of curiosity is attained by the glimpse of nature's beauty. In order to preserve this eternal source of pleasure and rarest of all types of pleasures, humanity has to work towards identification of the beauty spots, on this earth. These spots are the wealth of mankind irrespective of their physical location. Mount Everest, whether owned by Nepal, China or India, it is a constant source of inspiration and beauty pleasure to entire humanity. The lush green panorama of mountain ranges, hilly ridges, precipitous valleys, lake basins, extended meadows, snow-clad peaks, the round about mountain roads, the strange and captivating wild life, the world of the birds and insects, the wonderful waterfalls, and fast-rushing river water of Himalaya are the rarest of the beauty reserves of the earth. We have to keep them well-protected and preserved for ever.

Reconciliation of Ecology, Economics and Aesthetics

The issues of economic progress, sophisticated technology, and sustainable growth patterns have long occupied the attention of great thinkers. Early in 1970, the limits to growth were identified. Brundtland Commission (1987) internationalised the vital issues of sustainability. How human race could ensure meeting the present needs entirely without, of course, compromising the ability of future generations to meet their needs. The ideas of ecological sustainability, social sustainability and economic sustainability emerged from these discussions. The non-declining utility generation is possible of resource use round the globe by worldwide collaboration. It also calls for inter- and intra-generation equities. The taste of the beauty of nature has to go to the future generations as well. This can be ensured by common agreement globally to preserve nature, its beauty, its order, interdependence, ecological balance and by agreement for control on the rapid degradation in the quality of resources. Barbier (1987), Golgan (1987), Hinterberger and Schmidt (1997) have extensively discussed the need and implications of the approach to sustainable development and the preservation of resources for sharing with the coming generations to ensure intergeneration equity. The overall present consumption of scarce resources need regulation and management together with the policies to promote the supply of rare resources. This need active search for alternatives and putting limits to the consumption. The bio-diversity, forest wealth, beauty resources, protection of wild life and natural ecological systems, replacement of timber use by the substitute, new energy sources, greater sharing between the nations and collaboration in preserving resources can help the objective. Meadows *et al*. (1972) had adequately warned the world against the catastrophes to emerge for want of proper resource use planning. M.V. Nadkarni (1996) re-emphasized the urgent need for collaborated efforts of nations for resource preservation and sustainable development policies.

Well before the entire beauty-edged landscape vanishes from the earth, the global protection has to be expedited for the splendour resources of the earth. These may be used for 'tourism' for the entire humanity. These can afford the economic resource for the local governments as well as afford aesthetic fulfilment of humanity at large. The ecological balance shall be restored which can ensure the sustainability as well Himalayan beauty and grandeur constitute a rare resource which can be extensively utilized for the promotion of international tourism.

When Tourim Spoils the Resource-base

The main danger to resources, both capital assets and natural assets, is caused by the human interference. The floods devastate the arable agricultural areas, standing crops, roads and pavements, culverts and even the hutments. Only resource management device can save such loss. For instance, national highway 21 takes more than 7 lakh tourists every year. It has to serve as military movement route to Leh. This is flooded by Beas river due to spate. In 1995 alone the flood-led loss was worth Rs.106 crores. The upsetting of ecological order has emerged from the unplanned constructions to accommodate rush of tourists which has been expanding fast in Himachal. There are more than 750 hotels, several lodges and stay houses in Kullu-Manali. Heavy constructions have led to deforestation in large scale in 1,200 sq. km. area. The rocks have been broken and quarried from Beas river bank which promoted the flooding. The forests are fast disappearing. The mountain ridges are sliding down and eroded top soil is blocking Beas river bed. Deforestation has played havoc with natural weather cycle. The rainfall period has been shifting. The blastings in rocks by hydro-electric projects and cave tunnel making has also created danger to resources. The illegal quarrying has led to weakening of the hill sides. The eco-fragile region of Manali is losing arable land every year. Tourism has turned Kullu-Manali into a vast polythene bag sea. Unless we resort to protection of resources the erosion of valuable resources is likely to go on.

2

The Uttaranchal Himalaya: Environment, Resources, Economy and Society

Features of the Tract under Study

The Uttaranchal state of the Himalaya is a well-recognised regional entity – a physical as well as a socio-cultural unit. It includes the two principal revenue divisions – (1) Kumaun Division, and (2) Garhwal Division – with one separate district of Haridwar. It is situated between latitudes 28° 43' 24" and 31° 27' 50" north and longitudes 77° 34' 27" and 81° 02' 22" East and ecompasses an area of 53,485 sq. km. (equal to about 22.20 per cent area of the former UP state) with 70,50,634 population as per 1991 and 84,79,562 population as per 2001 censuses. This region makes a compact geographic entity with Nepal in the east, Tibet in the north and Himachal state of India in the west. In the east, a natural water divide is formed by Kali to separate Nepal from this tract. In the north another water divide separates this area from Tibet. To the western side, Tons river constitutes the water divide between Himachal and Uttaranchal states. To the western direction of Kali river six districts – namely Almora, Bageshwar, Nainital, Udham Singh Nagar, Pithoragarh and Champawat – constitute Kumaun division. This is eastern part of Uttaranchal state. On the western part, the districts of Chamoli, Uttarkashi, Pauri-Garhwal, Tehri-Garhwal and Rudraprayag constitute the hill districts of Garhwal. Dehradun to the south, is the foothill areas of Garhwal. District Haridwar comes under the tarai plains. The Chamoli and Pauri districts of Garhwal are separated by traverse mountain spurs from

Almora and Bageshwar districts of Kumaun Division. Formerly the term 'UP Himalaya' comprised of the twin revenue divisions – Kumaun and Garhwal. Presently the Uttaranchal state includes the district of Almora, Bageshwar, Pithoragarh, Champawat, Nainital, Udham Singh Nagar, Dehradun, Uttarkashi, Chamoli, Rudraprayag, Tehri, Pauri and Haridwar. The term 'Himalaya' covers all the human habitations settled in the lap of Himalayan ranges between Gilgit to Arunachal and twisting southward to Nagaland in the eastern wing of India. The administrative divisions included in 'Himalaya' are: (a) Gilgit, (b) Laddakh, (c) Kashmir, (d) Himachal Pradesh, (e) Uttaranchal, (f) Nepal as a sovereign land, (g) Sikkim, (h) Darjeeling, (i) Jalpaiguri of West Bengal, (j) Bhutan, (k) Assam, (l) Meghalaya (m) Arunachal Pradesh, and (n) Nagaland.

The observation of the physical map of Himalaya shows that nine countries have their share in Himalaya in some measure. These countries are; Afghanistan, Pakistan (Baluchistan part), USSR, China, India, Nepal, Bhutan, Bangladesh and Burma. The former hill areas of UP are also termed as "Garhkum Himalaya". The study area, i.e. the Uttaranchal state includes the twelve districts of Kumaun and Garhwal (former UP Himalaya) with one adjacent district of Haridwar (Map 2.1).

Regarding the area and population of the nine Himalayan states of India, Jammu and Kashmir stands first (in both) in ranking hierarchy; while the Uttaranchal state stands fourth and second place in respect of area and population-wise respectively. Sikkim is the smallest state with 4,04,000 persons in 7,596 km.^{2} as per 1991 census (Table 2.1).

Physical Divisions of the Himalaya

The geological structure of the Uttaranchal Himalaya is quite complex, complicated and unique. Geologists have classed the region into three principal categories:

(a) The Sub-Himalayan on Siwalik zone,
(b) The Middle or Lesser Himalayan zone, and
(c) The Greater or Inner Himalayan zone.

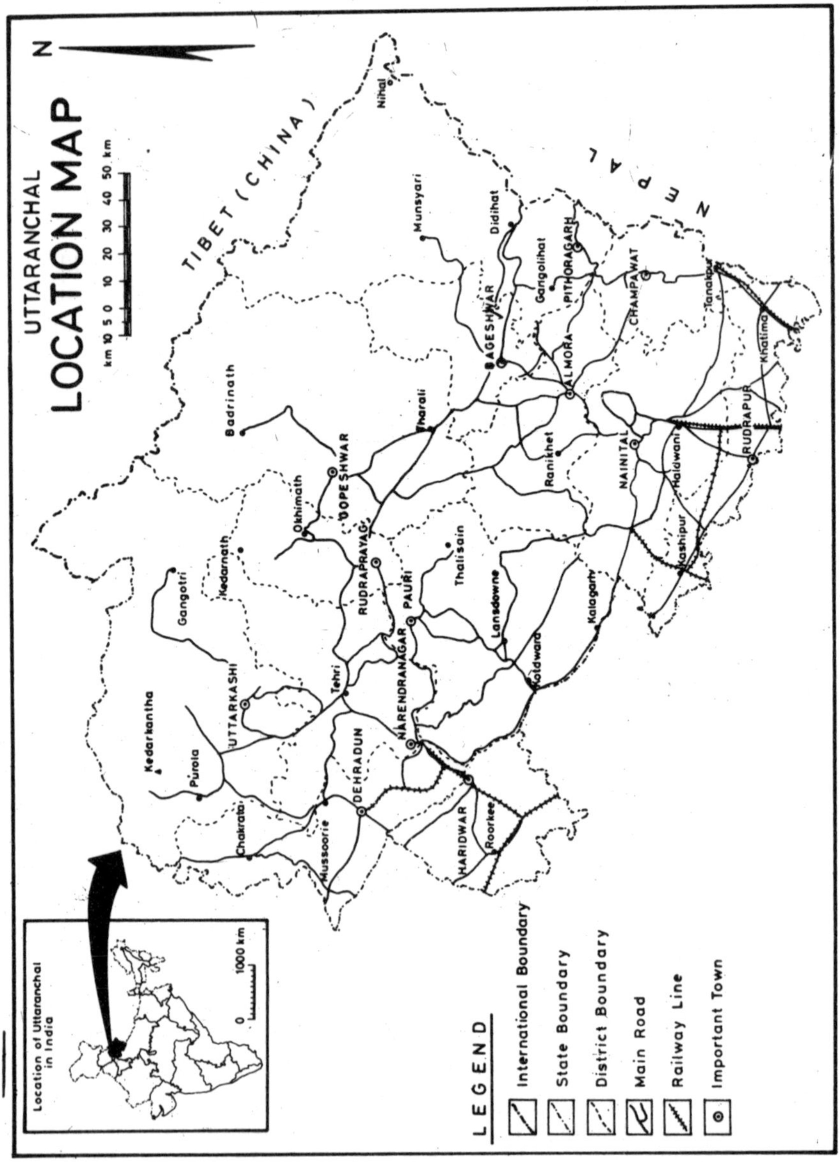
UTTARANCHAL
LOCATION MAP
N
km 10 5 0 10 20 30 40 50 km
TIBET (CHINA)
NEPAL
Location of Uttaranchal in India
0 1000 km
LEGEND
International Boundary
State Boundary
District Boundary
Main Road
Railway Line
Important Town
Nihal
Munsyari
Didihat
Badrinath
Gangotri
Kedarnath
Kedarkantha
Purola
Chakrata
Mussoorie
DEHRADUN
HARIDWAR
Roorkee
UTTARKASHI
Tehri
NARENDRANAGAR
PAURI
RUDRAPRAYAG
GOPESHWAR
Okhimath
Tharali
Thalisain
Lansdowne
Kotdwara
Kalagarh
BAGESHWAR
ALMORA
Ranikhet
NAINITAL
Haldwani
Kashipur
RUDRAPUR
Khatima
Tanakpur
CHAMPAWAT
PITHORAGARH
Gangolihat

FIG. 2·1

TABLE 2.1: Area and Population of the States Located in Himalayan Region, 1991

State	Area (km.^{2})	Population
1. Jammu and Kashmir	2,22,236	77,19,000
2. Uttaranchal	53,485	70,50,634
3. Himachal Pradesh	55,673	51,11,000
4. Sikkim	7,596	4,04,000
5. Arunachal Pradesh	83,743	8,58,000
6. Nagaland	16,579	12,16,000
7. Manipur	22,327	18,27,000
8. Mizoram	21,081	6,86,000
9. Tripura	10,186	27,45,000

The Outer Himalaya or Sub-Himalayan zone (Siwaliks) commences from upper Ganga plain. Geologists claim that this vast belt has been formed by tertiary and upper tertiary sedimentary river deposits. The most striking feature of this zone is marked in great thickness of rocks consisting detrital material, clay and conglomerates. The bed-part of this area is formed by sand stone and shale. Geological features have a great importance in shaping the economy and settlement patterns of the area.

Lesser Himalayan zone of this region is separated by a boundary fault line between Outer or Sub-Himalayan zone and central part known as Lesser Himalayan zone. Granite and crystalline rocks of poorly fossiliferious types of sediments coupled by complex tectonics represent the Lesser Himalayan zone. Tej Veer Singh (Singh, 1975, 8) claimed that these rocks have been metamorphosed to a larger extent and represent the age from Algonkian to the Eocene. They present lithological variations in the pattern of mosaic of colours – buff, cream, white, purple, pink, grey, yellow and slaty. Uttarkashi district of Garkhum has the most wide range of variety so pronounced and distinct. In its structural features, the area is an extension of sima krol belt with its upper layers of enfra krol sand stone, krol lime and tal quartzites. The krol belt in Lesser Himalayan zone constitutes the most striking tourism resource sites in the entire Himalaya.

The belt of Greater Himalaya is divided from the Lesser

Himalaya by the Main Central Thrust of Himalaya. Simple tectonic features are notable in this belt. The analysis of rock composition in this belt suggests that it bears quartzites, gneiss, garnet schists and several other types of rocks. At a glance, above 4,800 m. to the north is the innermost part of Himalaya and has a width of around 50 kms. Nanda Devi and Kamet peaks are at a height of 7,817 m. and 7,756 m. respectively settled in Greater Himalaya. Other notable peaks in this belt are Gangotri (6,614 m.), Kedarnath (6,950 m.), Chaukhamba (7,138 m.), Trisul (7,120 m.) and Bunder Punch (6,315 m.). The glaciers and snow-laden peaks in this area constitute a great scenic splendour. The great river valleys like Bhagirathi, Alaknanda, Dhauli Ganga and other rivulets present a very captivating landscape. Glacier lakes are the other great attractions in this belt from the angle of approach of tourism development. Hemkund, Rupkund and Chaukhamba glacier lakes are prominently known.

Chastity of Waters in the Craddle of Mountains

The next belt to the south of Greater Himalaya is of the Lesser Himalaya which comprises a large number of mountain ranges, hilly ridges, valleys and lake basins which adorn the area with great scenic beauty. The width of this belt may be around 75 kms. and the height ranges between 1,500 and 2,700 m. The entire belt has some remarkable features and lakes are one of them. The lakes are not well-distributed round the belt. These lake basins are confined to a well-demarcated belt of nearly 25 kms. in length and 4 kms. in width occurring near the outer fringe of Lesser Himalaya in Nainital district of Kumaun region. The hill ranges and peaks in Garhwal are more steep and sharply gazing to the skies intercepted by very deep ravines abound with fast-flowing rivers. Slope in the hills is relatively gentle in Kumaun. Garhwal region has comparatively lesser number of lakes yet the beauty of Gahna lake and Diuri lake are the wonders in themselves. Lakes have adorned the Garhkum region with rare natural beauty. Having been linked by good vehicular facilities and roads these beauty spots are available to the commoners. Lesser Himalayan belt has several locations of great tourist importance and in recent years, these have found popularity among domestic and foreign tourists.

Foothills and Duns: Gateways to Himalaya

Southward, we come across the Siwalik zone which comprises a long chain of narrow and low hills which seem to run somewhat parallel to the ranges of the Lesser Himalaya. Height of these hill ranges varies very widely between locations and the lowest height is around 750 m. while the highest points may measure around 1,200 m. To the interior hills these slopes are well-covered with dense forests. Some of the slopes seem to have been well-terraced and brought into cultivation while the most rugged parts are also covered with some kinds of trees. To the southern slopes these mountain ranges have some notable steep scarps. To the north they seem to be descending gently to flat-floored structural valleys. These are the *duns* covered with recent gravels of Lesser Himalaya to the height of 350 m. to the north of wider plains. Dehradun in Garhwal is one of the most open and beautiful part among the other *duns* like Patti, Chaukhamba, Kahtri and Kota. Dehradun is around 35 kms. long and nearly 25 kms. wide and has a most developed human settlement dressed with relatively developed modes of transport and tourist sites. In the eastern part of Uttaranchal, the Siwalik is separated from the Lesser Himalaya by the main boundary thrust and the fault zone is marked by extraordinarily wide valleys like Ladhiya, Gaula-Balia, Mandal, Kosi and Ramganga. These are typically characterised by fans and cones of landslide debris and by fault-cut triangular facets on spurs of recent and sub-recent origin. Kumaun Himalaya (Division) which is eastern part of 'Garhkum' has interesting settlements of Johar, Chaundans, Darma, Byans, etc., in Greater Himalayan belt. The Lesser Himalayan part of this sector covers the settlements in Danpur, Katyoor, Sira, Gangøli, Sore, Salt, Pali, Kosiyan, Baramandal, Chhakhata, Kali Kumu, etc. In the Siwalik part of Kumaun Patti Dun, Kota Dun, etc., are placed. Still southward the Outer Himalayan area covers the Tarai region. It is this Outer Himalayan tract which covers the belt of known settlements of Jaspur, Kashipur, Bazpur, Rudrapur, Kichha, Sitarganj and Khatima, as we proceed west to east. In Garhwal region the famous human settlements known through the annals are Chakrata, Puranla and Dehradun bordering with Himachal Pradesh. Moving towards east we come across the settlements of Rajgarh,

Tehri, Dunda, Bhatwari, Pratapnagar, Ukhimath, Joshimath, Narendranagar, Devprayag, Pauri-Garhwal, Gopeshwar, Karnaprayag and Lansdowne. In the outer Siwalik we find Dehradun, Haridwar, Kotdwar, and their neighbouring human settlements in Garhwal.

Drainage System

The tourist attractions are formed in the Kumaun-Garhwal area by the beauty of mountains, snow-clad peaks, lush green forests and the typically evolved river systems and their tributaries. In fact if we scan at the map of this tract west to east, we find 'Trans River' bifurcating Himachal from Uttaranchal in the extreme west. This collects water from north-east by its several tributaries and merges into Yamuna system while flowing down. Then, Bhagirathi having been subscribed by various rivulets right and left flows from north to south and then twisting to east it merges into Ganga. Ganga is contributed by a large number of rivers like Vishnu Ganga while in the north, Pindar and Alaknanda and Mandakini with its several tributaries. Ganga drains the region in the central part flowing east to west and then twisting its course to south. South-eastern part of Uttaranchal is drained by Ramganga being aided by a large number of local tributaries. To the extreme east, the region is drained by Kali, Saryu flowing east to south-west. This is aided by Sarda and Gori rivers and several other big drainage channels (Map 2.2).

It is the network of rivers and rivulets which makes the landscape very interesting to anybody who happens to visit this region. Broadly, the region is abound with three systems: (a) Ganga system, (b) Yamuna system, and (c) Kali system.

Ganga emerges from ice-cave of Gaumukh of Gangotri glacier – which measures around 30 kms. long and nearly 4 kms. wide. The meeting of Kedar Ganga in the wider Bhagirathi nearly 17-20 kms. southward of the glacier makes a wonderful natural scenery cutting a picturesque gorge. The mighty river travels across shaking hands with its dozens of sisters to Deoprayag where the confluence of Alaknanda and Bhagirathi is a known beauty spot and centre of pligrimage. Alaknanda river presents a very fascinating look flowing down the majestic rocks. It appears in its mighty force

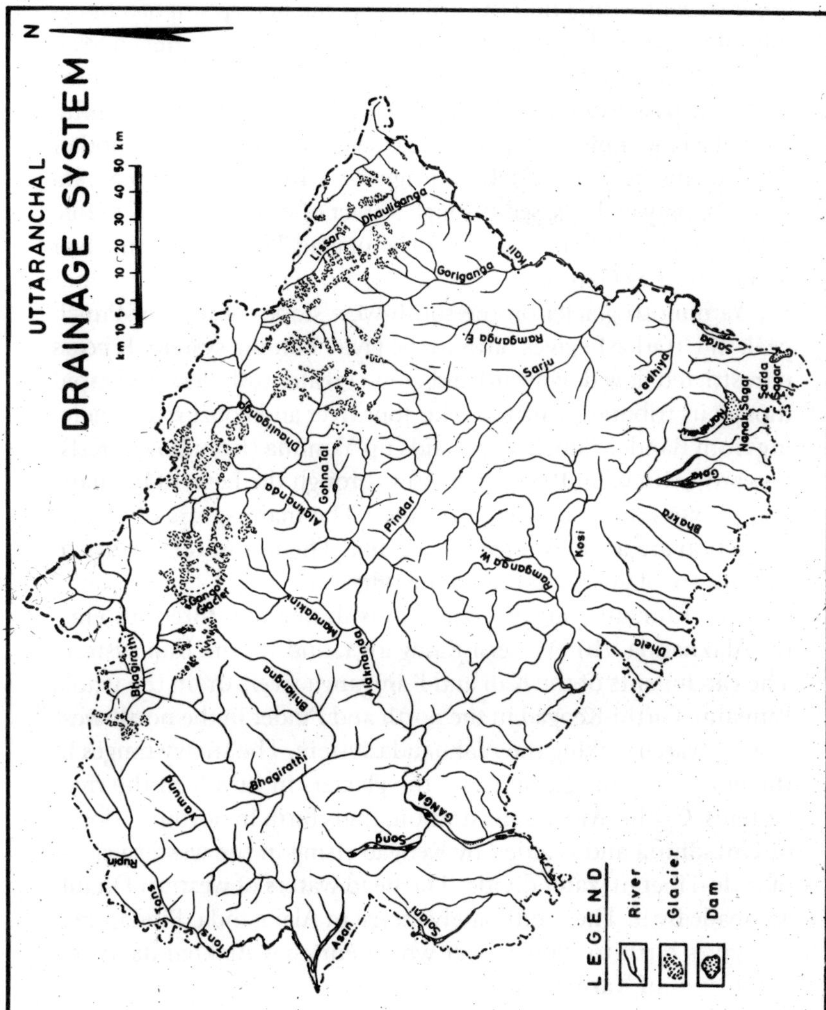
UTTARANCHAL
DRAINAGE SYSTEM
N
km 10 5 0 10 20 30 40 50 km
LEGEND
River
Glacier
Dam
Dhauliganga
Lissar
Goriganga
Kali
Ramganga E.
Sarju
Ladhiya
Sarda
Sarda Sagar
Nanak Sagar
Gola
Bhakra
Kosi
Dhela
Ramganga W.
Pindar
Gohna Tal
Alaknanda
Dhauliganga
Mandakini
Gangotri Glacier
Bhagirathi
Bhilangna
Yamuna
Rupin
Tons
Asan
Song
Solani
GANGA

FIG. 2·2

after emerging from the twin glaciers of Kharak and Sato Panth, drawing from Chaukhamba slopes. The famous waterfalls 'Vasudhara' and 'Sahastradhara' subscribe to the flow of Alaknanda. At Badrinath, Rishi Ganga merges into the main stream. The scenery is so captivating that the visitor gets the perception of a hanging valley. Near Hanuman Chatti, Khiraon Ganga renders herself into Alaknanda which is extremely beautiful. Ganga comes down from Nitipass to join Alaknanda at Vishnooprayag. The confluence of Mandakini and Alaknanda is seen in Nandprayag. Another river having been aided left and right by which meets Alaknanda at Rudraprayag. It passed through a tract of nearly 70 kms. before meeting the mighty Bhagirathi at Deoprayag. Henceforth, the river names itself as Ganga.

Yamunotri glacier on the south-west slopes of Bander Punch peak in Uttarkashi gives birth to the great Yamuna system. It bears unrestricted flow downward and grows greater turbulent and rapid though its tributaries are few. The Tons river and Pober river emerging from Bander Punch slopes aids up Yamuna (from Lower Kalsi onward) with great flows. It crosses through the Lesser Himalaya and plunges down to the Dun valley. The main sports of tourist attraction are at the source of Yamuna. The hot water springs of the site are of great interest to the pilgrims.

The Kumaun part of Garhkum is drained by three systems: (a) Alaknanda, (b) Western Ramganga, and (c) the Kali system. The catchments of the Kali and Ramganga rivers drain the whole Kumaun. Girthi-Keogad in the north and Pinder in the north-west work towards making the Alaknanda system. The snowy ranges in the north feed the glaciers and the glaciers in turn feed the river systems. Girthi river, for illustration, finds birth in northern slopes of Untadhura and is aided by Keogad rising in the western slope of Indo-Tibetan water divide. The head waters of western Dhauli are made by it. These ultimately merge in Alaknanda. Pindari glacier gives birth to Pinder river which enriches Alaknanda at the confluence of Karnaprayag.

Kali constitutes the largest water drainage system in Kumaun and works as bifurcating line between India and Nepal in Kumaun. This mighty river receives its water from Kalapani in the slopes of Indo-Tibetan water divides very close to Lipulekh pass at the height of nearly 4,266 m. Kuti river, a tributary of Kali system, emerges in the glacier at the base of Lampia Pass at 5,455 m. of height. These meet at a height of 4,801 m. and rushes down through Garbiang to Tanakpur. Eastern Dhauli river joins Kali at Tawaghat and Gori river merges in Kali river at Jauljibi at 590 m. height. The river grows all the more powerful having met Saryu at Pachheshwar at the height of 422 m. above the sea level. Dhauli in the eastern part originates from Dawe glacier at 5,058 m. and meets Lissar river to become 'Darma' river. Gori river emerges from Milam glacier (at 3,463 m. height) and becomes stronger by meeting Gunikhagad coming from a glacier on Untadhura slope. Having emerged in southern slope of Nandakot Saryu is fed by tributaries like Kanal, Pungar, and Lahaul before reaching Bageshwar (at 943 m.). At Bageshwar the Saryu is met by Gomti. Eastern Ramganga has its source in Namik glacier at the depression of Nandakot. It meets Saryu at Rameshwar. Another river Lohawat collects all waters from Kali Kumaun region and merges in Kali system. Lodhiya, a rivulet coming from Mornaula side flows to east and merges in Kali at Chukka. Kali river with its masterly drainage intrudes the Bhabar area at Brahmadeo where it gets the nomenclature of Sarda. It crosses through the human settlements of Tanakpur, Banbassa, Khatima and leaves Kumaun at Melaghat. To the western part of the tract, western Ramganga emerges in slopes of Dudhatoli mountain in Garhwal and flows north-eastward to reach Almora district through a gorge at Giwar and flows south-westerly through Bhikiasen having met Binau and Ganga rivers on way. Various small rivers are originating and merging into bigger systems ultimately.

The river systems in Uttaranchal as a whole constitute one of the great wonders and exciting scenery for the visitors who tour in the region with unending and unsatiable curiosity. The entire region has not yet been covered with network of roads and convenient vehicular reach. The typical landforms and scenic grandeur constitutes a great potential for development of tourism in this region.

Climatic Conditions

Wide variations in the altitude, slopes and the surroundings spatially cause great climatic differences. Micro-climatic conditions tend to vary widely between regions wherein the roles of factors like direction of ridges, slope-variation, shady and sunny slopes, the forest cover and closeness to glaciers predominant. Temperature, however, varies due to the varying elevation while direction of the relief has a great influence on temperature. It is widely experienced that the south-facing slopes receive sun for a greater span of time and also receive greater rain as compared to those facing north. It is reported that slopes behind the high ridges present a picture of rain shadow. In Garhwal Himalaya Bhagirath Kharak glacier constitutes an example. While to the north the temperature is near zero and no vegetation thrives there, the southern parts are quite warm and a good lot of grass and junipers grow there. Still another important factor in determination of temperature is the wind pressure and the direction of wind flow. The pace of flow has also much to bear on temperature level. Greater precipitation lies between 1,200-2,100 m. In Uttaranchal the gravity winds have very close impact on the climatic state. The gravity wind disturbance is created by vertical movement of air due to rise in temperature with the advancement of the day. When the sun sets, the moist air moves downward and consequently the mist rolls down to the deeper ravines and valley areas. When the mist settles in depressions, the sky gets more or less clear. Such open sky with moonlight makes the scenery of hills and snow-clad peaks extremely beautiful and captivating for the tourists. A large number of addicts of fun and frolic and trekking visit the hills during the winter when it grows too much hazy in plains. The hill areas of Garhkum, specially the northern parts, keep clad with thick or thin layers of snow from December to March. It snows quite frequently in February. Even during the later week of March, these regions often experience snowfall and hailstorms. The summer starts in April and by the month of June (middle) the rain commences which lasts till September. The rains do not stop abruptly in autumn. In October and November the weather is usually good, sweet cold, with clear sky and enjoyable sun during the day. The tourists have the finest weather during mid-September to mid of November after which the cold becomes a bit more biting and disturbing during the night.

Generally, the temperature tends to vary according to the elevation levels, in Uttaranchal Himalayas. In the areas closer to subtropical tract below 900 m. height, it is quite warm. Moving further to an upper zone 900-1,800 m., the climate becomes a sort of warm temperate nature. Beyond 1,800 m. upwards, the temperature dwindles and it becomes somewhat cool-temperate climate. To the further heights, climate is cold ranging till 4,000 m. when it abruptly changes to permafrost climate where temperature keeps at freezing level for most of the time of the day and night.

The level of temperature helps the process of precipitation in hills specially when followed by local thunderstorms and cyclonic events. It is in fact, the south-west monsoon which brings rains in this region. Major part of rains is the result of sourth-west monsoon while nearly one-fifth of the rains is the consequence of thunderstorms and cyclones. The monsoonal invasion enters from outer barriers where the first shower falls, specially in the areas above 2,000 m. Greatest rainfall is always in such areas of higher elevation at the outer barriers. The average in such areas reaches between 250 and 270 cm. per year. The *duns* do not receive good rain and Bhabar areas get rains not beyond 140 cm. per year as per past experience in records. The stations situated at the lap of Greater Himalayas find greater precipitation per year. Generally the rain is in greater measure in lofty ranges of the north till the snow line is reached. Around 3,500 m. of height above sea level, there is greater rain. Above this level, the incidence of snow is in greater measure. Ranikhet, Lohaghat, Almora, Pithoragarh, etc., receive rain between 90 and 150 in. annually while the interior parts like Berinag, Askot, etc., have an average rain of 150 cm. per year. The winter rains are usually followed by cyclones and in upper Uttaranchal tracts it snows well due to cyclonic impact. During the late summer, precipitation is due to local thunderstorms caused by atmospheric instabilities and sudden variations in temperature (Table 2.2).

It is noticeable that the higher elevation level has the lowest temperature in winter. In greater rainfed areas the minimum temperature drops still beyond even in the elevation level is less high. Usually higher determinants of rainfall prevent this occurrence. Seasonal winds do play a great role in determination of rainfall level and general climatic conditions. Some of the hill stations receive relatively low rainfall inspite of being placed in greater

TABLE 2.2 : Temperature Level in Altitudes

Altitude recorded (m.)	Station	Temperature level (degrees celcius)			
		Summer		Winter	
		Minimum	Maximum	Minimum	Maximum
2,005.5	Mussoorie	10.0	28.6	2.2	6.7
2,135.0	Chakrata	5.0	23.0	1.8	5.0
640.0	Dehradun	16.7	36.7	5.2	23.4

Source: Meteorological Data 1988-89, *Bulletin of Statistics*, UP, 1989.

height. Overall shape of the ridge and surrounding structure matters in precipitation. The rainfall level in various stations and their elevation level is shown in Table 2.3. Climatic conditions have a direct imprint on the distribution of natural vegetation in this region.

Types and Texture of Soils

It is known that soil composition in the region marks extensive spatial variations at short intervals which weaves the network of a very large variety of plant life growing in the region. Generally there

TABLE 2.3: Levels of Rainfall in Altitudes

Altitude (m.)	Stations marked	Level of rainfall (cm.)
1. 1,934	Nainital	270
2. 1,676	Almora	104
3. 1,636	Pithoragarh	122
4. 884	Karnaprayag	136
5. 778	Tehri-Garhwal	80
6. 682	Dehradun	212
7. 550	Srinagar	93
8. 457	Devaprayag	70

Source: Meteorological Data 1988-89, *Bulletin of Statistics*, UP, 1989.

are three grades of soil, easily identifiable, and bearing different characteristics:

(a) Alluvial drift soils of valley-lying area;
(b) Intermixed sedentary-cum-alluvial soils in deep situations of land in upper elevations; and
(c) Sedentary soils.

The valley-plains of mountainous region are often irrigated and bear high amount of humidity in the soil. The top layer of soil is dressed by particles of fine soil brought to the site by drains across the slope. It is mostly less-slopy land which retains the soil particles flowing down with dashing rainwater. The particles do not settle unless the downward flow of water is checked. In the immediate depth of about 8 in., these fields have gravels and pieces of disintegrated rocks. At the top layer the fine soil is intermixed with humus content. This may contain twigs of wood, disintegrated litter, pieces of grass-roots, etc. Water flowing from heights also carries pieces of bones, excrete of worms, insects, animals and ordinary cow-dung dropped by grazing animals. This strange admixture makes the soil more porus and prevents clodding of soil. The colour of the soil depends on these contents and colour of the disintegrated rocks which contribute these fine soil particles. Such type of soil affords a very good plant growth.

Soil found in deep situations of upper elevations from the valley-based beds, bear slightly different characteristics. In some bowl like formations of land and broad terraces sloping to hill side and slightly elevated to the valley side, the dashing rainwater gets little chance of drifting away the finer soil particles. Flow of water from the higher sloppy walls of the ridge carries with it the drift soil as well as humus content and deposits in the bowl like land formations. Such locations are much lower than the hill top and, perhaps, used to be the valley lying alluvial soils some generations ago. Due to deepening of the river bed and gorges these are left considerably higher than the river bed. The continuous process of land erosion and drifting of soil, such field formations have some features of alluvial soil while the features of predominant parent rock are no less evinced. The cultivators have to sortout the sizeable rock-pieces, stones and gravel from such fields every year. Such soils are not as rich in moisture content as the soil of the riverbeds yet the humidity is retained by the soil till late summer due to the deposits and intermixture of humus content. These fields are usually not irrigated, being remote and placed in higher elevation from the streams of water flowing in the gorges down.

The third category of soils is found in the terraced hill tops which are slightly precipitous. These soils bear the features of the parent rock. Being at the top of the ridge, these are not intermixed with drift soils with the flow of water. The finest soil particles are swept away by heavy rush of water downward. The rocks and stones are washed well by the water. The gravels and rocks get naked. Such soils are containing stones and rock pieces. The humus content of such soil is also very negligible and these lack phosphorus content. In 1964 Indian Council of Agricultural Research reported the depth of forest soils in this region. It was found that generally the soil was 2 to 8 in. in depth and consisted 5.94 per cent coarse sand, 29.53 per cent fine sand, 33.15 per cent silt and 22.40 per cent clay. Moisture content of the soil was 2.86 per cent. It consisted 2.73 per cent organic carbon and 0.25 per cent organic nitrogen. The phosphorus content grew greater to the deeper depths. Nearly 78 per cent of the soil content was insoluble matter. Percentage of clay content increased with greater depth beyond 17 in. so also the silt content.

The crop sustaining capacity varies from place to place by the nature of the soil, moisture, exposure to sun, closeness to forest, general configuration and also by the nature of crop chosen for cultivation. Alluvial and semi-alluvial soils are better for raising crops.

The Himalayan region has experienced a vast change over the last few decades regarding the closeness of water table to the surface. The elimination of forest cover and blasting of rocks for road construction, etc., have led to sinking of the water table to still deeper layers. This have resulted in relatively greater dry soil status in upper elevations where the forest cover has been removed. The human habitations have also tended to shift to downward locations in valleys in recent generations. Rocky and hilly terrain of Kumaun and Garhwal leave only little possibility of installing pumpsets in large-scale, draw tubewells or extending long distance canals. Natural fountains which are met within short intervals constitute the main water source for a small-scale irrigation. The deepening water table has deserted many a natural fountains in hill areas. Irrigation by storage of waste-water of rivulets is possible in some areas but the device has not been exploited in adequate measure. The flow of water is reduced in summer and some of the water springs get dried up in May-June and water again appears in the rainy season. The low-lying areas fetch water from the rivulets, wherever possible. The river beds and valleys have highly fertile land and perennial irrigation. These are *talaon* or low lands locally called 'Sera'. In lands situated in higher locations, where the irrigational channels do not command a hold yet due to greater humus content of the soil, the moisture is retained by the soil. Such land is cultivated for single or double seasons towards raising crops. Lands closer to forest area present a higher moisture and humus content in the black soil. It grows both *rabi* and *kharif* crops with encouraging results. Such crops, as cultivated in these lands are largely rainfed. The land in the tops or close-by, are usually full of gravel and unyielding rocks. As the scorching heat of sun grows, the rocks retain heat and help in evaporating the moisture of the soil faster. With lesser humus, these soils lose humidity faster and get completely dry in summer. Even in the monsoon season these grow only coarse crops like Kulthi, and are kept fallow in the summer. If the fields are deep in soil layer and retain moisture inspite of exposure to sun, these can host good crops even in the *rabi* season. Agriculture in hills is stylish and interesting and makes the curious tourist observer wonder struck. Due to the precarious nature of the terrain, the average life of a hill-farmer is tedius, and full of deprivation and drudgery. It is more so for the women-folk who eke-out a living in niggardly nature.

Singh (1989) makes a sweeping remark about the soil composition of hill areas. "Soil in this region is not a significant thing. Mostly stony and immature types of soil is found here. It does not have any system nor it forms a compact block. It differs from valley to valley and slope to slope according to ecological conditions. On the foothills of mountains, deposits of gravel and coarse sand are found which are very poor as far as fertility is concerned" (Singh, A.P., 1989, 60-61). There is a system of soil empire spread over the rocks in hills which needs proper surveys and studies. Along the river beds where the breadth is adequate and slope is eliminated some narrow strips of alluvial soils are found everywhere in hills. Red loam soils are evinced in patches here and there in the valley areas. Most of the areas in the top elevations have glacial type of soil. If we analyse the soils by pedo-ecological zones, it is evident that above 3,000 m. sea level, glacial soils are commonly met with. Between 200 m. and 3,000 m. which makes the Alaknanda zone and parts of upper Bhagirathi, the soils are frost soils, brown in colour, deciduous brown to grey coniferous soils are common. The texture of the soils is good for paddy growth. Towards the lower tracts drained by Bhagirathi and Alaknanda between 1,000 and 2,000 m. from sea level, the soils are of brown-frost type. These thrive good crops in adequate soil depth. To the still lower parts, Siwalik and *dun* tracts, situated below 1,000 m. or so, the soils are largely alluvial and wherever these are cultivated aided by irrigation, these afford bountiful crops.

Geology and Minerals

The rocks and minerals in this area need a mention to introduce the reader with the economy and potentialities of development in the area. Development of tourism is a part of a wider development process. The mountainous terrain ranging from the head of plains to the northern peaks displays a great sequence of thickness of upper tertiary age aggregating 17,000 ft. in thickness and composed in ascending order of lower Siwalik or Nahan sandstone with subordinate shales after which come the middle Siwalik soft sand rocks and upper Siwalik conglomerates. "In the narrower part of this zone, mostly Nahan sandstone is found, the wider parts, on the other hand involve the younger rock stages and probably, given very frequent repetition by folding and reverse faulting in high measure. To the southern half the highlands are having slates and massive limestone. They are sometimes succeeded by bands of mesozonic limestone tol beds and numilitic shales" (Wadia, 1961, 82). Northern half is associated with schistose slates, quartz-schists and basic lava flows. The schistose slates pass into mica schists with the isolated patches of gneissose granite (Walton, 1910, 7-8). Ordovician and Silurian rocks are known to exist in Garhwal and

Kumaun south-east of Spiti (Krishnan, 1949, 221-40). Pankhanda has some dissimilarities from Spiti type rocks. In Pankhanda ladinic stage dwindles down to insignificance and upper trias is much less thick. In the whole of the central Himalayan gigantic south-facing escarpments including Simla in Himachal, Spiti; Kumaun and Garhwal the stratigraphy of northern and Tibetan zone of Himalayas is typically displayed. The rocks that occur towards shore region display primitive clay state which is oldest and constitutes the basis of this part of rocks of the district. Higher ascends have primitive transition and floetz limestone which occur in succession (McClelland, 1885, 35-36). Towards eastern part there are fine distinct tectonic units with separate stratigraphical formation. From Tanakpur to Jauljibi in Kumaun the stratigraphical pattern can be easily seen. The foothill is composed of the piedmont type of accumulations of gravels and constitutes the presently forested belt of Bhabar. Towards the Sukhidhang range the rock is built mainly of highly dipping lower Siwalik of Nahan series. These comprise sandstones and purple shales and silt stones (Valdiya, 1962, 14). McClelland classified the rocks of this area in four categories (McClelland, 1885, 34-37):

(a) Primitive rocks,
(b) Transition rocks,
(c) Floetz rocks, and
(d) Alluvial rocks.

Towards Kumaun the rocks mark a variation. In Almora, rocks are of Cambrian, Ordovician, Silurian, Devonian, carboniferous, Permian and somewhere of Vindhian types. Towards south of this tract, a strange admixture of different types; Vindhian, Pleistocene, tertiary, Eocene, Oligocene, Miocene, pleccent and Cambrian-Ordovician, Silurian, carboniferous and Permian type. To Tehri side it is again Vindhian, Pleistocene and Cambrian type. In most parts of Garhwal the same formation is met with. Towards Dehradun the features are that of Nainital type (Government of India, 1965, *Regions, Resources and Development*, 169).

The mineral wealth of a region is also a part of the overall geological formation. The development potential depends much on the availability of minerals and their economic viability. The region of Garkhum has been known for mineral deposits. In fact some mineral-based industries flourished in the past in the region basing on the local mineral sypply. Scale of extraction in the past has, of course, been meagre. Walton (Walton, 1910, 5-8) had reported that in Gorkha regime Kumaun and Garhwal had an annual income of Rs.50,000 from mineral extraction. Several old copper sites in Garhwal district including those in Pokheri-Chamethi, Mohankhal and Dhanpur Dobri areas were explored recently and those in Dobri were proved promising (Rao, 1958, 4). Even during British period investigations had been carried out. Among the known mineral deposits of the area are magnesite, arsenic, lignite, sulphur, soapstone, quartzs, schists, copper ore, iron ore, gold, calcite, marble, galena, and mica. These deposits need further detailing and scaling for exploitation viability. Even in early decades of 19th century Captain Herbert (1826), Captain Drumand (1838), Rockendorf (1845) and European syndicate (1909) had worked in this direction. District Nainital, Tehri and Pithoragarh have minerals of a larger commercial scale awaiting exploration. Dolomite, lead, gypsum and slate are evinced in Tehri. In other parts of Garhwal, gypsum, treatile, limestone, asbestos, copper, dolomite, and graphite are found. Talc deposits have been traced in large measure. Sulphur and pyrite deposits of Garhwal are ascertained. Manganese (Mn) and magnesite exploration has attained advanced stage. In Mahankhal magnesite chlorite schists suggest a high quality ore but in a limited measure. In Tehri district, Bhagirathi basin and Dhanpur in Garhwal, Pokhri Chhammethi, Mahankhal and Dobri areas have assured good results for further examination. In Almora, Phalanti hill range near Dhirauli at the bank of Saryu, Thela Patan village near Bageshwar and Tamakhani and Dhungi Dhank forest range have been investigated for copper, and stray samples have proved good results to suggest deeper investigations ahead. Deposits of limestone and gypsum in Kumaun-Garhwal region are well-established which suggest potentialities of portland cement industry, soda ash, calcium cynamide nitroleum, etc. Horsi, Agarkhal, Nagini, Narendranagar are found rich in limestone. Nilkanth, Pundarsu, Toli, Basi villages closer to Rishikesh have yielded samples of high silica content. Dehydrated silicate of magnesium or soapstone are found in some places of

Almora (Jakhera close to Baijnath). Industrial activity making electronic equipment, crayons, paper, rubber, pottery, roofing, ceramic tiles, saphalt tiles, paints, cosmetics, insecticides and chemicals can emerge on this basement. Dehradun area offers good deposits of gypsum. Deposits near Manjhara (Sahastradhara) and deposits of Saklana Patti are workable and large (Rao, 1958, 9-10). Deposits of Nangargaon, Sera village, area near Lakshmanjhula, in Garhwal, and Dhapila in Nainital are in large quantity as well as economically viable. Asbestos is also found in Garhwal and Almora. Near Nandprayag in Garhwal, good deposits of sulphur have been located. Similarly Gohantal area has the occurrence of pyrites in limestone. Overall, the mineral wealth hidden below the surface needs adequate scaling and economic evaluation.

Impact of Topography in Socio-Cultural Pattern and Economic Setting

Geographic setting is the mother of human habits, and attitudes. Any attempt at studying the problems encountered by man in his bid for betterment quite naturally calls for a cursory look into the geographical setting of the habitat. Great geographers like Ellen C. Sample (Sample, 1932, 2) very aptly remarked, "Man can no more be scientifically studied apart from the ground which he tills or the land over which he travels". The economic significance of different forms of earth's surface lies in so far they determine human habitation, occupations and lines of movement. Plains and fertile valleys weave a suitable set of physical conditions for an easy communication, human settlement and the best of agricultural and industrial activity. Though natural facts alone are not the sole determinants yet the role of physical frontiers of agriculture like temperature, seasons, heat and the frost, moisture, rainfall, humidity and evaporation, topography, landforms, configuration, degree and duration of slope roughness and smoothness of land, physical, chemical and bacteriological characteristics of soil and such other natural set of factors woven around man goes a long way to suggest the pattern of economic life. Tourism is by no means an exceptional occupation which could evade the impact of topography. The truth is that topography has an important role in suggesting the game and romance of the tourists.

It is a fact that genius of humanity adopts itself with the rare versatility to the most dissimilar facts and even the most adverse conditions are adjusted with. But the topographical features bear a stamp on the behavioural characteristics of inhabitants. In region, this human life is a continuous struggle against the odds of nature. Somewhere the nature yields to human effort as is evinced in tedius conditions of hill agriculture, elsewhere man adjusts his taste, fashions, habits, and tradition to the given conditions of nature. The practice of life evolves the most appropriate mode of occupation and living in all geographic conditions. The terms and line of human compromise with a given geographic state weaves a pattern of human civilization appropriate to the conditions while the process keeps on refining itself in new situations internal and external (Pande, 1968, 27-28).

Topography suggests the availability of land resource which in turn determines the suitability of an area to support man with crops. As is generally evinced in slopes the soils are shallow and unworthy. This state imposes a great limitation on the economic activity insofar farming is concerned. Man seeks evasions and even in the state of light rainfall and abundant grass he chooses for obvious opportunity for nomadic career associated with flocks and herds as evinced in northern Himalayas (Pant, 1935, 1-10). Human zeal for finding new vistas is unending. He seeks to efface the impact of natural conditions and vagaries of climate on human life. This generates a special quality in man to struggle against nature and given course of conditions (Mukherjee, 1938, 36). Marwaris and Gujaratis are the rarest risk takers and Himalayans are the sturdy gallant population. Both seek fortunes outside their homeland. Those who fail to migrate have to work with unyielding soil at subsistence level without any possibilities of marginal marketable surplus (Pande, 1968, 29). Eminent geographers like Dubey (Dubey, 1963, 16-17) opined, "...Success of tillage may require more toil in an uneven topography as compared to the levelled land. Nature denies agricultural prosperity in a rugged mountainous region while the only low lands which man shuns are those blighted with hostile climates, poor drainage, unproductive soils, remoteness or inaccessibility". Regions of undulating topography are conspicuous by their economic backwardness and cultural isolation. Such areas everywhere are largely inhabited by the tribal communities who take pride in avoiding competition. Such areas are devoted to lumbering and herding unless accessible deposits of minerals and hydel power potentialities provide them with adequate mining and manufacturing investments. Forestry, for long, has provided these areas with manageable meagre living. Until the recent transport revolution and emergence of roads, the mountainous tracts with their rugged relief features faced very unsurmountable costs of ecnomic operations. Dubey states that "mountains and uneven topography as a solid barrier to transportation, pose a formidable obstruction to any commercial intercourse" (Dubey, 1963, 17). Ellen Churchill Sample felt, "These natural blockades (mountains) conspire to foster the isolation which in turn leads to undue satisfaction with mediocre and limited achievements on the part of the man" (Sample, 1932, 569-71). Srivastava (Srivastava, 1951, 2) feels that the role of uneven topography is as negative as a deterrant climate which explains the backwardness of Tharu in Sitarganj and Khatima. This suggests the role of physical environment in economic life. A very analytical account of how topography influence human life is evinced in Gregor's (Gregor, 1963, 79-101) *Environment and Economic Life*. This Himalayan tract has a heterogeneous topography. To the north the tract has a wrinkle topograpy. Then follows the Bhabar region heading towards south. It is a small belt at the foothills and is characterised by moderate slopes. Crossing the Bhabar belt of around 20-30 kms. breadth, the tarai belt starts where the slope diminishes considerably. It is around 8 ft. per kilometre. After the slope is eliminated, the wider Indo-Gangetic plains start. The four types of topography, thus, are as under:

(a) Mountainous;
(b) Bhabar tract;
(c) Tarai; and
(d) Wider plains.

The mountainous region has a long geological history. It is believed that the mountainous region of Himalaya of which Kumaun-Garhwal (Garkhum) is a part, was the site of shallow

Tethys sea. Later in the tertiary era of geological past, powerful compressive forces folded and thrust marine deposits which rose out of the waters in gigantic earth waves, and under the erosion of water and ice, became a land of broken and irregular mountain masses. The crustal movements of this type have resulted in development of a series of longitudinal valleys. In the post-tertiary period in geological history, further changes raised the central portion of these ranges together with foothills into a vast mountain system. The features of surface in this mountain area are that the mountains are high while valleys are also equally deep. The nature of rocks also marks frequent spatial variation and the typical feature is that the mountains have preponderance of length over breadth. Towards the north the hills are well-clad in forests till the snow line. Facing southward from the hills one crosses over the rapid transitions through curious phenomena in Bhabar and Tarai and then to the wider alluvial plains.

The Bhabar region which is between 28° 56' 46" and 29° 35' 22" north latitudes; and between 78° 57' 40" and 80° 01' 8" east longitudes has some typical features which differentiate it from rest of the types. It is known for its thin covering of the alluvial soil on the dry bed of boulders where every drop of rain or river water sinks rapidly to the deepest layer of boulders. This region strips along foothills throughout. Its formation varies at different directions from 8 to 20 kms. across the base of mountains where torrents, streams and rainwater carried through rivulets in its downward dash through the slopes have accumulated a wide bank of coarse diluvial deposits (Atkinson, 1882, 117). This region has a southward slope of about 15-45 ft. per kilometre. The phenomena of formation of Bhabar tract is very interesting for the tourists who are really so curious about the typical area. In fact, rivers bring with them boulders, gravel, and silt and as the slope is moderated, heavy matter starts stationing. The heavy matter settles at the lowest layer and on that layer, another layer of silt gets settled. The process has continued for centuries past. The top layer is of the fine silt, therefore, the top part of the soil is rather porous, arid and waterless. All water that drops on the top gets sunk deepest to the down layer of heavier boulders. The upper deluvial soil supports a luxuriant and tropical vegetation particularly, the trees with deep roots. In between the deep layer boulders water gets accumulated and support of the moisture keeps the trees alive. The slope makes the water to flow down to Tarai underground. During the odd summer the trees here receive moisture from vapour-laden air. Tropical heat in combination with considerable rain weaves good climate for vegetation. Bhabar area is known for its dry climate.

Descending still further southward across the Bhabar region, we come across a broad belt of jungle grass and swamps. The belt has a breadth of around 15 kms. and it runs parallel to the foot of outer Himalayan region. The notable feature of the table land in this area is that it marks difference in the slope of its bed. The slope cannot be marked so clearly while moving north to south and one feels that the slope in the surface is smoothed and reduced. The slope gets reduced not abruptly but at a very gradual pace. In this long descent of 15-22 kms. all along in Bhabar areas the slope is reduced from 44.8 ft. per kilometre at immediate foothills to nearly 15 ft. per kilometre at the southern ends of Tarai (Atkinson, 1882, 97). The slope dwindles further to 8 ft. per kilometre or less, as we proceed ahead towards the Rohilkhand region from Bhabar area across the Tarai. At such a smooth slope of around 5 ft. per kilometre, the hidden water in the deeper earth layers, in between the boulders below the surface in the Bhabar tract, percolates. Streams which dive deep in Bhabar, ooz and flow again on the surface or it forms stagnant pools. Marshes and ferns, sluggish streams and water logged, chocked morasses are very frequently met with in Tarai. Water table is very close. A little digging of the surface makes the moisture in the soil evident. Batten in his report on Tarai observed, "water in Tarai is so near the surface that whenever a buffalo rolls in the mud or a stick is pushed into the soil or bulls fight, a spring gushes out" (Batten, 1871, 146). The state has changes little bit now due to removal of forests and wild grasses. Most of the region has now been branded with intensive tillage and cultivation of commercial crops. The belt has a narrow breadth of 20 kms. and a length of nearly 137 kms. running between the forest belt of Bhabar and plains. The total area of Tarai tract may be around 1,380 sq. kms. and is situated within 28° 43' and 29° 26' north latitudes and 78° 53' and 80° east longitudes. The tract has a tropical climate. Since "... the streams carry away only a portion of superfluous moisture and they run only sluggishly in the tortuous channels doubling back constantly in their course. The soil here consists of moist alluvial matter without a sign of rock either in fragments or in site" (Atkinson, 1882, 83).

Tarai presents a special feature with regard to its moist atmosphere. "At close to night the moist raised from saturated ground by the fierce heat of sun is seen like a pullover the landscape" (Batten, 1871, 146). The natural impact of these physical conditions is that the region is highly malarious and unhealthy for human habitation but is "exceptionally suitable for agricultural purposes specially for crops requiring greater humidity" (Pande, 1968, 33). Anti-malaria drive in the '50s and '60s in this tract has greatly reduced the toll on human life due to malaria as compared to the state of affairs at the advent of Independence. Area Development Committee (1947) had noted, "Life in Tarai is but a continual struggle for existence against the depredation of wild animals luxuriant vegetation, depressing climate, a high death rate and bad communication..." (Government of UP, Report, Tarai and Bhabar Development Committee, 1947, 86). Since Independence much has been done to eliminate the vagaries of climate and the hazardous living conditions in this area. Bazpur, Gadarpur, Khatima, Sitarganj, Nagina, Dhampur and the areas in the periphery of Garhwal, Bhabar had hostile climate few decades ago. Population has tended to multiply fast and modern cultivation methods have come up in this area. Sarda river in the east to Kashipur in the west, Tarai spreads its green carpet. Parganas of Bazpur, Gadarpur, Rudrapur, Kilpuri, Nanakmatta, and Baheri are the areas of dense population now. Tourists enjoy their trips to the lush green agricultural farms in Tarai.

Kashipur presents a slightly different climate as compared to Tarai and Bhabar areas. This subdivision resembles the plains of Rohilkhand in topographical description. To the north it is more similar to Tarai while to the south it changes its character gradually as the soil loses its marshy features and slightly different type of vegetation emerges. It is not as malarious and damp as Tarai but it holds this characteristic more than the plains of Rohilkhand.

The topographical particulars can be marked in the fact that the mountainous terrain, as viewed from south, displays a tendency to ascend facing north. The table land rises gradually upward but only in a conspicuous manner. Ridges at the foothills are higher (5,000'-7,000') but later to the north elevation of mountains is slightly reduced to the site of upper-most elevations in extreme north connecting the table land which links Tibet. The mountain system extending throughout is drawn from the southern extremity of snow-clad spurs of varying heights in every direction. The peaks are separated by depressions in between lower depressions have been lent to agriculture wherever the slope is moderate and soil is worth that. The extremes are covered with wild forest or with snow. The gaps in between the forests and agriculture are seen as eroded naked hills due to land slips occurring very off and on, in recent decades. The topographical diversities are to the disadvantage of the local inhabitants but afford the tourists a good feast of variety and enjoyable landscape. The curiosity regarding this heterogeneous topography and variety of vegetation attracts the tourists to this part of Uttaranchal from all over the globe.

Nature has adorned the Uttaranchal state with several beautiful water bodies like lakes, rivers and waterfalls. It has carried a high repute for hypnotic splendour and tourist attractions. Entire Garhwal division is beautiful due to its forests, hilly ranges and fast-flowing rivers. It is the abode of peace and aesthetic values. Chhakhata pargana of Nainital district is named as 'West

TABLE 2.4: Length, Breadth and Depth of Chosen Lakes in Kumaun Region

Lakes	Height (ft.)	Greatest length (ft.)	Greatest breadth (ft.)	Greatest depth (ft.)	Area (sq. ft.)
1. Nainital	6,407	4,733	1,518	93	51,49,000
2. Bhimtal	4,500	5,580	1,490	87	49,00,000
3. Naukuchiatal	4,000	3,120	2,270	132	48,49,500
4. Malwatal	3,400	4,480	1,833	127	49,09,600

Gazetteer of Himalayan Distt. of NWP, 1882, Vol. I, p. 89.

TABLE 2.5: Geographical Area and Population Pattern in Uttaranchal Himalaya

District	Geogl. area (km.²) 2001	Population				
		1961	1971	1981	1991	2001**
1. Nainital	3,422	5,74,320	7,90,080	11,36,523	15,40,174	7,62,912
2. Udham Singh Nagar	3,055	–	–	–	–	12,34,548
3. Almora	3,689	5,52,843	6,48,622	7,57,373	8,36,617	6,30,446
4. Bageshwar	1,696	–	–	–	–	2,49,453
5. Pithoragarh	7,169	3,44,143	4,15,163	4,89,267	5,66,408	4,62,149
6. Champawat	2,004	–	–	–	–	2,24,461
Kumaun division	21,035	14,71,306	18,53,865	23,83,163	29,43,199	35,63,969
7. Tehri	4,421	3,47,736	3,97,385	4,97,710	5,80,153	6,04,608
8. Uttarkashi	8,016	1,22,836	1,47,805	1,90,948	2,39,709	2,94,179
9. Chamoli	9,125	2,53,137	2,92,571	3,64,346	4,54,871	3,69,198
10. Pauri	5,440	4,82,327	5,53,028	6,37,877	6,82,535	6,96,851
11. Rudraprayag	–	–	–	–	–	2,77,461
12. Dehradun	3,088	4,29,014	5,77,306	7,61,668	10,25,679	12,79,083
Garhwal division	30,090	16,35,050	19,68,095	24,52,549	29,82,947	34,71,380
13. Haridwar	2,360	–	–	–	11,24,488	14,44,213
Uttaranchal	53,485	31,06,356*	38,21,960*	48,35,712*	70,50,634	84,79,562

*Excluded Haridwar district.

**2001 – Provisional data.

Notes: 1. District Udham Singh Nagar included under old Nainital district, Bageshwar included under old Almora district, Champawat included under old Pithoragarh and Nainital districts and Rudraprayag included under old Pauri and Chamoli districts.

2. Formerly Haridwar district was a part of old Saharanpur district of UP.

3. Rudraprayag town was a part of Pauri district in the recent past but a greater part of newly formed Rudraprayag district lies in old Chamoli district.

Source: Census Handbooks of respective years.

Moreland of Kumaun'. Grandeur of lakes, peaks, bracing climate, smoothing green quilt and scenic lure is of singular interest to tourists in Garhkum. Lakes offer golden avenues for fish culture. Chhakhata pargana is hosting a number of important lakes, the details of which may be seen in Table 2.4

The view of Sattal lakes is really so captivating that tourists get spell bound by the hypnotic beauty of nature all around. The area is close to Bhimtal lake.

TABLE 2.6: Decadel Growth of Population in Uttaranchal Himalaya

District	Decadel growth (in per cent)				
	1901-11	1961-71	1971-81	1981-91	1991-2001*
1. Nainital	–0.15	32.14	38.26	29.87	32.88
2. Udham Singh Nagar	–0.13	–41.30	–41.16	–44.35	27.79
3. Almora	15.88	15.14	15.80	9.43	3.14
4. Bageshwar	15.88	–12.98	–15.80	9.43	3.14
5. Pithoragarh	15.88	12.98	16.38	14.11	10.92
6. Champawat	13.23	–51.39	–25.34	–36.38	17.56
7. Tehri	11.88	14.20	25.25	16.60	16.15
8. Uttarkashi	11.88	20.33	29.19	25.50	22.72
9. Chamoli	11.69	15.58	28.83	21.97	13.51
10. Pauri	11.96	14.66	15.34	9.05	3.87
11. Rudraprayag	11.74	12.71	24.68	17.40	13.44
12. Dehradun	15.25	34.57	31.93	34.66	24.71
13. Haridwar	–5.85	32.93	32.72	28.44	26.30
Uttranchal	13.26	24.44	27.45	24.23	19.20

* – Provisional data.

Himalayan Habitat: The Cultural Setting

Human Resource Development

The population of this identified Himalayan region has marked a tremendous growth over the years. Inspite of that growth the average density per square kilometre in this area is lower in the state. The district-wise growth figures indicate a rising trend over the decades at varying rates because population from the upper ridges is migrating to lower parts of Himalaya and its foothills, besides the large scale immigration occurring in southern part (Tables 2.5 and 2.6).

(a) *Socially Lagging Social Groups (Scheduled Castes and Scheduled Tribes)*

The priority based population of Scheduled Castes in the Uttaranchal Himalaya, is highest in Uttarkashi and lowest in Pauri-Garhwal as percentage of total population. It may be remembered that their proportion in former Uttar Pradesh was 21.16 per cent while it accounts for 17.48 per cent for Uttaranchal state as per 1991 census. The tribals, constitute hardly 0.21 per cent in total population of Uttar Pradesh. In the Uttaranchal Himalaya the precentage is 3.76. If we subtract the population of tribes based in Tarai areas, then it is 3.60 per cent. The population percentage in the districts may be noted from Tables 2.7 and 2.8.

The figures depicted in Table 2.5 speak of the fact that Uttaranchal Himalaya has considerably lesser proportion of the lower

TABLE 2.7: District-wise Percentage Share of Scheduled Caste and Scheduled Tribe Population (1981) and Density of Population in Uttaranchal Himalaya, 1991 and 2001

District	Scheduled Caste			Scheduled Tribe			Density of population	
	Rural	Urban	Total	Rural	Urban	Total	1991	2001*
Nainital	18.09	12.21	16.47	8.88	0.26	6.51	149	198
Udham Singh Nagar	–	–	–	–	–	–	332	424
Almora	21.01	13.84	20.56	0.26	0.58	0.28	198	205
Bageshwar	–	–	–	–	–	–	99	108
Pithoragarh	19.72	14.81	19.45	3.29	7.83	3.54	59	65
Champawat	–	–	–	–	–	–	107	126
Tehri-Garhwal	12.93	8.91	12.88	0.01	0.03	0.01	128	148
Uttarkashi	22.71	11.46	21.93	0.99	0.39	0.95	30	37
Chamoli	17.31	16.67	17.26	1.96	8.85	2.52	43	48
Rudraprayag	–	–	–	–	–	–	106	120
Pauri-Garhwal	11.75	11.65	11.72	0.17	0.19	0.17	124	129
Dehradun	12.68	11.15	11.93	19.30	0.24	9.99	332	414
Haridwar	–	–	–	–	–	–	485	612
Uttaranchal	16.87	11.95	15.97	4.42	0.78	3.76	133	159
UP	23.09	12.33	21.16	0.24	0.05	0.21	–	–

* – Provisional Data.

TABLE 2.8 : Scheduled Caste and Scheduled Tribe Population in Uttaranchal, 1991

District	SC population		ST population	
	No.	Per cent	No.	Per cent
1. Nainital	2,43,314	15.80	90,020	5.84
2. Udham Singh Nagar	–	–	–	–
3. Almora	1,84,237	22.02	2,739	0.33
4. Bageshwar	–	–	–	–
5. Pithoragarh	1,15,832	20.45	18,313	3.23
6. Champawat	–	–	–	–
7. Tehri	82,384	14.20	615	0.11
8. Uttarkashi	54,594	22.78	2,300	0.96
9. Chamoli	79,572	17.49	10,273	2.26
10. Pauri	92,261	13.52	1,502	0.22
11. Rudraprayag	–	–	–	–
12. Dehradun	1,37,464	13.40	84,076	0.08
13. Haridwar	2,42,658	21.58	2,026	0.18
Uttaranchal	12,32,316	17.48	2,11,864	3.00

Source : Distt. Census Handbook, 1991

classes as compared to the UP state while the tribal population in these tracts is greater than the UP state's average.

(b) *Urban Population*

The urbanisation in the region is recent origin in modern context. Though historically the region had several urban centres yet now those towns are non-existent or the names have changed. The British forces developed some areas as cantonments, some were the capitals of local ancient kingdoms, and the rest are the transport centres, trading areas or tourist places. Some towns have developed as district headquarters of administration and centres of the social services like education, health and justice. The region has small size of towns and these usually function as transit centres for rural exports and rural imports from other regions. Table 2.9 shows the urban and rural population in districts of Uttaranchal Himalaya.

TABLE 2.9: Distribution of Urban and Rural Population in Uttaranchal Himalaya

District	Rural population		Urban population	
	1981	1991	1981	1991
1. Nainital	8,24,080	10,37,210	3,12,443	5,02,964
2. Udham Singh Nagar	–	–	–	–
3. Almora	7,09,777	7,83,110	47,596	53,507
4. Bageshwar	–	–	–	–
5. Pithoragarh	4,62,248	5,24,295	27,019	42,113
6. Champawat	–	–	–	–
7. Tehri	4,77,164	5,47,258	20,546	32,895
8. Uttarkashi	1,77,676	2,22,448	13,272	17,261
9. Chamoli	3,35,172	4,14,331	29,174	40,540
10. Pauri	5,75,208	6,01,353	62,669	81,182
11. Rudraprayag	–	–	–	–
12. Dehradun	3,89,527	5,10,199	3,72,141	5,15,480
13. Haridwar	–	7,76,346	–	3,48,142
Uttaranchal	–	54,16,550	–	16,34,084

Source: District Census Handbooks of the respective years.

The urban population in the region is only little and less than the percentage of urbanites in Uttaranchal. The townships are too small and unviable for municipal management and financial resources. The towns are clean, charming and well-situtated to form an attraction for the tourists. The town-wise population figures in the urban sector of Uttaranchal Himalaya may be studied at length from Table 2.10.

Cultural Environment

Prof. Kassas of Cairo University explained economic development by the changes in the following types of environments:

$$G = f(BSTC)$$

where, G stands for Growth, B stands for Biosphere, S stands for Sociophere, T stands for Technosphere and C stands for

Capitosphere. It is now commonly agreed that economic change is a by-product of an overall socio-cultural change, technological growth and network of the capital structure. Development of tourism as an industry is an economic enterprise but it entails changes in social and cultural environment suitable to the growth of tourism industry. Certain level of infrastructure is also necessary for promoting tourism. The cultural environment covers the biosphere and socio-sphere together. It embraces wide issues of human habitations, their infrastructure and amenities of living, the pattern of settlements, size, nature and growth trends of population, the occupational pattern and aspiration levels. The adaptive temperament, response pattern, and psycho-pathology of inhabitants have a bearing on the levels of growth in each sphere of life.

The nature of the economy, society and culture of the Himalayan region can be diagnosed by the identification of the nature of the habitat and size of the settlements besides the other parameters. Economically and culturally the region's lag may be measured by the remoteness from the norms like national average as applied by B.D. Pande Commission on backward areas. Venkatachelam Committee (1960) also treated these areas as backward by national norms as the region stood 20 per cent below national norms and 10 per cent below the state norms. The other criteria usually accepted are as below:

(i) A high ratio of agricultural population;
(ii) Absence of industry;
(iii) Low per capita gross value of output;
(iv) Under-utilised natural resources;
(v) Low urban population;
(vi) Low availability of roads, and vehicles;
(vii) Low consumption of energy per capita;
(viii) Low per capita income;
(ix) High birth and death rates;
(x) Greater incidence of disguised unemployment;
(xi) Low literacy, education and training.

The region distinguishes itself from the geographical tracts of Uttar Pradesh, insofar as the physical constraints on the size of

TABLE 2.10: Urban Population

District/Urban agglomeration	Area (in sq. km.)	Population		
		Person	Male	Female
(1)	(2)	(3)	(4)	(5)
Uttarkashi	17.16	17,261	10,255	7,006
Uttarkashi (MB)	12.02	13,919	8,288	5,631
Barkot (TA)	5	3,214	1,846	1,368
Gangotri (NA)	0.14	128	121	7
Tehri Garhwal	55.91	32,895	21,045	11,850
Tehri (MB)	35.05	20,226	13,127	7,099
Narendra Nager (MB)	10.36	4,928	3,130	1,798
Muni-ki-Reti (NA)	2.82	4,519	2,926	1,593
Dev Prayag (NA)	5.18	2,164	1,189	975
Kirti Nagar (NA)	2.5	1,058	673	385
Dehradun	198.37	5,15,480	2,82,320	2,33,160
Harbertpur (TA)	7.33	8,571	4,494	4,077
Doiwala (TA)	1.91	7,476	4,006	3,470
Vikas Nager (MB)	1.4	10,991	5,854	5,137
Dak Patthar (CT)	1.25	10,271	5,629	4,642
Chakrata Cantt. (CB)	15.98	4,670	3,539	1,131
Raiwala (CT)	4.73	4,115	2,214	1,901
Rishikesh (MB)	12.12	71,704	39,411	32,293
(a) Rishikesh (MB)	2.59	44,487	24,960	19,527
(b) Virbhadra (NA)	1.78	15,982	8,477	7,505
(c) Rishikesh (CT)	7.75	11,235	5,974	5,261
Massoorie (UA)	67.65	29,629	17,619	12,010
(a) Massoorie (MB)	64.75	26,722	15,942	10,780
(b) Landour Cantt. (CB)	2.9	2,907	1,677	1,230
Dehradun (UA)	86	3,68,053	1,19,554	1,68,499
(a) Dehradun (MB)	35.17	2,70,159	1,43,805	1,26,354
(b) FRI & College Area (CT)	4.69	4,716	2,634	2,082
(c) Adhoiwala (CT)	1.5	13,378	7,195	6,183
(d) Dehradun Cantt. (CB)	20.98	43,031	25,014	18,017
(e) Clement Town Cantt. (CB)	7.03	18,237	11,095	7,142
Rajpur (CT)	14.59	18,532	9,811	8,721
Pauri-Garhwal	67.75	81,182	47,618	33,564
Kotdwar (MB)	2.59	21,378	11,425	9,953
Pauri (CT)	41.44	20,397	11,560	8,837
Kalagarh (CT)	5.98	10,527	5,649	4,878
Sri Nagar (MB)	7.77	18,791	12,913	5,878
Lansdowne (Cantt.)	6.09	7,106	4,415	2,691

in Uttaranchal, 1991

Scheduled Caste	Scheduled Tribe	No. of occupied residential houses	No. of house-holds	Literates	
				Male	Female
(6)	(7)	(8)	(9)	(10)	(11)
2,239	60	4,064	4,145	7,901	3,884
1,777	51	3,234	3,310	6,424	3,321
457	8	739	742	1,360	559
5	1	91	93	117	4
3,371	67	7,920	8,350	15,830	6,345
1,681	52	5,245	5,354	9,940	3,737
888	4	1,048	1,088	2,398	1,038
364		–850	1,126	2,122	787
299	11	496	501	851	538
139		–281	281	519	245
60,177	3,071	1,00,970	1,02,024	2,12,157	1,45,263
1,114	41	1,519	1,522	2,776	1,781
560	23	1,360	1,367	2,888	1,986
1,490	210	1,909	1,924	3,998	2,920
1,188	148	2,368	2,402	4,443	3,020
626	550	821	821	3,106	630
506	331	876	882	1,449	851
7,295	230	14,930	15,039	28,969	19,073
4,005	81	9,226	9,335	17,653	10,983
2,074	86	3,255	3,255	6,987	5,295
1,216	63	2,449	2,449	4,329	2,795
4,456	240	5,998	5,998	13,467	7,182
3,955	130	5,232	5,232	12,294	6,530
501	110	766	766	1,173	652
42,942	1,298	71,189	72,069	1,51,061	1,07,820
31,231	785	52,726	53,438	1,07,601	82,181
816	94	1,043	1,043	2,079	1,334
2,085	116	2,720	2,720	4,771	3,245
4,456	158	7,887	8,037	20,222	11,494
1,908	28	3,054	3,054	8,381	3,614
2,446	117	3,763	3,763	8,007	5,952
8,621	144	16,105	16,433	32,884	20,091
1,236	7	4,050	4,065	7,846	5,657
2,280	38	4,607	4,618	9,034	5,610
1,844	–	2,266	2,266	4,028	2,595
1,866	66	3,038	3,340	6,859	3,602
860	19	1,461	1,461	3,762	1,758

(*Contd.*)

(1)	(2)	(3)	(4)	(5)
Dogadda (MB)	2.59	2,444	1,349	1,095
Bah Bazar (CT)	1.29	539	307	232
Almora	32.75	53,507	30,826	22,681
Ranikhet Cantt.	21.75	16,874	10,319	6,555
Dwarahat (NA)	2.97	2,810	1,538	1,272
Almora (UA)	8.03	28,051	15,784	12,267
(a) Almora (MB)	7.36	26,001	14,228	11,773
(b) Almora (Cantt.)	0.67	2,050	1,556	494
Nainital	38.08	2,21,940	1,21,803	1,00,137
Ramnagar (MB)	2.46	37,281	19,911	17,370
Bhowali (MB)	1.32	4,364	2,396	1,968
Lalkuan (TA)	4.25	5,310	3,038	2,272
Kaladhungi (TA)	1.16	4,663	2,607	2,056
Bhimtal (TA)	3.95	4,225	2,241	1,984
Nainital (UA)	14.32	30,951	17,530	13,421
(a) Nainital (MB)	11.73	29,837	16,826	13,011
(b) Nainital (Cantt.)	2.59	1,114	704	410
Haldwani-cum-Kathgodam	10.62	1,04,195	56,550	47,645
Haridwar	64.58	3,48,142	18,90,080	1,59,062
Manglaur (MB)	1.32	34,161	18,208	15,953
Laksar (TA)	3.3	15,622	8,620	7,002
Landhaura (TA)	0.75	12,195	6,794	5,401
Jhabera (TA)	0.09	7,633	4,054	3,579
Roorkee (UA)	17.04	91,139	49,570	41,569
(a) Roorkee (MB)	7.74	80,262	42,846	37,416
(b) Roorkee Cantt.	9.3	10,877	6,724	4,153
Haridwar (UA)	42.08	1,87,392	1,01,834	85,558
(a) Haridwar (MB)	15.07	1,49,011	81,412	67,599
(i) Haridwar (MB)	11.91	1,47,305	80,206	67,099
(ii) Gurukul Kangri (OG)	1.09	1,454	983	471
(iii) Jwalapur Mahavidyalaya (OG)	2.07	252	223	29
(b) BHEL Ltd. Ranipur (NA)	26.94	38,381	20,422	17,959
Udham Singh Nagar (MB)	84.9	2,92,293	1,36,116	1,05,760
Kashipur (MB)	5.46	69,870	37,447	32,429
Rudrapur (MB)	12.43	61,280	10,819	38
Jaspur (MB)	4	30,831	16,343	14,488
Kichha (MB)	4.02	21,131	11,395	9,736
Bazpur (MB)	2.62	16,857	9,403	7,454
Sitarganj (MB)	2	16,704	8,960	7,744
Nagla (CT)	28	22,072	12,787	9,285
Khatima (MB)	8.4	11,245	6,121	5,124
Gaderpur (MB)	3.4	9,487	5,077	4,410
Shaktigarh (MB)	1.8	3,845	2,068	1,777

(6)	(7)	(8)	(9)	(10)	(11)
470	14	548	548	1,101	714
65	–	135	254	254	155
3,217	45	10,695	11,665	22,383	15,451
2,610	15	3,397	3,534	8,496	4,191
607	30	664	670	1,237	777
4,047	425	5,618	6,140	12,650	8,975
3,602	272	5,373	5,820	11,400	689
445	153	245	320	1,250	286
30,157	735	34,090	43,091	81,872	54,208
3,377	2	6,227	6,612	11,650	7,557
1,025	27	836	995	1,834	1,330
634	6	1,106	1,180	1,843	874
442	5	904	904	1,458	781
799	6	782	835	1,634	1,306
6,974	155	4,480	6,976	14,006	9,195
6,803	151	4,331	6,775	13,446	8,871
171	4	149	201	560	324
9,932	379	15,275	18,613	35,433	23,970
37,272	22	63,694	63,711	1,24,918	82,914
797	–	5,069	5,069	5,395	2,720
3,000	–	2,979	2,982	5,536	3,072
1,887	–	1,946	1,960	2,079	792
883	–	1,035	1,035	1,979	1,012
8,529	4	16,235	16,235	37,697	25,237
7,587	1	14,334	14,334	32,190	22,691
942	3	1,901	1,901	5,507	2,546
22,176	18	36,430	36,430	72,232	50,081
17,622	9	28,341	28,341	54,943	37,041
17,469	9	28,070	28,070	53,883	36,722
150	–	238	238	850	295
3	–	33	33	210	24
4,554	9	8,089	8,089	17,289	13,040
52,721	29,873	48,408	51,040	88,453	52,462
2,715	5	10,230	11,225	24,206	16,161
32,655	28,625	11,947	12,352	16,448	10,166
1,934	–	4,376	4,521	8,513	4,548
3,279	12	3,321	3,478	5,682	3,539
2,043	2	2,929	3,014	5,431	3,339
1,511	992	2,903	3,071	4,764	2,884
2,821	18	4,411	4,609	8,758	4,550
883	83	1,830	1,931	3,802	2,310
624	132	1,538	1,629	2,945	1,819
123	–	693	700	1,177	601

(Contd.)

(1)	(2)	(3)	(4)	(5)
Sultanpur (TA)	2	5,866	3,169	2,697
Mahuakhera Ganj (TA)	0.27	6,614	3,552	3,062
Kelakhera (TA)	4	5,025	2,731	2,294
Dineshpur (TA)	4.5	6,099	3,161	2,938
Mahuadabra Haripura (TA)	2	5,367	3,083	2,284
Champawat	11.26	26,098	14,460	11,638
Lohaghat (NA)	4.5	3,891	2,252	1,639
Champawat (TA)	5	2,525	1,410	1,115
Tanakpur (MB)	1.01	13,110	7,259	5,851
Banbassa (CT)	0.75	6,572	3,539	3,033
Chamoli	73.13	38,998	23,955	15,043
Chamoli Gopeshwar (MB)	15.02	15,378	9,207	6,171
Joshjmath (MB)	11.19	11,488	7,648	3,840
Karnaprayag (NA)	25	5,169	2,943	2,226
Gauchar (TA)	15	4,422	2,412	2,010
Badrinath (NA)	2.01	978	742	236
Nand Prayag (NA)	2.16	1,262	702	560
Kedarmath (NA)	2.75	301	301	–
Rudraprayag	1	1,542	1,008	534
Ukhmath	–	–	–	–
Jakholi	–	–	–	–
Augustmuni	–	–	–	–
Pokhri	–	–	–	–
Pithoragarh	25.3	35,697	19,961	15,736
Pithoragarh (MB)	8.99	27,708	15,593	12,115
Dharchula (TA)	15.19	4,475	2,401	2,074
Didihat (TA)	1.12	3,514	1,967	1,547
Bageshwar	5	5,772	3,185	2,587
Kapkot	–	–	–	–
Garur	–	–	–	–
Takula	–	–	–	–
Bhisiyachana	–	–	–	–
Bageshwar (MB)	5	5,772	3,185	2,587
Total	675.19	16,70,807	26,02,632	7,18,758

human habitations is concerned. Villages and towns in hills are invariably smaller as compared to those in the wider plains. Why the hill-based habitations are invariably smaller is explained by the fact that in hill areas the level land is very rare and is usually in deeper valleys wherever it is found. The percentage of good arable land is not beyond 16-20 per cent. While the main source

(6)	(7)	(8)	(9)	(10)	(11)
826	–	856	898	1,335	485
2,158	–	945	947	1,351	371
274	4	604	742	824	281
196	–	1,027	1,034	1,541	875
679	–	798	889	1,676	533
3,419	120	5,678	5,778	9,432	5,779
556	6	954	974	1,742	1,023
475	21	619	623	1,010	587
1,555	41	2,593	2,640	4,433	2,648
833	52	1,512	1,541	2,247	1,521
6,563	2,316	8,946	9,125	18,936	8,337
2,403	978	3,774	3,854	7,157	3,731
1,489	1,073	2,141	2,157	6,153	1,987
1,091	112	1,197	1,256	2,288	1,149
1,103	7	1,048	1,053	1,902	1,070
32	7	325	336	636	115
432	138	310	310	514	285
13	1	151	159	286	–
172	18	415	415	755	326
–	–	–	–	–	–
–	–	–	–	–	–
–	–	–	–	–	–
–	–	–	–	–	–
5,567	3,146	5,930	8,734	15,771	10,034
4,109	630	4,064	6,584	12,348	7,892
721	1,897	1,112	1,217	1,888	1,193
737	619	754	933	1,535	949
1,271	225	1,016	1,321	2,401	1,508
–	–	–	–	–	–
–	–	–	–	–	–
–	–	–	–	–	–
–	–	–	–	–	–
1,271	225	1,016	1,321	2,401	1,508
2,11,396	39,842	2,74,331	3,25,832	6,33,693	4,06,602

of livelihood continues to be cultivation and population grows regularly, land for cultivation cannot expand. All arable land is used very economically and with greater intensity. Valleys are not safe for settlement. Villages settle in relatively higher elevations closer to the natural springs wherever possible. The firmness of the hill rock is an essential condition for sheltering population.

All arable land of the hill areas is not available at a single site. It is scattered in few patches here and a few there. The area available for cultivation at a place is only little which can support a given mass of population at a given level of agricultural technology and given occupational choice. If population grows incessantly there is no other option but to migrate from one site in order to make a comfortable living. Thus, addition to population results in shifting of a few households to another patch of land. The habitations are intercepted by big barriers of communication and day-to-day contacts. These barriers are the deep ravines, change of the ridge which means long spatial distance, rocks and forests. The farming occupation in hills requires very active vigil and guard against the wild animals, therefore, household has to shift its habitation in order to guard a distant farming land. All places in hills are not equally safe and stable. The joint line ridge is usually unsafe for house building. Each and every site cannot get natural water spring, therefore, the choice for the site of house construction is dictated by some other conveniences also. If population multiplies rapidly, no village can afford sheltering any number of households, because each household needs some arable agricultural land to settle upon. The slope of the land in hills being greater, the breadth of the fields is only narrow. The total land essential for supporting a household spreads over a greater area than the actual land put to cultivation. The wall area of the terraces depends on the slope of the hill. Even the best village finds it impossible to feed more than one thousand or nearly 250 households. Each household requires a piece of land for making a cowshed and growing some fruit trees, vegetables and some fodder trees besides the land for cultivation purposes. Every household tries to settle at a place where it can fetch firewood and water. The topographic constraints are thus more imposing and a limiting factor in the size of the village (Pande, 1968, 162-63). The census of 1961 found that nearly 96.9 per cent villages in Pauri-Garhwal, 96.6 per cent in Tehri-Garhwal, 96.5 per cent in Almora and 86.9 per cent in Nainital district have a population of less than 500 which is nearly 80-85 families (Census of India, UP, Part II(A) 1961, 164).

Economic Structure and Labour Utilisation

The balanced economic development process involves understanding of economic structure of each region so as to ensure (a) best utilisation of resources, and (b) minimising human costs which inevitably accompany the unbalanced styles of growth. The regional organs should approximately conform to the features of the major entities. Any major deviation in this regard is indicator of the regional discriminations in creating economic opportunities vis-a-vis resource potentials. The policy correctives can help out the smoothing up process. Market imperfections can be removed to all equal opportunities. The discrimination may also arise for the personal, demographic, inter-personal or family relations, traditions or the geographical barriers (Mathur, 1980-2-11).

The region has some peculiarities in respect of the topography, terrain, natural resources, agro-climatic conditions, forest coverage, and the overall cost structure of production. The density is still very low and the size of the habitations, cities, townships, villages and the isolated settlements in the forest areas, all are small and do not compare with the general characteristics in the state as a whole.

Poor transport and communications are the distinguishing features of this region. Significance-wise the area constitutes border with two neighbours, with whom the relations at the moment are far from being good.

Qualitatively the population is peaceful, hard-working, law-abiding and featured by greater literacy and education (Tables 2.11, 2.12 and 2.13). It constitutes an egalitarian society and inter-household property and income differentials are not as great as in the wider plains of UP. Percentage of Scheduled Caste population is less than that of UP except in Uttarkashi. The Scheduled Tribes are centred in this region yet these constitute around 3 per cent. Scheduled Caste and Scheduled Tribe groups together make the almost same percentage of lagging groups as it exists in the state of UP. The percentages of literates account for 18.93, 33.26, 57.75 and 72.28 for the years 1951, 1971, 1991 and 2001 respectively in Uttaranchal. The sex-ratio accounts for 936 in 1991 and 964 in 2001 in the state as a whole.

TABLE 2.11: Pattern of Literacy in Uttaranchal Himalaya, 1991

District	Literates				
	Rural	Urban	Male	Female	Total
1. Nainital	4,39,609	2,64,643	4,56,500	2,47,752	7,04,252
2. Udham Singh Nagar	–	–	–	–	–
3. Almora	3,59,424	40,235	2,57,247	1,42,412	3,99,659
4. Bageshwar	–	–	–	–	–
5. Pithoragarh	2,42,952	30,167	1,84,770	88,349	2,73,119
6. Champawat	–	–	–	–	–
7. Tehri-Garhwal	2,05,256	22,175	1,62,980	64,451	2,27,431
8. Uttarkashi	80,214	11,785	70,134	21,865	91,999
9. Chamoli	1,96,926	28,354	1,50,423	74,857	2,25,280
10. Pauri-Garhwal	318569	52975	225863	145681	371544
11. Rudraprayag	–	–	–	–	–
12. Dehradun	2,39,968	3,57,420	3,67,114	2,30,274	5,97,388
13. Haridwar	2,29,650	2,07,832	2,93,950	1,43,532	4,37,482
Uttaranchal	23,12,568	10,15,586	21,68,981	11,59,173	33,28,154
In per cent	69.49	30.51	65.17	34.83	100.00

Note: Literates include the persons above six years.

TABLE 2.12: District-wise and Sex-wise Literacy percentage in Uttaranchal in 1991 and 2001

District	Total literates		Literate male		Literate female	
	1991	2001	1991	2001	1991	2001
1. Nainital	68.36	78.60	80.42	87.39	54.51	70.98
2. Udham Singh Nagar	49.29	65.76	60.47	76.20	36.02	54.16
3. Almora	59.83	74.53	80.78	9015	41.32	61.43
4. Bageshwar	54.54	71.94	76.52	88.56	34.22	57.45
5. Pithoragarh	61.38	76.48	80.31	90.57	42.41	63.16
6. Champawat	55.81	71.11	77.63	88.13	32.62	54.75
7. Tehri-Garhwal	48.46	67.04	72.09	85.62	26.31	49.76
8. Uttarkashi	47.23	66.58	68.74	84.52	23.57	47.48
9. Chamoli	60.40	76.23	80.85	89.89	39.66	63.00
10. Pauri-Garhwal	65.53	77.99	82.57	91.47	49.65	66.16
11. Rudraprayag	57.47	74.23	80.36	90.73	37.08	59.98
12. Dehradun	69.50	78.96	77.95	85.87	59.26	71.22
13. Haridwar	47.97	64.60	59.28	75.06	34.37	52.60
Uttaranchal	57.75	72.28	72.79	84.01	41.63	60.26

Note: 1. Literates include the persons above six years.
2. Data for 2001 are provisional.

TABLE 2.13: District-wise Sex Ratio, Literacy and No. of Inhabited Villages in Uttaranchal Himalaya, 1981, 1991 and 2001

District	Sex ratio			No. of inhabited villages
	1981	1991	2001	1991*
1. Nainital	847	881	906	1,806
2. Udham Singh Nagar	841	863	902	–
3. Almora	1,095	1,099	1,147	3,024
4. Bageshwar	1,031	1,055	1,110	–
5. Pithoragarh	1,027	992	1,031	2,186
6. Champawat	947	945	1,024	–
7. Tehri-Garhwal	1,081	1,048	1,051	1,959
8. Uttarkashi	881	918	941	678
9. Chamoli	1,020	982	1,017	1,569
10. Pauri-Garhwal	1,091	1,058	1,104	3,205
11. Rudraprayag	1,121	1,094	1,117	–
12. Dehradun	811	843	893	746
13. Haridwar	817	846	868	503
Uttaranchal	936	936	964	15,676

Source: Distt. Census Handbooks, 1991 and provisional data of 2001.
*No. of inhabited villages of the districts as per Sl. Nos. 2, 4, 6 and 11 are already included in their respective parent districts.

The dependency ratio and workers' ratio is nearly similar in UP and this area. Workers' participation rates are greater in Uttaranchal. As we proceed upward from the districts at foothills, we get greater participation rates among the workers. Table 2.14 makes the features more clear.

Occupational Structure and Dependency

There does exist a similarity in the proportion of population engaged in different occupations in U.P. and Uttaranchal. Some of the districts in the lower ranges of Himalaya have features of the UP state as a whole, e.g. Nainital and Dehradun. But when only hill region is counted there exists a similarity in the hilly tract which can be separated easily from the plains tract of former UP. There is greater concentration of workers in agriculture in hills of

TABLE 2.14: Workers Dependant Ratio per 100 Persons in Working Force and Population in Productive Age Groups in Uttaranchal Himalaya

District	Number of dependants		
	Per 100 workers	Per 100 population in 15-59 years	Work force participation rate
Uttarkashi	57	66	63.54
Chamoli	72	93	58.02
Rudraprayag	–	–	–
Tehri-Garhwal	94	101	51.48
Pauri-Garhwal	120	95	45.40
Dehradun	187	80	34.83
Pithoragarh	149	95	40.14
Champawat	–	–	–
Almora	157	97	38.84
Bageshwar	–	–	–
Nainital	198	90	33.53
Udham Singh Nagar	–	–	–
Haridwar	–	–	–
Uttaranchal	138	91	41.93
Uttar Pradesh	223	96	30.94

Source: Census of India, Census figures, 1971-1981, Districtwise Data.

Uttaranchal due to the fact that in miserly nature of the precarious hilly tract, nothing can be obtained without intensive use of labour unlike on the fertile Indogangetic plains. Female participation in agriculture is greater in hills because the land does not yield well till all labour available is deployed. The careful observation of the data, drawn from census 1971-81, makes the idea clear about activity-wise participation of workers in the Uttaranchal Himalaya (Tables 2.15 and 2.16).

It is notable that the percentage of the workers engaged in manufacturing and proceeding is smaller in this tract as compared to the state as a whole.

This Himalayan tract has some notable features regarding its

TABLE 2.15: Sex-wise Workers Engaged in Economic Activities in Former UP Himalaya

(Percentage)

Districts	Persons (P) Male (M) Female (F)	Manufacturing			Constru-ction	Trade and commerce	Transport, storage and com-munication	Other services
		Primary sector	House-hold	Non-household				
(1)	(2)	(3)	(4)	(5)	(6)	(7)	(8)	(9)
Uttarkashi	P	88.49	0.73	1.09	1.37	1.05	0.15	7.12
	M	79.92	1.08	1.71	2.47	1.94	0.28	12.60
	F	98.60	0.30	0.36	0.07	0.01	0.05	0.64
Chamoli	P	87.16	1.71	0.34	0.40	0.90	0.32	9.17
	M	74.12	2.17	0.69	0.87	1.95	0.69	19.41
	F	98.29	1.31	0.03	0.00	0.01	–	0.36
Tehri-Garhwal	P	92.22	1.09	0.51	0.23	0.87	0.21	4.87
	M	84.02	2.09	1.07	0.50	1.86	0.45	10.02
	F	99.28	0.24	0.03	0.00	0.01	–	0.43
Dehradun	P	39.09	2.47	6.80	1.42	7.94	3.84	38.46
	M	36.85	2.53	7.14	1.56	8.74	4.21	38.97
	F	57.82	2.00	3.99	0.22	0.22	0.71	34.11
Pithoragarh	P	81.59	2.10	0.47	1.00	1.69	0.58	12.59
	M	70.93	2.46	0.74	1.68	2.83	0.97	20.40
	F	97.27	1.56	0.07	0.01	0.03	0.00	1.06

(*Contd.*)

(1)	(2)	(3)	(4)	(5)	(6)	(7)	(8)	(9)
Almora	P	85.16	1.12	0.77	0.52	1.79	0.69	9.95
	M	76.34	1.62	1.26	0.86	2.93	1.14	15.85
	F	98.47	0.35	0.03	0.01	0.07	0.02	1.04
Nainital	P	68.93	2.05	5.15	1.81	6.34	3.60	12.12
	M	66.84	2.13	5.62	2.00	6.97	3.97	12.46
	F	87.29	1.32	0.96	0.21	0.75	0.39	9.09
Uttaranchal Himalaya	P	77.06	1.51	2.15	0.89	3.02	1.44	13.93
	M	65.80	2.01	3.25	1.39	4.70	2.24	20.61
	F	96.58	0.64	0.25	0.03	0.10	0.05	2.35
Uttar Pradesh	P	78.04	3.66	3.62	0.61	4.07	1.73	8.27
	M	76.95	3.64	3.91	0.67	4.42	1.91	8.50
	F	87.64	3.92	1.03	0.10	0.89	0.19	6.23

Source: Census of India, 1971-81, Districtwise figures.

TABLE 2.16: Category of Main Workers

District/City/Town	Main workers			Cultivators	Agricultural labour	Live-stock, forestry	Mining and quarrying	Construction	Trade and commerce	Transport, storage and communication	Other services	Marginal workers			Non-workers		
	Persons	Male	Female									Persons	Male	Female	Persons	Male	Female
(1)	(2)	(3)	(4)	(5)	(6)	(7)	(8)	(9)	(10)	(11)	(12)	(13)	(14)	(15)	(16)	(17)	(18)
Uttarkashi	0,05,941	0,05,113	00,828	0,842	00,019	0,179	002	0,409	00,882	0,188	02,023	0,285	134	0151	0,11,035	0,05,008	0,06,027
Uttarkashi (MB)	4,747	4,171	576	405	15	126	2	339	748	176	2,608	200	73	127	8,972	4,044	4,928
Barakot (TA)	1,123	871	252	412	4	52	–	70	134	11	371	33	16	17	2,058	959	1,099
Gangotri (NA)	71	71	–	25	–	1	–	–	–	1	44	52	45	7	5	5	–
Tehri	13,005	12,118	887	440	207	595	11	4,472	1,583	596	4,513	380	147	233	19,510	8,780	10,730
Tehri (MB)	8,654	8,049	605	430	206	341	5	3,510	1,140	314	2,393	129	53	76	11,443	5,025	6,418
Narendra Nagar (MB)	1,925	1,776	149	4	1	110	–	478	109	60	1,132	4	2	2	2,999	1,352	1,647
Muni-ki-Reti (NA)	1,373	1,311	62	–	–	81	5	316	200	167	401	236	86	150	2,910	1,529	1381
Dev Prayag (NA)	673	625	48	3	–	19	–	112	85	31	402	11	6	5	1,480	558	922
Kirti Nagar (NA)	380	357	23	3	–	44	1	56	949	24	185	–	–	–	678	316	362
Dehradun	1,54,452	1,40,188	14,264	1,989	2,818	4,926	308	8,944	30,311	9,883	69,751	1,209	395	814	3,59,819	1,41,737	2,18,082
Hartbertpur (TA)	2,444	2,199	245	434	569	108	–	119	310	113	528	77	4	73	6,050	2,291	3,759
Doiwala (TA)	2,225	2,018	207	150	239	49	–	68	429	111	526	94	24	70	5,157	1,964	3,193
Vikas Nagar (MB)	3,316	2,986	330	98	248	48	2	105	1,391	177	755	142	39	103	7,533	2,829	4,704
Dak Patthar (CT)	2,768	2,599	169	29	40	1,316	–	46	146	72	1,057	9	5	4	7,494	3,025	4,469
Chakrata Cantt.	31,168	2,947	169	6	2	30	–	26	200	19	2,789	4	–	4	1,550	592	958
Raiwala (CT)	1,212	1,089	123	180	178	58	–	51	240	74	338	14	2	12	2,889	1,123	1,766
Rishikesh (UA)	20,668	19,008	1,660	301	183	817	28	1,427	4,454	1,940	5,619	342	126	216	50,694	20,277	30,414
Rishikesh (MB)	13,546	12,554	992	63	48	169	28	1,229	4,061	1,711	3,450	189	79	110	30,752	12,327	18,425
Virbhadra (NA)	4,103	3,625	478	87	–	10	–	58	126	24	447	39	12	27	11,840	4,840	7,000
Rishikesh (CT)	3,019	2,829	190	151	135	638	–	140	267	205	722	114	35	79	8,102	3,110	4,992
Massoorie (UA)	10,055	9,058	997	124	13	175	136	1,150	2,091	425	5,374	17	7	10	19,557	8,554	11,003
Massoorie (MB)	9,026	8,132	894	123	13	166	132	1,043	1,899	368	4,837	15	6	9	17,681	7,804	9,877
Landaur Cantt.	1,029	926	103	1	–	9	4	107	192	57	537	2	1	1	1,876	750	1,126

(Contd.)

(1)	(2)	(3)	(4)	(5)	(6)	(7)	(8)	(9)	(10)	(11)	(12)	(13)	(14)	(15)	(16)	(17)	(18)
Dehradun (UA)	1,08,648	98,284	10,364	667	1,346	2,325	142	5,952	21,060	6,952	53,765	510	188	322	2,58,895	1,01,082	1,57,813
Dehradun (MB)	76,564	68,278	8,286	291	759	1,846	127	4,748	18,873	6,034	32,446	406	162	244	1,93,189	75,365	1,17,824
FRI & College (CT)	1,584	1,409	175	-	-	11	-	176	25	8	1,323	17	7	10	3,115	1,218	1,897
Adhoiwala (CT)	3,752	3,421	331	19	16	58	10	406	480	208	1,557	6	-	6	9,620	3,774	5,846
Dehradun Cantt.	14,688	13,722	966	57	65	275	1	207	1,127	387	11,396	13	5	8	28,330	11,287	17,043
Clement Town Cantt.	7,117	6,939	178	117	355	28	1	234	196	117	5,826	2	1	1	11,118	4,155	6,963
Raipur (CT)	4,943	4,515	428	183	151	107	3	181	359	198	1,217	66	13	53	13,523	5,283	8,240
Pauri	26,975	24,848	2,127	736	82	2,051	7	2,549	4,192	1,680	13,784	485	73	412	53,722	22,697	31,025
Kotdwar (MB)	5,935	5,538	397	49	34	194	-	526	1,754	777	1,703	96	7	89	15,347	5,880	9,467
Pauri (MB)	6,775	5,766	1,009	640	13	507	-	589	962	377	3,394	302	18	284	13,320	5,776	7,544
Kalagarh (CA)	2,436	2,318	118	33	30	1,033	-	147	188	59	767	44	26	18	8,047	3,305	4,742
Sri Nagar (MB)	8,299	7,918	381	4	2	142	6	1,076	870	348	5,486	8	3	5	10,484	4,992	5,492
Lansdowne Cantt.	2,744	2,584	160	2	1	114	-	134	264	54	2,092	11	9	2	4,351	1,822	2,529
Dogadda (MA)	642	585	57	8	2	54	1	73	128	58	251	24	10	14	1,778	754	1,024
Bah Bazar (CT)	144	139	5	-	-	7	-	4	26	7	91	-	-	-	395	168	227
Almora	16,810	14,702	2,108	457	34	637	48	810	2,922	718	10,468	1,710	477	1,233	29,215	12,462	16,753
Ranikhet Cantt.	6,542	6,096	446	138	24	151	13	168	868	242	4,770	1,000	292	708	9,332	3,931	5,401
Dwarahat (NA)	974	618	356	311	7	14	-	38	213	22	332	109	40	69	1,727	880	847
Almora (UA)	9,284	7,988	1,306	8	3	472	35	604	1,841	454	5,366	601	145	456	18,156	7,651	10,505
Almora (MB)	7,747	6,561	1,086	8	3	472	35	604	1,841	454	3,819	515	116	400	17,738	7,451	10,287
Almora Cantt.	1,547	1,327	220	-	-	-	-	-	-	-	1,547	85	29	56	418	200	218
Nainital	55,487	51,174	4,313	916	692	2,794	70	4,928	14,144	5,287	19,974	1,028	352	676	1,34,474	52,747	81,727
Ramnagar (MB)	9,960	9,407	553	309	66	728	-	1,125	2,482	799	3,115	13	4	9	27,308	10,500	16,808
Bhowali (MB)	1,407	1,223	184	20	16	64	-	87	265	99	784	11	5	6	2,946	1,168	1,776
Lalkun (TA)	1,671	1,616	55	12	3	190	24	102	405	359	162	627	182	445	3,012	1,240	1,772
Kaladhungi (TA)	1,493	1,358	135	141	189	215	-	38	409	47	343	159	26	133	3,011	1,223	1,788
Bhimtal (TA)	1,325	1,073	252	185	170	39	-	22	122	69	571	1	-	1	2,899	1,168	1,731
Nainital (UA)	9,847	8,581	1,266	20	21	536	15	593	1,885	551	5,737	85	48	37	21,019	8,901	12,118
Nainital (MB)	9,124	8,068	1,056	20	21	500	3	581	1,864	527	5,138	19	16	3	20,694	8,742	11,952
Nainital Cantt.	723	513	210	-	-	36	12	12	21	24	599	66	32	34	325	159	166
Haldwani-cum-Kathgodam	29,784	27,916	1,868	229	227	1,022	31	2,961	8,576	3,353	9,262	132	87	45	74,279	28,547	45,732
Haridwar	95,319	89,439	5,880	2,417	3,323	3,029	281	5,839	20,684	6,538	29,124	999	155	844	2,51,824	99,486	1,52,338
Manglour (MB)	9,317	8,817	500	553	1,130	222	88	1,131	2,379	473	1,700	206	9	197	24,638	9,382	15,256
Laksar (TA)	4,469	4,262	207	286	220	33	-	154	1,031	727	931	164	10	154	10,989	4,348	6,641
Landhaura (TA)	3,766	3,671	95	565	435	36	-	226	330	151	475	450	55	395	7,979	3,068	4,911

Jhabera (TA)	2,089	2,017	72	323	631	17	8	54	403	40	356	14	–	14	5,530	2,037	3,493
Roorkee (UA)	24,820	23,101	1,719	415	170	1,232	71	905	5,481	1,116	12,182	53	33	20	66,266	26,436	39,830
Roorkee (MB)	20,419	18,817	1,602	415	169	1,230	71	897	5,336	1,102	8,003	51	31	20	59,792	23,998	35,794
Roorkee Cantt.	4,401	4,284	117	–	1	2	–	8	145	14	4,179	2	2	–	6,474	2,438	4,036
Haridwar (UA)	50,858	47,571	3,287	275	737	1,489	114	3,369	11,060	4,031	13,480	112	48	64	1,36,422	54,215	82,207
Haridwar	41,080	38,518	2,562	270	732	1,479	112	3,247	10,748	3,884	11,851	100	41	59	1,07,831	42,853	64,978
Haridwar (MB)	40,646	38,116	2,530	269	732	1,473	112	3,247	10,742	3,852	11,483	700	41	59	1,06,559	4,249	64,510
Gurukul Kangri (OG)	397	367	30	1	–	6	–	–	6	32	331	–	–	–	1,057	616	441
Jwalapur Mahavidyalaya (OG)	37	35	2	–	–	–	–	–	–	–	37	–	–	–	215	188	27
BHEL Ltd. Ranipur (NA)	9,778	9,053	725	5	5	10	2	122	312	147	1,629	12	7	5	28,591	11,362	17,229
Udham Singh Nagar	81,218	76,580	4,638	6,486	13,441	1,024	3	3,757	15,947	4,733	21,292	2,100	625	1,475	2,08,975	80,741	1,28,234
Rudrapur (MB)	18,281	16,664	1,617	702	5,707	274	2	649	3,337	1,191	3,767	109	17	92	42,890	15,974	26,916
Kashipur (MB)	19,006	18,119	887	1,006	744	276	1	1,163	4,557	1,585	5,322	344	157	187	50,520	19,165	31,355
Jaspur (MB)	7,741	7,427	314	597	913	158	–	641	1,591	494	1,672	40	15	25	23,050	8,901	14,149
Kichha (MB)	5,935	5,678	257	391	1,196	49	–	154	1,334	471	1,373	24	14	10	15,172	5,703	9,469
Sitarganj (MB)	4,751	4,582	169	558	598	31	–	265	1,344	188	1,416	193	28	165	11,760	4,350	7,410
Gadarpur (MB)	2,465	2,321	144	305	322	77	–	103	661	72	557	1,184	376	808	5,838	2,380	3,458
Bazpur (MB)	4,938	4,768	170	234	325	46	–	205	951	255	1,061	1	–	1	11,918	4,635	7,283
Khatima (MB)	3,129	2,989	140	68	106	42	–	137	1,062	175	858	8	–	8	8,108	3,132	4,976
Nagla (CT)	5,582	5,035	547	11	516	39	–	125	252	129	4,322	22	13	9	16,468	7,739	8,729
Shaktigarh (TA)	1,094	999	95	274	320	7	–	46	223	25	131	52	2	50	2,699	1,067	1,632
Sultanpur (TA)	1,546	1,521	25	581	579	–	–	21	112	34	166	–	–	–	4,320	1,648	2,672
Mahuakhera	1,790	1,693	97	616	542	8	–	153	62	20	101	75	–	75	4,749	1,859	2,890
Kelakhera (TA)	1,399	1,376	23	359	572	7	–	49	161	28	183	19	1	18	3,607	1,354	2,253
Dineshpur (TA)	1,782	1,657	125	381	702	8	–	36	262	40	198	10	–	10	4,307	1,504	2,803
Mahuadabra Haripura (TA)	1,779	1,751	28	403	299	2	–	10	38	26	165	19	2	17	3,569	1,330	2,239
Champawat	8,180	7,497	683	531	86	311	5	688	1846	1,045	3,069	489	78	411	17,429	6,885	10,544
Lohaghat (NA)	1,220	1,125	95	30	2	81	2	112	329	66	497	114	23	91	2,557	1,104	1,453
Champawat (TA)	943	700	243	251	–	55	1	87	187	35	263	59	17	42	1,523	693	830
Tanakpur (MB)	4,049	3,872	177	23	30	117	2	178	1,166	794	1,424	13	2	11	9,048	3,385	5,663
Banbassa (CA)	1,968	1,800	168	227	54	58	–	311	164	150	885	303	36	267	4,301	1,703	2,598
Chamoli	15,611	12,894	2,717	2,683	203	822	1	1,467	1,603	434	7,502	308	83	225	23,079	10,978	12,101
Chamoli Gopeshwar (MB)	5,279	4,263	1,016	834	3	455	–	644	504	213	2,239	142	26	116	9,957	4,918	5,039
Joshimath (MB)	5,905	5,114	791	950	49	148	–	299	393	70	3,721	45	22	23	5,538	2,512	3,026
Karnaprayag (NA)	1,508	1,350	158	119	32	88	–	191	287	107	594	49	16	33	3,612	1,577	2,035
Gauchar (TA)	1,515	958	557	661	1	84	–	255	106	22	335	22	2	20	2,885	1,452	1,433

(Contd.)

(1)	(2)	(3)	(4)	(5)	(6)	(7)	(8)	(9)	(10)	(11)	(12)	(13)	(14)	(15)	(16)	(17)	(18)
Badrinath Puri (NA)	685	583	102	36	117	1	–	1	161	6	323	8	7	1	285	152	133
Nandprayag (NA)	429	336	93	70	–	45	–	75	85	13	97	39	7	32	794	359	435
Kedarnath (NA)	290	290	–	13	1	1	–	2	67	3	193	3	3	–	8	8	–
Rudraprayag	664	645	19	2	–	19	–	19	257	36	220	1	–	1	877	363	514
Ukhimath	–	–	–	–	–	–	–	–	–	–	–	–	–	–	–	–	–
Jakholi	–	–	–	–	–	–	–	–	–	–	–	–	–	–	–	–	–
Augustmuni	–	–	–	–	–	–	–	–	–	–	–	–	–	–	–	–	–
Pokheri	–	–	–	–	–	–	–	–	–	–	–	–	–	–	–	–	–
Pithoragarh	10,674	8,960	1,714	839	67	528	153	840	2,301	609	4,471	683	69	614	24,340	10,932	13,408
Pithoragarh (MB)	8,256	7,011	1,245	735	60	414	151	644	1,741	542	3,529	237	52	185	19,215	8,530	10,685
Dharchula (TA)	1,392	1,081	311	69	4	44	2	81	356	44	479	413	8	405	2,670	1,312	1,358
Didihat (TA)	1,026	868	158	35	3	70	–	115	204	23	463	33	9	24	2,455	1,090	1,365
Bageshwar (MB)	2,012	1,655	357	195	17	85	–	186	590	95	663	420	114	306	3,340	1,416	1,924
Kapkot	–	–	–	–	–	–	–	–	–	–	–	–	–	–	–	–	–
Grur	–	–	–	–	–	–	–	–	–	–	–	–	–	–	–	–	–
Takula	–	–	–	–	–	–	–	–	–	–	–	–	–	–	–	–	–
Bhaisiachhana	–	–	–	–	–	–	–	–	–	–	–	–	–	–	–	–	–

Source: District Census Hand Books, 1991.

greater female participation which is partly explained by the fact that the size of holding and irrigation content is meagre (10-11 per cent). The land is very rocky and yields only little except in the rare fertile valleys which have alluvial soils and good amount of moisture. These situations suggest that not much can be expected in yield from these holdings. Therefore, work has to be searched outside agriculture by migration of males and burdening the females with the sweating drudgery of rainfed agriculture on terraces.

Out-Migration of Earners from Himalayan Habitat

Migration constitutes a major constraint. Except in the districts in the close proximity of the foothills and where the topography and slope is much less, the out-migration exceeds the in-migration process. This leads to the thinning of the male workers in agriculture and greater sex ratio per thousand miles. The figures shown in Table 2.17 present the sex ratio in age-groupwise population and the extent of migration in Uttaranchal. The extent of migration is actually greater than the figures recorded in census. The extent tends to vary extensively. It may be around 6.2 per cent in central Almora, 12.0 per cent in north Pithoragarh and more than 13.7 per cent in western Almora among the male workers.

Poorer resource base is the fundamental reason why the workers are constrained to migrate. The arable land in the region is already overladen and the margin of extending agricultural cultivation is absent. The population growth leads to greater out-migration for making a livelihood. Districts like – Uttarkashi, Chamoli, Tehri and Pithoragarh deserve considerable aid in the establishment of alternative occupations. The resource-base in Nainital and Dehradun is better specially in the Bhabar and Tarai tracts. Planning Institute of UP had made the general categories of the districts regarding the resource base, institutional structure, level of development, agricultural status, industrial state and the infrastructure.

The clustering shown in Table 2.18 has the bias of the assumed priorities towards developmental frame. Transport and communications had been given low priority in view of the fact that this region had long continued under disregard and it is only during Third Plan onwards that this region has been attended to the needs

TABLE 2.17: Age-groupwise Sex Ratio and Migration in Former Himalaya

(Percentage)

District	Sex ratio in age-groups								Net migration (–) out-migration (+) in-migration (percentage)
	0-14	15-19	20-24	25-29	30-39	40-49	50-59	60+	
Uttarkashi	1,006	702	963	925	947	867	757	807	Negligible
Chamoli	998	1,190	1,149	1,228	1,176	1,078	984	931	–8.00
Tehri-Garhwal	970	1,839	2,231	1,852	1,298	1,165	1,109	995	–14.09
Pauri-Garhwal	1,013	1,113	1,469	1,497	1,154	1,296	1,112	961	–10.77
Dehradun	920	739	738	654	728	643	634	957	+8.62
Pithoragarh	957	1,071	1,233	1,175	1,294	1,037	936	838	–6.72
Almora	970	1,121	1,446	1,310	1,322	1,130	963	872	–8.87
Nainital	892	790	765	805	766	654	655	656	+6.82
Former UP Himalaya	954	997	1,100	1,056	1,022	931	871	822	–3.32
Uttar Pradesh	968	806	1,012	977	934	855	798	818	–

TABLE 2.18: Districts of Uttaranchal Himalaya in Hierarchical Clusters

District	Placed into cluster according to criteria					
	Resource base	Institutional structure	Level of development	Agricultural resource utilisation	Industrial resource utilisation	Infrastructure and social facilities
Uttarkashi	II	I	V	VI	I	II
Chamoli	II	I	II	IV	I	I
Tehri-Garhwal	II	II	V	VI	I	VI
Pauri-Garhwal	II	II	II	IV	III	II
Dehradun	VIII	III	IX	VIII	VIII	VIII
Pithoragarh	II	I	II	VI	I	I
Almora	II	II	II	VI	I	VII
Nainital	VIII	II	VIII	IX	IV	IX
Bageshwar	–	–	–	–	–	–
Champawat	–	–	–	–	–	–
Udham Singh Nagar	–	–	–	–	–	–
Rudraprayag	–	–	–	–	–	–
Haridwar	–	–	–	–	–	–

Source: Tewari, R.T. (1980), A Tentative Regional Framework for Balanced Economic Development of Uttar Pradesh, Area Planning Division, State Planning Institute, Government of Uttar Pradesh, Lucknow.

under grants from the centre. In some districts irrigation and modern methods of cultivation have begun (Papola, 1980). Some industrial activity has emerged in Dehradun and Nainital districts due to their being extended to Tarai, Bhabar and Dun areas. Factory employment has improved the terms of percentage in recent decades. The districts like – Tehri-Garhwal, Pauri-Garhwal, Almora have recorded a fall in this reference in last few decades. The share of small-scale and cottage works in the production of Uttaranchal Himalaya is 3.5 per cent. The per capita development outlay in Uttaranchal Himalaya has risen consistently over the decades due to central share in development of backward regions (Singh, A.K., 1981, 12). During 1974-79 it claimed hardly 7.6 per cent of UP's spending. During 1978-83, the share rose to 10 per cent. Most of

TABLE 2.19: Plan-wise Expenditure on Uttaranchal (excluding Haridwar District)

Plan	Expenditure (Rs. in million)		
	Central assistance	State plan	Total
1. Fifth Five Year Plan (1974-79)	1,040.00 (51.00)	1,000.20 (49.00)	2,040.20 (100.00)
2. Sixth Five Year Plan (1980-85)	3,500.00 (53.00)	3,088.70 (47.00)	6,588.70 (100.00)
3. Seventh Five Year Plan (1985-90)	6,791.90 (56.00)	5,339.10 (44.00)	12,131.00 (100.00)
4. Eighth Five Year Plan (1992-97)	10,050.00 (47.70)	11,000.00 (52.30)	21,050.00 (100.00)
5. Ninth Five Year Plan (1997-2002)	12,750.00 (28.80)	31,550.00 (71.20)	44,300.00 (100.00)

Note: Figures in parentheses are in per cent.
Source: Statistical Diary, Uttaranchal Division, 1995, U.P. State Planning Institute Lucknow and Ninth Five Year Plan, Uttaranchal and Sub-Plan, (1997-2000).

the spending was on Minimum Needs Programme. The backlog of development is so much in this tract that a small bit-by-bit expenditure is not likely to transform the economy. Most of the resources have been consumed in building roads in the difficult terrain. This has, however, considerably added to the development of tourism in some patches while the general state of backwardness and tedious life in Uttaranchal Himalaya has remained neglected under the tourism development. Its impact on rural sector has not been noticed.

It is very much clear from Table 2.18 that from 5th to 9th Five-Year Plans, central assistance alloted to the former UP Himalaya (presently Uttaranchal) to meet out its expenditure was the lowest in 9th Plan (i.e. 28.80 per cent); while it was 56 per cent in Seventh Five-Year Plan (Table 2.19).

Mini-Fields and Terrace-Culture

This Himalayan tract, excluding Bhabar, Tarai and Dun belts, has homogeneity in respect of the size of holdings and their scattered nature.

It may be observed that the holdings tend to concentrate in the smaller size-groups and there is lesser occurrence of holdings in higher size groups. Most of the holdings are marginal cultivating units below 2.5 acres or 1 hectare. The unirrigated lands with rocky composition and thin layers of soil in uplands do not yield enough for family consumption round the year. There is no question of a marketable surplus which can find market in the wake of tourism growth.

The landholdings have a typical composition of plots. Approximations in the field studies show that on an average each holding has 12-58 plots or terraces scattered over a very wide area in each direction. The cultivation, supervision, guard, and care of crops in these directions is tedious task for anybody to attempt. Some plots in the sunny areas known as *taail* lands. These are featured by hours a day at a stretch. The other category is of the shady lands where the exposure of sun is for less than four hours a day. These have different productivity levels and a different set of crops which grow there. The maturity of crop takes more time in shady lands so the cropping period extends to longer time span. Some of the hilly terraces are odd placed in the surroundings of rocks and bullocks cannot be taken to these for ploughing. The width of the plots at times is so poor that a pair of bullocks cannot turn with plough, therefore, the land has to be tilled by manual labour. Some areas receive a good rainfall and have good irrigation from rivulets but most of the fields are without any irrigation. Some of the tracts are known drought prone areas which receive low rain and the land gets completely dry in summer.

Levels of Farm Yield and Income Composition

Productivity-wise quality of land varies extensively over the hills. The yields are low in uplands while these are better in valley areas. Table 2.20 shows the crop-wise productivity of selected crops of Rabi and Kharif.

The productivity rates are the averages and tend to differ very sharply during the consecutive years. Usually the fourth year one

TABLE 2.20: Crop-wise Productivity Rates in Uttaranchal

(Quintal per hectare)

District	Wheat	Barley	Massoor	Paddy	Maize	Jhongra
1. Dehradun	17.73	17.41	6.60	17.36	10.43	10.10
2. Tehri-Garhwal	14.33	10.87	5.00	14.03	10.44	11.00
3. Pauri-Garhwal	12.73	10.86	5.10	10.32	10.56	9.00
4. Chamoli	13.96	16.12	6.60	13.45	11.68	6.50
5. Uttarkashi	18.19	18.04	4.00	16.49	10.93	4.20
6. Pithoragarh	15.47	14.09	6.60	13.62	12.20	11.70
7. Almora	11.61	10.40	6.60	12.31	19.89	9.30
8. Nainital	26.39	14.45	9.82	29.27	12.19	10.00
9. Haridwar	24.50	26.46	6.80	25.27	13.50	–
10. Bageshwar	NA	–	–	–	–	–
11. Champawat	NA	–	–	–	–	–
12. Udham Singh Nagar	NA	–	–	–	–	–
13. Rudraprayag	NA	–	–	–	–	–

Source: UP Govt., Roster Survey, Econ. & Statistics, UP, Lucknow, 1995-96.

crop comes-up nicely and 2 crops in five years are bad. Two crops in every five years are normal.

The income levels in the tract are a composite affair. The inhabitants follow a large number of occupations so as to meet their needs. They combine crafts, agriculture, animal husbandry, dairying, honey-making, forestry, hunting, labour on construction activity and forest works, lending, services in public and private employments, and also receive the transfer incomes from migrants, state subsidies, etc. Table 2.21 presents an approximation of incomes under the expert surveys in the region (1971 prices).

Deficient Transport and Communication Gap in Uplands

Transport is the interlink between the factors of production to bring them together and between sectors who makes the system smoother. The development of trade, commerce and industry is dependent on the transport interlinks. Himalayan region being a tract of folded mountain chains, steep slopes, unstable rocks and infrequent fertile arable area offers low possibilities of effective and easy

TABLE 2.21: Income Composition of Rural Households in Uttaranchal

(Rs. per year)

Source of income	Garhwal division	Kumaun division	Total
1. Agriculture	1,179	1,421	1,300
2. Animal husbandry and dairying	590	1,010	800
3. Poultry and honey	40	100	70
4. Forestry and grass; fuel and fodder	354	270	312
5. Hunting	–	20	10
6. Labour in construction work	300	124	212
7. Porting and coolie; horses and mules	150	50	100
8. Financial gains, interest and dividends	32	80	56
9. Services	484	152	318
10. Trade and commerce	200	400	300
11. Industry crafts	220	80	150
12. Transfer incomes	117	55	86

Source: Pande, G.C., *Economy of Kumaun and Garhwal Divisions*, Lucknow University, 1968, pp. 437-482.

transportation. This has an impact on the economy and culture of the area. British government built few roads which helped it in mobilising personnel for armed forces and forest products to the railway heads from Uttaranchal Himalayas. The Chinese aggression in 1962 in the northern borders constrained the government to build some roads even in the inner Himalaya. The development efforts in the third decade of planned era built roads mostly for the promotion of economic activities and reaching civil and military supplies to the remoter areas in Uttaranchal Himalaya. After 1975, the region received greater attention to the purpose of tourism development to the interiors of the area. The cost of making and maintaining roads in hill areas is greater for the uneven topography and unstable rocks in the area. Rail heads are in the foothills and have not been extended in the planned era. NER metre gauge and broad gauge lines connect the plains to Lalkuan, Kathgodam, Ramnagar and Tanakpur in the foothills of Kumaun. Northern Railway connects Kotdwar, Rishikesh, Haridwar and Dehradun by broad gauge in foothills of Garhwal region. There have not been adequate attempts to make railway line to the hill areas because the hill areas are not the major exporting area of sizeable production like agro-products or industrial products. The major export from these areas are fruits, timber, spices and labour, of which labour export is the main part. By far, roads serve the interlink between wider plains and the interior hills. Highways, district roads and village roads are the three types of roads found here. While railway line stretches north to south-east and south to north-east parallel to the foothills, the roads interconnect the railway stations with penetrating roads into Himalaya. State highways (6, 29, 37, 45, 47, 53, 55, 57) pass through Uttaranchal Himalaya. Tanakpur rail head in eastern strip is linked by road to Lepulekh. Kathgodam railway station is linked by roads to inner Himalayan region. The network of roads in lower parts of Himalaya is now quite well-woven and motor transport in the tract is quite satisfactory. From Kathgodam one route goes to Almora via Bhimtal and another via Jeolikote meeting together at Bhowali. Kathgodam is linked straight via Jeolikote to Nainital hill station, which is connected with Almora, Ranikhet, Baijnath, Gwaldam, and also to Pithoragarh eastward. In the western part Uttaranchal. Himalaya is linked with Rishikesh, Kotdwar, Haridwar and Dehradun rail heads. There are mainly major road links to Mussoorie, Yamunotri, Gangotri, Badrinath and Kedarnath. Rishikesh to Yamunotri, the route extends to Hanumanchatti, at around 220 km. In order to reach Yamunotri, a pedestrian journey has to be undertaken for more than 12 kms. In another route from Rishikesh to Gangotri, one has to cross 245 kms. Trek route leads to Gaumukh from Gangotri at nearly 18 kms. Rishikesh is linked with Badrinath route. The pilgrims also take-up trek route via Govind Ghat and Hemkund. The route has a trekking advantage through valley of flowers. The interlinks between tiny human habitations and towns in the lap of Himalaya have been built in Fourth and Fifth Plans. Transport vehicular service is offered by Garhwal Motor Owners' Union, Tehri Motor Owners' Union, Kumaun Motor Owners' Union, UP Parivahan Nigam in these areas. Vehicles are also given on hire by Regional Vikas Nigams in Kumaun and Garhwal. Various private tourism agencies in these tracts run their package tours on their own vehicles. In foothills air service by Vayudoot is given up to Dehradun and Pantnagar stations, the latter being 75 km. from Nainital.

Potential-based Prospective Strategy of Development

The regional economy of Uttaranchal is by no means very different from the other hill areas in the Himalayan fold. The natural conditions here are similar to Himachal, Kashmir, Assam and rest of the backward areas of Himalayan fold. Relative distribution of the necessities of life over time and over space, across geographical regions are a useful means of focusing on living conditions. A large portion of the population in Uttaranchal Himalaya is still below poverty line and a quarter of it survives under abject poverty. The sources of living are in dearth due to very acute scarcity of the arable area and absence of alternative means of livelihood for an increasing labour force. The region faces unemployment as well as lack of purchasing power even for the essential things of daily life. Large-scale luxuries which are common among vested classes in the greater part of Indian plains are unknown in this area. The natural resources of the area have not been explored, scaled and utilized. Most of the areas in this Himalayan tract are unsuitable for agriculture and actual arable area, worthwhile, is about 16 per cent. For the absence of any alternative occupation, the economy is basically agrarian by character. The other combined occupations are forestry, animal husbandry, sheep and goat keeping, cottage industries, etc. The labourers have to migrate to the wider plains for employment as labour, porter, menial service and other unskilled works.

The entire tract of Himalaya is not satisfactorily usable for agriculture and human settlement. The unculturable land in Pithoragarh in the extreme east of Uttaranchal Himalaya, is 3.87 per cent while it is 19.40 per cent in Chamoli, 4.32 per cent in Almora, 0.54 per cent in Dehradun and 2.10 per cent Tehri. The land is shown as covered by forest or land meant for forests to the extent of 88.88 per cent in Uttarkashi, nearly 69 per cent in Tehri, 62 per cent in Pauri-Garhwal and 57 per cent in Nainital district. Even in Pithoragarh nearly 51 per cent area is devoted to forests. The actual green cover of forests is far too less now due to deforestation in recent decades, yet the area devoted to forests is not shiftable to cultivation. Net cultivated area, however, does not exceed 13.18 per cent in Pithoragarh, 5.50 per cent in Chamoli,

4.20 per cent in Uttarkashi, 12.43 per cent in Tehri-Garhwal and 16.97 per cent in Dehradun. Even in Almora district, the net cultivated area is only 15.66 per cent and in Nainital district it is 28.35 per cent while it also covers the Bhabar and Tarai parts of Udham Singh Nagar. The overall net cultivated area in this tract is around 15 per cent. Overall irrigated area in this tract is nearly 12.50 per cent which shows that good agriculture is not possible here (mountainous tract) in the background of poor soils, lack of irrigation, lesser arable land and dearth of transportation. Horticulture, dairying and poultry can, however, thrive if proper atmosphere for these is created (Table 2.22).

The region had some small-scale cottage units of industrial activity in the remoter past. Woollen, cotton textiles, mineral-based units, woodcraft and timber-based units, agro-based cottage level works, existed here even in the British regime. The opening of the area to wider competition with well-placed units in the wider plains by roads led to elimination of cottage units due to higher costs and low quality of the products and service. The official efforts to boost up cottage level industrial activity could not stimulate such works due to overall lack of demand in the area and competing units which came-up rapidly in the foothills, taking the advantage of low costs and availability of skill and raw-material there. In this sense this area survives as a colony for the developed areas of the state. Like other hill areas of India, namely Assam Hills, West Bengal Hills, former UP Hills have the problem of high costs for heavy industrialisation which relate to transport costs, environmental costs, skill compensatory costs and the marketing costs. The assembling type industries can thrive well in the region. Horticulture-based, vegetable-based, forest-based, consumer-based, fibre-based, mineral-based, leather-based, and engineering-based works can be developed in the area depending on the accessibility and availability of raw-material. The conventional industries in this tract were river water driven flour mills, oil crushing units, rope-making, tea industry, mat-making, cane works, wood-ware, crafts, woollen-textiles, metal-based ware, soap, phenyle, honey making, leather goods, vegetable fats, earthenwares, slate works, iron smithy, etc. But the new wave of competition and migration orientation eliminated this base. The new direction in which industrial activity has emerged

TABLE 2.22: Land Use Pattern in Uttaranchal, 1994-95

(In per cent)

District	Reporting area (Ha)	Forest	Barren and uncul-turable land	Land under non-agricul-tural uses	Waste land	Net area sown	Perma-nent pas-tures and other grazing land	Area under trees and groves	Current fallow land	Other fallow land
(1)	(2)	(3)	(4)	(5)	(6)	(7)	(8)	(9)	(10)	(11)
1. Nainital	7,03,097	57.42	0.66	4.79	4.52	28.35	0.18	2.63	0.43	1.02
2. Udham Singh Nagar	–	–	–	–	–	–	–	–	–	–
3. Almora	7,28,701	54.06	4.32	2.35	8.08	15.66	8.15	6.24	0.09	1.05
4. Bageshwar	–	–	–	–	–	–	–	–	–	–
5. Pithoragarh	6,37,200	51.84	3.87	2.26	8.04	13.18	12.17	6.59	0.17	1.88
6. Champawat	–	–	–	–	–	–	–	–	–	–
7. Tehri	5,74,544	69.13	2.10	1.89	12.51	12.43	0.49	0.003	0.007	1.44
8. Uttarkashi	8,17,631	88.83	2.28	0.78	1.03	4.20	1.58	0.86	0.004	0.44
9. Chamoli	8,41,382	61.93	19.40	2.13	3.92	5.70	2.57	4.16	0.01	0.19
10. Pauri	7,20,657	62.62	4.76	2.43	6.17	12.34	0.62	8.56	0.02	2.48
11. Rudraprayag	–	–	–	–	–	–	–	–	–	–
12. Dehradun	3,07,377	68.87	0.54	5.61	4.08	16.97	0.03	1.40	0.93	1.57
13. Haridwar	2,01,466	18.62	1.06	15.45	1.31	59.56	0.04	0.40	1.92	1.64
Uttaranchal	55,32,055	62.78	5.29	3.01	5.69	14.68	3.26	3.88	0.21	1.20

Source: Statistical Diary of the respective districts, 1995.

now is the kind of works employing electricity as power, e.g., cold storage, saw mills, furniture, hosiery, printing, etc. Carpet industry which was a conventional mode still survives with state help. Mineral works like magnesite, limestone powder, cement bricks, talcum powder, etc., are growing. Soap, wax, paints, varnishes, medicines and related chemicals are the new phases. Most of the units shown in this Himalayan hills are either financially weak and slow or are operating in Tarai belt with offices in hills. Television, radio, electric works, etc., have come-up in some areas. Bakeries and consumer-based works have gained some popularity due to tourist demand. Recently tourism industry has marked progress in the urban localities of hills and the catering industry has gained momentum. UP Financial Corporation, Pradeshiya Industrial Investment Corporation, State Industrial Development Corporation, Small-Scale Industries Development Corporation and the Regional Vikas Nigam for Kumaun and Garhwal, have tried to aid the entrepreneurs in the area.

Economy of Uttaranchal Himalaya, has evinced greater growth of tertiary occupation in urban sector. The area has been affected by tourism and state-promoted development. Thus, the employment in state sector has grown very rapidly. Education, health and related services have swelled the figures of tertiary growth. Infrastructural growth has also helped this. Trade, transport, commerce, security, peace, health, education, research, etc., are growing faster than manufacturing.

The guiding principles, on which the hill area programmes have been designed, are for the promotion of a secure basic life support to the people and the nature together. Geographers have emphasized the principle of complementarily between interests of hills and plains areas of the country. The preservation of ecology, environment and stability against landslides, floods, pollution, etc., is the theme of modern policy governing the hill areas. Hill areas are expected to function all in the interest of other areas, therefore, cultivation of terraces for crop raising is being discouraged. Landslides and floods in plains cause misery of millions.

Basic Needs Approach in development has diverted the attention of the state from the long-term area planning to immediate relief projects of civil supplies, energy supply, water, kerosene, health services, education and the local political development. Seventh Five Year Plan has observed, "since our understanding of the eco-system in these altitudes is limited, a sound data base has to be established for understanding of hydrology, climate, tectonics, seismology, flora and fauna and safe population carrying limits of each area. Even in more populated lower altitudes and regions, growing population concentration including tourists traffic seasonally, industrial projects and road building, promoted access, beyond safe carrying capacities have caused ecological strains and accelerated degradation, the ill-effects of which can be felt not only in middle mountain ranges and foothills but also in the plains below." (Government of India, Seventh Five Year Plan, 1985-90, Vol. II, 341). Hill areas are particularly suited to industries which require pollution-free atmosphere, cold climate, high skills and high value addition, e.g., electronics, watch making, optical glass, collapsible furniture, etc., handloom, carpet industry, food industries, processing and tourism, plantation, sericulture, agro-based works, etc., are suitable for hills.

3

Geography of Transport and Tourism: Background to the Subject Matter

Distribution of human, capital and entrepreneurial resources over the space and exploitation by combining them with diverse natural resources of the globe is possible by transport interconnections. Wilfred Owen (1964) in *Strategy for Mobility* remarked that transport interjoins the producing sectors and thus forms a process of production itself. In the context of vast geographical landmass, significance of this interlinking process is all the more significant. In the remote, distant, diverse and fragmented land parts, the sole factor in retardation is immobility. This results in major hurdles constituting deterrants to economic growth. S.K. Ray (1983) in *Economics of Third World* treats transport network as *sine qua non* of economic development.

Transport Geography is that branch of learning which relates to physical organisation of transport routes and constraints of landforms on movement of people and the goods and information necessary to maintain man and the superstructure built by him. Deserts, forests, mountains and rivers have an impact on free movement of people. How best the mobility of men and goods can be kept unrestricted under different forms of earth worries a geographer inclined to study the transport systems. Considerable potential of carrying very bulky commodities in great measures have been traced by transport geographers in river and other water transport systems. The Amazon, Nile, Ganges, Niger, Mekong rivers offer such illustrations. Commercial growth in ancient days was marked by this system. Even the heaviest wooden logs were carried undeterred in the river streams incurring only low costs. Great geographical explorations of continents were possible by the river stretches through the great distances. Similarly the railways afforded a great sustenance to the move for industrialisation in the early phases of nineteenth century. The geographers were able to interlink the coal mines and metallic mineral deposits with great manufacturing centres which ultimately led to the modern industrialisation. Military movements through the extended geographic frontiers could be possible by extension of railways. The remoter inlands have now been interconnected for free movement of people and goods by road transport.

The history of human civilisation can be spelt out by the developments in Transport Geography. The subject deals with the spatial possibilities and potentialities to help man in this search for the optimum travels at low costs. It is undeniably true that growth in economic, social and cultural terms and its rate of change hinges *inter alia* on national transport network. The role and significance of transportation in the space, earth or waters is exceedingly important on considerations like: historical, economic, environmental, social and political developments. Transportation governs trends of events as foundation for communication, trade, commerce as well as defence. The hinterlands are laid open by the transportation network and market dimensions are explored by this network. The relative levels of use and over-exploitation of national resources depend on transport and affect the ecology and environment. Urbanisation and population transfers depend again on transport. The railways, for instance, were extensively geared primarily to promote exports in favour of colonial empires in eighteenth and nineteenth centuries leaving the tracts through which the railway passed unaffected and unstimulated for economic betterment. The inflexibilities of the railway transport system were covered up by the introduction of road transport system and proved more successful in serving the local movement needs. These modes encouraged transport as an industry consisting millions of small-scale vehicle operators and petty entrepreneurs unlike a giant railway system. Smaller, fragile and perishable commodities also find the avenues of inter-regional transfer by the road transport and smaller places, towns and villages, in the nooks and corners, are conveniently served for human traffic as well as for goods traffic by the road transport. Geographers have suggested the complementarity of transport systems wherein a coordination emerges between them setting aside the unhealthy competition. Road transport involves high costs as compared to railways in maintenance of routes as well as in haulage. The marketable surplus from remote production centres is mobilised by roads as complementarity service to the huge structure of railways which operate more efficiently in carrying bulk-loads on long distances. Railways make the nations to keep united and varied parts interconnected for the purposes of administration and control. Rail network of Russia and India are important for their unity among geographically different parts. *Indian Railways Year Book* (1984-85) reads that it has Rs.10,377 crores of investment, it operates over a route of 61,850 kms., it employs 16.03 lakh employees and feeds the industrial demands as well as passenger flows together with aiding the trade and commerce of the vast economy. Nearly 38,585 vehicular coaches run on the tracks interconnecting the whole of the country. The annual revenue generated by the vast Indian Railways is to the order of Rs. 5,358.77 crores. Steam, diesel and electric locomotives total to 10,128 in 1986. Nearly 334 crore passengers travel by the railways and 26.5 crore tonnes of load is carried to remote corners. This suggests how important is the role of transport network.

Indian shipping transport is not yet so developed as is desirable and as the potentialities suggest. India has hardly 436 ships and handle 7,500 thousand tonnes (GRT) of load. Hardly 30 per cent of the cargo traffic in Indian overseas trade is done by Indian fleet. Nearly 11.3 hundred crore of rupees are earned by Kolkata port only. Nearly 44 hundred crore rupees are earned by Chennai port annually. Similarly 39.6 crore rupees are earned by Vishakhapattnam port per year. 11.6 crore passengers are embarked per year in Mumbai port. Nearly 67.7 crore tonnes of load is imported annually through Calcutta port and 19.8 crore tonnes of load is exported from this port. This suggests the role of transportation network in India alone. While India is a very poor nation in terms of foreign trade. Overall, sophistication of container vehicles, tankers, cellular ships and dearth of organisational discipline in India sea transport are eminent. When Indian shipping attains its gloom, it would be one of the world's biggest shipping system. Where and how the ports can be developed to the optimum benefit of the trade is suggested by the expertise of Transport Geographer.

Air transport is rather a costly mode of transport for under-developed areas and less resourceful part of the people, yet time resource saved, wherever it is scarce, is more than compensating for the greater monetary costs in the air transport. For such landforms, where the road and railway cannot emerge or are time consuming, air transport affords a handy service of movement of people and freight. Separated, secluded, fragmented and remote areas are served with well-proned advantage by air transport. Passenger and freight traffic by air is of considerable importance for national cohesion (Barke and O'Hare, 1984, 160-71). The transport modes have helped the development of tourism and world trade. Tourism has relatively low costs when compared with trade and even the tiny and less resourceful and less developed countries have the benefit of greater income creation. It is hence proved to be labour intensive industry and created employment potential. Thus, Transport Geography covers the field of accessibilities and making the approaches to the remotest resources with the objective of utmost utilisation by man. The transportation and communication networks should allow people, goods and messages to flow efficiently at low cost, higher accuracy, better speed, safety and comfort. Clumsy and inefficient transport structures do not deliver the service with greater satisfaction. The right type of networks are suggested by a Transport Geographer. Thus, there are three components in Transport Geography: (a) the network of linkages, (b) the study of interlinks between linkages and flows, and (c) the study of flows themselves. Flows cover a very wide range of things that emerge due to the flows. Society itself is the cause and result of flows. Various cultural patterns are the products of flows. Economic development is both a cause and consequence of flows of goods, men, materials and resources. The trade, commerce, communication and exchange involve the flows (Yeats, 1968, 113-14).

A brief idea of the role of air transport can be formulated by taking an example of Indian economy. Indian Air Lines and Air India, the two air corporations carried 68,25,000 revenue passengers in 1981, taking flights over 1,400.3 million revenue tonne kilometres. Indian airways will attain their target of 23.6 billion passenger kilometres business by 2000 AD. International transportation has greater role of maritime shipping and air transport. As the tourist grows and trade flourishes the roles are bound to mount-up in context of India.

Objectives of Transport System

The systems are devised to reduce the user's cost of movement in a given set of traffic flows. The cost of developing and building the structure of the transport network and facility building has to be minimised while the utility offered to the user has to be optimised. This is possible by keeping the building costs, operating costs, choosing the closest route and working on choicest of convenient designs. A sort of normative structure is conceived as a model of networks and flows in the imaginative form. The practised system, at times, exactly matches to the model and sometimes it deviates causing the cost to vary. Geographers study the origins and flows, directions and spill over in the spheres of movement geometry. The movements are not in a parallel time-bound traffic flow but are marked with variations quite off and on. For analytical purposes the flows are mapped and, lower and upper boundaries of fluctuations are portrayed in origin and destination end points. A geographer ignores actors and activities for the sociologists and economists, but take-up the basic spatial dimensions of movement with reference to the relief system. The movements identical and similar are isolated and marked point-to-point which comprise the geographer's transportation and communication media. Breaking down the complexity of almost infinite number of movements on the basis of spatial structures of the origin and destination points is helpful in isolating each movement within demarcated points. Several combinations and permutations emerge from the four spatial structures and all directions of the flows are covered. The computational possibilities rate searched to digest and formulate an ideal structure. The transport systems have the objectives of delivering service of movement at lowest user's cost and keeping the operating costs at the lowest ebb and offering the choicest of the convenient designs by choosing an ideal structure of transport network to cater the needs of the innumerable simultaneous flows of traffic to different directions.

Tourism and its Rationality

Tourism is the process by which the unsatiable lust of the tourist to visit new places, enjoy and see the bountiful nature and human-makes, is satisfied. The process is attained through travel that he undertakes. The bent of mind which makes the tourist move and the philosophy which motivates him to the journey is tourism. There may be several objectives behind. Sometimes these may be undiagnosed and unknown to the person who undertakes the journey or he may not express it within his gripped vocabulary. Tourism, in fact, explains the cause of movement affecting the current of traffic flows, time schedules and directions. When the bent of mind of the people, in general, favours trip-making, holidaying outside the normal place of residence, site seeing, enjoying travel in different landforms and water bodies, etc., the movement of the people grows to greater numbers and the traffic flows emerge to demand transport network. Thus, tourism covers, both, the activity of travel and the bent of mind which causes it.

Travel Consciousness

When the sustained bent of mind of the people motivates large-scale travel consciousness and movement place-to-place, spatial mobility becomes the token of higher ways of living, it has some obvious implications (Robinson, 1976, xxvi). How people move? When do they choose to move? Which directions they opt to move? What are the purposes of movement, etc., are the questions emerging before the analyst. He observes the entire activity of movement and makes his measurements and derives some general tendencies. Thus, tourism is studied by the analyst as a phenomenon. When these are studied in various dimensions to satisfy more than one curiosity or question, it makes the entire phenomena under study. To the person who undertakes a journey for his satisfaction, it is an activity. To the sociologist, it is a social activity indicating mobilities and bearing upon the social behaviour and interaction. Economist may choose to classify this movement as having some involvement of cost and gain in hedonistic angle of thought. Geographer concerns himself to analyse whether the movement flows along the space work-out to his ideal structure of optimality.

Socio-Cultural and Economic Factors in Transport Development

Abler, Adams and Gould (Abler, Adams and Gould, 1971, 289) very aptly remarked, "... No where is this principle illustrated more dramatically than in instances where transportation and communication improvements have transformed isolated, self-sufficient, subsistence farmers into prosperous commercial producers.... For the fortunate one-third of the world's people, absolute space has been transformed into relative space by adjusting systems". Economists have found that immobility has bogged down the stagnant pools of traditionalism to staggering deprivation and tradition trodden techniques resulting in low performance. The dynamic elements have filtered gains from mobility and travel. Immobility retains inside the isolated walls of the habitations and technology of doing things and skills of solving the challenges of nature become crude in seclusion for want of mobility. What Wilfred Owen (Owen, 1956) emphatically established, "immobility perpetuates poverty...." Large-scale production and modernisation of techniques of output creation depends on international specialisation and trade across the national boundaries. The movement of goods is essential not only for exchange but necessary in order to organise production by transporting inputs and mass-scale haulage of fuels. The products of more than a million types move in different directions to find the consumers. The goods traffic flows, in a way, are more complicated to understand and the complexities are tending to multiply as new transport systems are devised. Forms and composition of output, are changing still faster. Social interactions and closer contacts are able to establish understanding, mutual appreciation and goodwill. The global unification of cultures is resulting from global movement of people in large-scale. In today's world, it is well-nigh impossible to imagine of a developed frame of human mind without undertaking tours and extensive travels. Therefore, the role of transport and tourism constitutes the very bed-rock of modernism.

Future Prospects of Transport and Tourism

The development of great metropolis centres and giant urban settlement complexes has rendered the life so fast and time-bound that the future depends on the efficiencies of transport and movement accuracies along space and time. The multidimensional growth of human civilisation has necessitated great articulation skills and combining of things to the precision and accuracy. Labour movement to work-places from hundreds of kilometres away from all odd directions, movement of goods and apparatus from continents across and time-bound connections of vehicular transport in multi-angular movement, revolutionizing networks of communications and transport structures, etc., are making the life so complicated that most sophisticated computers are at human service to monitor these systems. In such a growing process of complexities the role of transport structures, their forms, growth and efficiencies, alone, will solve human traffic flows and unending challenges of goods traffic management. So far the tourism and movement has only a small segment of population under its coverage. The future shall demand greater efficiencies at every count. As the marketing and scales of production will expand and new products are created, the consumption horizons expand, population shall multiply and their wants and aspirations mount up, challenges get by far more skill-demanding.

Outline of the Themes

The present endeavour is an attempt to diagnose the problem of role of transport network, modes and patterns in development of tourism. The study chooses to investigate into the different dimensions of the chosen problem with special reference to the development of tourism in the Uttaranchal Himalaya. The main identifying characteristics and distinct elements of tourism, which separate it from general flow of the traffic are: (a) involvement of travel by non-residents of the place; (b) stay of temporary nature in the area where the visit is made; and (c) the outdoor stay is not intended for the purposes of making earnings and practising professions. It is known that hill areas and their peripheral areas in foothills have a tourist flow primarily for merry-making, fun and frolic, rod and rifle romance, making health gains by climatic advantages of these areas, and aesthetic satisfaction besides the foremost gains of visiting pilgrim centres in the abode of Gods. The region had eminent temples and shrines of Hindus, Sikhs and other sub-communities. The devotees had been pouring in this tract on foot from various remote places within and outside the country for ages-past. But the emergence of modern efficient transportation systems and well-knit network of air transport, road transport, etc., have led to sudden growth of tourism within a decade to several folds. The emergence of the modern transport network has more than singular impact. It has offered the local economy and society a foremost ingredient of developmental infrastructure. The forward and backward linkages of the activity, in a long run, have created novel forces and waves of stimulations for other sectors to grow. The sectors which got more encouragement by the spurt in the traffic flow of tourists in the recent years may be the operation of vehicles commercially to cater to the growing passenger needs as well as the goods carriages, promoted by the demand for goods raised by the newly introduced tourism. The massive road building in this Himalayan tract in the post-Independence period prompted the intending traffic of devotees to the holy shrines of Badrinath, Kedarnath and holy Rupkund. The pedestrian pilgrimage was possible only by the physically stout and strong. Motor vehicle movement to these remote locations has persuaded even the weak, and even infants can be taken along the female devotees. Besides the pilgrims, there is a huge influx of tourists from abroad as well as the remotely placed parts of the country to the tourist centres in Kumaun and Garhwal divisions. A large number of new tourist centres have come-up in the recent decades. The private and public sector investments have shot-up in the region.

Tourism has its own typical culture featured by greater intermixing of people, cultural cocktail, face-lifting of the buildings, decorations on roads, and greater attention given to the sewage, sanitation, water supply and ensued electric supply, emergence of hotels and restaurants and greater proneness to money-making. Tourism is essentially a service-creating industry and develops the tertiary sector faster. The areas in the grip of newly emerging tourism culture have picked-up these traits and other sites on way are following suit.

In hill areas of Uttaranchal, the tract was treated as inaccessible and road building was believed to be exhorbitantly costly in view of the hard rocks, instability of the upper thin soil, involvement of too many bridges and culverts. The products of cottage industry, agriculture and creative arts had no market outside the tradition trodden tribal agriculture inside the rims of the mountain walls. The interlinks and contacts with outside world were practically restricted which in turn kept the technique of agriculture and industry backward and the inhabitants had been denied the basic services of education, health, electricity, water and communication. Transport network in the region developed in post-Independence period raised various new challenges, constraints, rivalries, competition, technical change and utilisation of factors, i.e. land, labour, capital and technology. New form of entrepreneurship entered the region. The tourism industry founds its access into the region due to the emergence of a modernised network of road transport. The difference is very clearly marked if we compare the state of areas linked by transport and the secluded areas unlinked by any mode of modern transport.

Tourism has activated the rest of the economy due to the injection of effective demand for the idle capacities. It has led to earnings not only in domestic currency but has turned this tract as earner of the rare foreign exchange in terms of dollars, guilders, sterling and marks. Transport has not taken the form of an organised industry along with tourism.

Tourism has, by far, changed the life style, status of women, dignity of the untouchables in the remote past, shifted the allocation pattern in consumption and saving. The architectural designs and materials have undergone a big change in the area due to the increased transport and large-scale haulage of cement, bricks and machinery to this end.

Tools and Techniques of Analysis in Transport Geography

The present study sets before itself the objective of investigating into these dimensions of change, assessing the impact of transport network measuring the nature and scale of transportation in various modes and trying to evaluate the extent of growth of traffic flows, and their directions. The study is designed to assess the overall existing pattern of transport, communication and tourism structure, establishments and their working over the past decades. The precise estimation of the growth of income, investments, employment and such other dimensions as a result of transport-communication and tourism is being attempted to confirm the general impressions enumerated in the set of hypotheses. The associative objectives of the study are the estimation of the growth of tourist accommodation, hotels, yatree niwas, their facility structures, their utilisation levels and yields in terms of earnings. The study, under the associative objectives, would go into the building costs of the hotels and overall frame of maintenance costs including the unutilized capacity.

Techniques developed in the sphere of transport geography to make such types of assessments of the state and status of transport network, traffic flows and related infrastructure shall be employed to reach the conclusion and pave a path for planning in a longer perspective.

Working Out Techniques and Literature Survey

The eminent geographers like W.L. Garrison and D.F. Marble (1961), K.J. Kensky (1963), W. Bunge (1966), E.J. Taaffe, R.L. Morrill and P.R. Gould (1963), J.P. Cole and C.A.M. King (1968), P. Haggett and R.J. Chorley (1969), R. Abler, J.S. Adams and P. Gould (1971), M.J. Beckmann (1967), Z. Prihar (1956), Jagdish Singh (1972), etc., have shown the beckon light towards studies on Transport Geography. A very large galaxy of writers have attempted the field of scaling the impact of transport in different references. This study has to draw its own methodology to pave a path for scientific assessment and analysis. Tourism is not an untouched area of analysis. Great many experts like – H. Robinson (1976),

A.J. Norval (1936), T.S. Yukic (1963), J. White (1967), A.J. Burckart (1975), J.M. Bryden (1973), T.L. Burton (1970), I. Cosgrove and R. Jackson (1972), J.E. Williams and W. Zelinsky (1970), R.I. Wolfe (1966), J. Naylon (1967), S. Sayer (1973), A.K. Bhatia (1982), P.N. Seth (1978), T.V. Singh (1979), R.N. Kaul (1985), etc., have worked extensively in this field.

The present study takes up the conceptual understanding as a basic task and tries to identify the precise definitional frame before reaching the theoretical interrelation established and proved so far by the thinkers in the past. The study, thereafter, stretches across the conceptual framework and phraseology adotped in the studies. How the various parts and sub-topics are believed to be interwoven and the causes, animators and consequences of tourism are proposed to be taken up by this study in order to proceed to the deeper analysis with reference to this area under reference. The socio-economic and cultural consequence of transport network building and tourism development are likely to be discussed at length in this study as based on the secondary sources and extensive survey of literature on these titles. The inter-relationships between the determinants and main variables shall have to be attempted in the context of resource utilisation and transport development, infrastructural strengthening and investment relationships as related to the transport network knitting. How the economic variables and cultural factors affect tourism development shall be given the analytical treatment with evidences found out by empirical methods. A detailed analysis of the physical and cultural environment in the region under reference shall be attempted so as to interrelate the gains of transport and tourism with the achievements of the local economy. The stimulation process and forces of modernisation unleashed by development of transport and tourism in local economy shall have to be analysed.

Under the procedures adopted in this research plan, a detailed analysis of structural designs of transportation network and pattern of development of tourism will be easier with these background studies before hand. The tools and techniques of Transport Geography are adequate to measure the accessibilities, cast the topographical properties and their bearing on the transportation network and analyse the transport connectivity in this reference. The impact of these on economic development and socio-cultural growth may be sorted out at this stage.

In depth studies on local road development pattern, traffic flows and traffic management with reference to the passenger and goods-movement, to and fro, shall penetrate into the growth of vehicular traffic and its administration. The dimensions of official, semi-official and private stimulating organisation of tourism shall constitute a large part of the analysis at this stage. In order to acquaint itself with the local morphology of the tourist potentials, a detailed study of the place, origin and destination ends and the way back will be done with the objective of assessing the optimality of development and transport network-catering. Towards the end, this study proposes to identify the large range of new problems, potentialities and prospects of development of tourism in the Himalayan tract. The road building and blasting of the unstable rocks, deforestation for consumption, clearance, cultivation, penetration of hostile population groups into the secluded mountain habitat, etc., have raised some distortions in the ecological equilibrium, disturbances in environment and underground water table, and socio-spheric challenges which shall constitute the policy prescription parts of this study.

The scope of the study, thus, summarises itself into the following major points:

(a) To study transport network and connectivity with reference to tourism development.
(b) To specify and correlate tourist movement patterns and flows.
(c) To mark and identify accessible and non-accessible areas and to analyse topological properties of transport network.
(d) To study the pattern of organisation, social and economic significance of tourism.
(e) To establish a correlation between the infrastructural facilities and tourism development.
(f) To conduct tourist measurements and surveys with the help of sample studies.

(g) To promote and develop the foreign tourist movement in the region.

(h) To study travel and tourist problems and potentialities in the region; and suggest necessary measures towards the growth of the regional tourist economy.

(i) To study the environmental degradation, planning challenges with reference to the new developments as a consequence of developments in transport and tourism in Uttaranchal.

The Profile of Information

The study runs along the path of the location analysis, morphological identification, mapping, indication and marking of routes and sites of tourist flows, and makes a vast statistical profile available to the world or researchers in the field. The compilation of data from a very large number of agencies on the issues and dimensions enumerated earlier is the objective herein. Primary, secondary and literary sources shall be carefully tapped on filter the evidences and references in the context of this study. In the primary data collection, discussions, reactions and experiences of the staff, tourism enterprises and pilgrims are being recorded. These shall go a long way in suggesting the problems and policy imperatives. The secondary sources like statistical agencies, expert mapping organisations like – Survey of India, Transport Department of the state, Tourism Development Corporation, Central Tourism Development Corporation, records of temple committees and related offices, hotel records and the municipal records have been carefully seen and necessary data to the specific evidences have been collected. The small as well as large scale topographical sheets (maps) of Survey of India have been used for the purpose of the study. Among the literary sources, analytical reports, tour notes, inspection reports, books, articles in the journals, data published in periodical bulletins, etc., are included. The utilisation of the surveys and studies attempted earlier in various related contexts shall also be ensured to make the study equipped and substantiated with up to date references and evidences.

Having collected the vast range of data from these sources the study has tried to verify the hypotheses and the general hunches developed in the initial chapters. The data have been processed, classed and categorised and interrelated to filter definite tendencies. The data profile have also been reduced to smaller tables to find the break-ups and regional statistical portrait.

4

Transport Linkages: Prime Analytical Dimensions

Spatial Linkages: The Connotation

Transport Geography has very precise and well-defined phraseology which makes the expression accurate to the needs without entering the realm of confusion. Hodder and Lee (Hodder and Lee, 1974, 148) treat transport network as – physical expression of integration within and between economies. They are both cause and effect of the movement demands induced by this integration. The functional integration between the places thus is the domain of transport. When one economy comes in direct contact of the other, a network of exchange is woven between them. This is, by and large, the result of spatial interaction. The generation and distribution of this interaction over the space calls for the exchange and movement. This movement can be understood as a demand for transport. The demand is met by the pressure and persuasions in the economy to weave the transport linkages. These linkages in turn take-up the burden of handling the job of movements whether men, materials or messages. The greater the integration between location and higher the intensity of contacts, more is the demand for transport which ultimately lead to inducement for weaving a network. Hodder and Lee have rightly remarked, "The demand for transport is not an independent variable affecting the supply of transport because both the generation and distribution movements are closely affected by the structure and efficiency of transportation" (Hodder and Lee, 1974, 148).

The eminent transport geographer, Kansky (Kansky, 1963, 3) found the transport networks lumpy and capital intensive for their being cost involving in initial stages specially the engineering costs and fixed costs of capital. Another great thinker on the subject, Gauthier (Gauthier, 1970, 612-19) claimed that transportation networks are problematic in developing nations for their being short of capital while 20-40 per cent of investments in them are for development of transport and communication networks. The authoritative contribution of Hirschman (Hirschman, 1958), economist favouring unbalanced growth patterns for developing economies, pleaded for huge concentration of investment on development of transport network which ultimately promote the directly productive activities in the economy. Similarly, Richmond (Richmond, 1957, 67-73) emphasized the interspatial transport inducements useful to the growth of the interlinked economics. Transport networks are the infrastructure, the basic minimum of the facility interconnecting the localities which promote the exchange and movement of passengers and goods. This ultimately leads to the social and economic growth besides the integration at all levels.

Transport is a compensatory process as a remedial measure for rectifying the anomalies of supplies at various locations. Its aim in case of goods transport is to set men free in respect of place-relations and to make these relations more elastic to social needs. Gould (Gould, 1960) opined that a sense of complementarity can be filtered from the transportation process undertaken inter-space. The alternative destinations in transportation offer attractiveness unfulfilled by the place of origin. Human needs to interact with rest of the population, see and observe the phenomena of nature, and use things not produced at the place of habitation generate the continued process of transportation. The economists place transportation in productive processes for their being related to enhancement of usefulness. This may involve the movement of goods or the factors themselves. The inherent difference between transportation and travel is marked by a 'feel' of the living thing experienced on way to the destination. Goods do not feel so these are transported by the passengers travel while being transported. Similarly 'trip' differs from a travel because the trip is marked for hurried round without involving any enjoyment on way. A businessman moves on a trip wherein he is dispatched on a mission for a destination for specified purpose and he has no inclination for enjoying the journey and experiences on way. In transport the obvious questions which arise relate to the mode of transport, speed, freight, efficiency in loading and unloading and the related efficiencies of services. Cost elements are highly relevant in transportation and in this context the shortest route and least effort-lowest cost criteria matters. In case of travel these considerations do not constitute as big a decisive role as they have in transportation.

Transport as an Instrument of Mastering Space

Ullman (Ullman, 1956, 862-80) has suggested threefold system to explain interaction development. According to him, the bases for transportation and interaction are: complementarity, intervening opportunity and transferability. Transport means "carrying interspace". Kurt Weidenfield defined it as "the technical instruments and organisation designed to enable persons, commodities and news to master space". In its technical connotation, transport includes the network of communications. It constitutes the very thread work of integration between the human habitations, space and the man. It is the route to the unification process. Goods, persons, ideas and skills flow interspace with the help of the systems created by men. This may include the human being, mastered animal force, vehicles, trains, air buses and aeroplanes, ships, postal system, telegraph system, wireless, television, newspapers, or the other complex of communication system. A telephone service represents a transport of ideas and messages. In the savage era, the human need of transport was only meagre and human force was enough to manage it. As the nomadic system gave way and the human civilisation came to settle itself in agriculture, the specialisation started growing more complicated. Emergence of market and exchange system led to intensification of dependence and societal cooperation. A felt need of network of transport emerged to reach the goods, men, ideas, messages and skill to various cores of production system. Growing needs and expanding horizons of human civilisation raised the need of transport in alarming scale. The emergence of state led to still greater need of integration within the human habitations and so also of the outer contacts. This multiplied the need for efficient modes of transport. All attempts to meet the scarcity challenges were practically ended with new inventions in the field of transport to win over the space. The growth of modern material civilisation was practically a continued war against the physical separation of men, material, resources, workers, consumers, producers and the other wings of production structure. Transport is the interlinking agent between these. Once these are brought together in touch, whether physical or otherwise, the production process starts. Having crossed over the stages of production, output has to cross through the processes of exchange and marketing which again requires the victory over the separating factors and obstacles to mobility. The transport system brings the exchanging parties together by physical or other contacts before transport system reaches the final products to the gates of the wider mass of consumers scattered over the globe.

Transport Combines Resources

Geographers and economists often believe that production in any form is with the help of the earth's resources. Production is the process of making an addition to utility of a good commodity, idea, situation, etc., to the welfare of man or to the satisfaction of human will. Since the human preference changes over time and space, therefore, production also varies over them. The usefulness of human gain can occur from goods and services in various ways are kept within the bracket of production. Geographers have for long emphasized and analysed production in terms of crop-raising. Economists have termed this as quantitative enhancement where one seed leads to production of several seeds in cooperation with nature. A geographer would not perhaps agree to the concept of quantitative growth by raising crop. Because the total resources and elements in the envelope of the earth including space are fixed and quite a bit measured. Nobody adds or reduces the total quantum of the contents of globe. A farmer to his best intentions only causes some changes wherein the resources of the nature are made to change forms. Thus, production is fundamentally a change causing suitability to human needs. Whether it is a case of forestry, multiplication of fish, poultry farming, dairying, cropping of cereals, or any such other form of production of primary sector, or it is the manufacturing sector, the concept of production finds a neat application. Growth in the ability and availability of a thing to satisfy human want is production. When a mineral exploration works towards extracting coal from a mine it only makes a thing, useful to man, available. Change in form promotes the availability. A manufacturer combines factors like raw materials, nature, labour, capital, skill and management, and thus, gives the initial raw materials a shape and merit more convenient for human use. Manufacturer does not create, he only combines and changes the form.

Usefulness of a commodity, person, information or skill also grows if these undergo a spatial change in the same way as the structural change, compositional change or temporal change would do. Transport as a process of production, renders this service. It shifts the commodity, person, message, skill and information from one point of space at a point of time to the other, so that its usefulness grows. This growth of usefulness is production. Some commodities are more desirable for human beings at some places than the other. This service of sending goods to the places of more desirability is the cause of addition to the usefulness of increased capacity to satisfy human want. In this sense transport causes the place utility creation. The production structure is located at a place where all types of raw materials are not produced. The materials are shifted from the sites of production at farmer's place to the factory. In the similar way, the labourers are carried to the factory site. The building materials which make the factory have to be carried to the place. Power, water and other amenities are reached to the site. The capital assets like machines and structures are shifted from other places to the factory site. Without all this, the production is not possible. Soil fertility does not allow production of all materials at a place. This necessitates the use of carrying mechanism. Things are equally useful everywhere because the need is relative to climate, total consumers, availability and the purchasing power. The varying need intensities are the cause of trade. A service of shifting the thing or commodity from the area of less intensity of need to greater intensity of need is transport and it is this shifting and presentation for consumption at a new place which fetches it higher price Transport covers the areas of power-transmission as well as communication of ideas whether by message on phone or by press. Combining factors for such change in forms which add to human utility is production and the combining depends on the transport of all the connected agents to the producer. Thus, production is made possible by transport. Drawing canal includes transport of water itself while the motor boats on the canals carry men which is human and goods transport. The transport system serves the economy of a country the same way as the veins and neuro-system serve a human body. It is the clue to the understanding of distribution of production in the economy. The equalisation of prices over the space is the resultant impact of transport system. The inter-space differential of need intensities and quantum of supplies explain the price-differentials. The traders with the help of the transport system create the space-utilities and, this way, redistribution occurs in an automatic way over the space according to the intensity and purchasing power of different areas. Prices get smoothened due to the transportation. Time utilities are created by the cold storage and warehousing services which redistribute the supplies over time.

Transport as a Sector of Production

Transport not only promotes and nourishes production, it is a production in itself. In the present day world, a very sizeable labour force, capital and entrepreneurship is devoted to the activities related to the manufacture of the structures, apparatus and equipment of the transport vehicles, roads, railway track, aerodromes, aeroplanes, ships, locomotives, rickshaws, bullock-carts, rope-ways, telephone systems, telegraph lines, wireless and television activity including all types of transmissions. The spread of gas supply pipes and petrol supply pipes is the transport service active in promoting production as well as consumption. The nations which pioneered in the production, development and application of efficient modes of transport are the richest and developed of all the countries of the globe. The disutility of spatial separation has been neutralised to a great extent by the development of transport. The utilisation of resources of the globe to the optimum welfare of man has been rendered possible by the growing efficiency of transport system. Remotely placed resources whether land, labour, capital, enterprise or others are in themselves useless till they are put to process of production for man. Transport is that mechanism which carries idle herbs of Himalaya to the remotest lands curing the ailing humanity in the form of medicines. Idle manpower of Bihar and West Bengal is reached Durgapur, Rourkela and Bhilai for steel making. Great warriors of Punjab, Haryana and hill states are taken to remote borderlands for protecting the motherland. The speciality of soil and its fertility are reached the remoter lands and foreign lands in the shape of agro-exports. The natural endowments of Bihar and Assam run the huge industrial complexes in distant parts of India as well as in remote parts of the globe which import these minerals from India. For the absence of transport human consumption levels would have been only meagre and living standard would have been by far negligible. It is the water transport facility which was first to helpout production in modern patterns. Most of the factory production came to be settled in river beds, sêa-shores and such other places. Movement of labour in all forms has been possible due to transport. The communication and banking systems have helped in shifting messages, news and information and mobilise capital. Communication again is a part of transport. Mobilisation of savings of the current production led to warehousing and generation of capital. The mangerial and administrative skill is shifted from the place of origin to the place of use by transport. The Gujaratis, Marwaris, Parsees and in a measure Punjabis have exhibited high level of spatial mobility due to the transport systems. Entrepreneurship is not distributed over the space in an equal measure. Opportunity costs shift the factors from one use to the other and mobility is made possible by the modern development of transport. The entire modern framework of international, inter-regional and intra-region trade is made possible by the various forms of transport facilities evolved by man. The speculative markets of the stock exchange and price work on the footing of the communication of information. Every dimension of human life depends on the information channels network of transportation.

Transport Animates Regional Specialisation and Trade

It is universally known that Ohlin (Ohlin, 1935) proved the fact that an international trade is a special case of inter-regional trade emerging from the differential in costs of production due to the varying proportions of factor endowments spatially. Regions have spatial advantages on some points and disadvantages on the other. The comparative costs of production suggest the line of optimum specialisation. The goods so produced under specialisation are exchanged between regions. The sole burden of exchange and commodity movement is borne by the transport which shortens all the distances. The international division of labour is rendered practicable due to the transport development. The credit of utilising even the marginal and sub-marginal lands for economic purposes goes to transport. Equalisation of wage rates and interest rates spatially is possible due to the increased mobility of factors owing to the transport. Inter-space mobility of capital and entrepreneurship equalises the profit rates. The investment opportunities and scope for expansionary trend in investment gets bright when transport opens up the avenues. Even the best locations do not find support of investors and industrymen if transport services are not available the overall mobility of men, material, skill and ideas is restricted.

Transport Network Promotes Cultural Inter-Mix

Transport creates mobility and inter-community contacts. Social and cultural links between communities are promoted by transport. This leads to breaking of isolation and seclusion. Unification process in technology, modes of exchange, styles of production, life-style, consumption pattern, thinking and philosophy ultimately integrates the society in a close-knit of common culture and language. The accumulated surpluses are collected together to constitute single social investible pool.

Transport animates merger of isolated cultural currents into the main stream. Breaking of isolation of rural sector and remoter human settlements, leads to prolonged and sustained process of urbanisation. The urban life styles penetrate deeper to the rural habitations and market-systems find birth in rural areas. Transport introduces new goods, new norms and new techniques in the remoter areas which keep untouched by modernism in absence of transport. In a sense the over-mobility caused by the transport creates the over-crowded cities. The international closer contacts today are due to transport of messages and news. International peace is generated due to such development. The unification process of the globe is the gift of improved levels of transport. Stability and effectiveness of law and order and government administration cannot run in absence of efficient transport system. This extensive review of the gains of the transport suggests that all human progress is largely to be ascribed to the credit of development of transport. It is yet a logic subject to doubt that all results of transportation progress have been unmixed blessing. There can be some situations more favourable to preservation of higher human values in a state without much of transport. The tribal communities have preserved some basic human values which the present day unified world has lost altogether. Specialisation and large scale production has not always been good. Global exchange and minutest division of labour has reduced human dignity to those of twigs of wood which are constrained to flow with the stream of water. Individual liberty, taste, dignity, character, crafts, etc., have been swept away in the general wave of large scale production and standardised norms. The areas which have failed in winning the favour of transport are lagging in the race of development and inter-region growth differntials have become too much evident now. Consumerism and futile waste of resources, inter-region exploitation and drain on the resources of some areas has been due to the transport development. Experience of the lagging communities and backward areas makes it evident that transport tends to put two unequal competitors at a 'duel' wherein the stronger is bound to win and conquer. Powerful oppresses the weak and less developed areas when compete with the developed, the former loses its industry as well as entrepreneurship. Transport breaks the monopoly positions of the meagre scale workers but strengthens the monopoly of large scale producers. It is, therefore, correct to conclude that the *laissez faire* is less than fair. But the drawbacks enumerated in the above paragraph are the failures of an economic policy and administrative system which should by all means protect the weak. Transport does not suggest this exploitation rather opens up the horizons of a new expansionary move. Transport is a system, an industry and a service network considerably helpful in human betterment.

Spatial Interlinks and Sectoral Coordination

It is an undeniable fact that the introduction of railways stimulated trade and movement of factors of production tremendously. The growth of industries and farm production rose considerably higher everywhere due to a cheap and comfortable mode of transport. The primary sector as mother of other sectors, was able to create raw material, surpluse of output and capital for other sectors. The inter-sectoral exchange is possible only due to the interlinking capacities of transport system. Cash crops on commercial scale would not have been produced without an efficient transport. Food could not have reached the non-agricultural producers of any economy if transport had not guaranteed the regular supplies. It is to the sole credit of the transport system that most perishable goods are also produced on a large-scale and consumed in very remote areas. The marketed surplus grows with the greater availability of transport and the process of specialisation gets strengthened. The industrial fuels are traded and transported intercontinentally and output is traded round the globe only due to transportation facilities.

Network of Linkages

Roads have worked as veins and arteries and helped in proper circulation of factors in each organ of the economy. Roads make the network of linkages rendering the essential services of inter-space transfer and passage of the flow of products of human-make as well as the natural resources like basic materials. Maurice H. Yeates (Yeates, 1968, 113) in his classic work *An Introduction to Qualitative Analysis in Economic Geography* categorised these flows in three parts:

(a) flow of goods;
(b) flow of services; and
(c) flow of ideas.

These may further include a separate category of flow of basic and human recources. In its practical meaning the transport geography is the study of the inter-spatial connections of trade, exchange and commodity links. The links are formed only by the aid of the transport systems. How one region gets in touch of the cultural patterns, traditions, practices of life and habits is to be found out in the linkages established by the transport systems. The manpower tends to shift from one location to the other as labourers, skilled men and organisers of activities or as other agents of production or as groups of consumers. Anyway, the links towards building an organised society are to the credit of the transport woven across the fragmented geographic regions. The production capacity of human race across the land surface depends much on the techniques which spread from one set of the population to the other. Innovations are carried inter-spatially by the transportation of the persons, their experiences and their skill. In the similar fashion the areas deficient in resources like minerals, water, power, etc., are fed with the resources with the help of transport. Transmission systems in this sense constitute a form of transport.

Regional Inter-Dependency, Specialisation and Transport

Human civilisation has grown on the foundation pillars of specialisation, division of labour and economic collaboration. The entire society undertakes to collaborate in production agreeing to a blue print of division of labour and specialisation at the first stage, and exchange collaboration at the second stage. The success of the collaboration depends considerably on the working of efficient transport network which alone can ensure the emergence of the situations of contact between producers and the buyers and a factor-market to feed the specialisation mechanism. Better transport interlinks, therefore, can well indicate a higher level of economic development and greater extent of specialisation in production of goods and services developed between the regions. The price equalisation mechanism over the space is spread by the transport network and the making of availabilities possible over the fragmented space is entirely to the credit of the network of transport in its various modes. Movement of goods, resources, and entrepreneurs over the space is the vital reason behind equalisation of costs of production as well as smooth distribution of the consumables. Standard of living of the humanity is equalised due to the cost equalisation and making the commodity flows possible. Spread of information, literature, skills and practices of life is rendered possible by the touch of the groups of population, the credit of which may entirely be ascribed to the development of transport network over the geographic entities.

Interaction of Transport and Tourism

The economists have long held the opinion that the economic growth always emanates from the leading sectors which emerge as pace-setters. The much talked strategy of unbalanced growth suggests that all sectors can not and need not grow together in view of the acute shortage of resources available for investment in the developing countries. Some pace-setter sectors which have greater linkages forward and backward are identified and developed initially. The external and internal economies generated in these chosen sectors, pave good avenues for other related productive sectors automatically in a due course of time. The initially unbalanced growth ultimately leads to balanced growth of economies in long run, as the initially developed major sectors prepare good avenues for the rest of the sectors. H.W. Singer, C.P. Kindleberger, and Paul Streeten are the leaders in this school of thought. A.Q. Hirschman (Hirschman, 1958) has taken strong side with this view, "... development has of course, proceeded in this way, with growth being communicated from the leading sectors of the economy to the followers from one industry to another, from one firm to the another...." In fact, the backward isolated and tradition-based economy has its own partial equilibrium and when there is no disturbance in it, it repeats its production, quantum and quality, in a routinised form without indicating any departure from stationary equilibrium. The initially stated investments in some leading sectors, add significantly to the layour of the structure and infrastructure. The external economies so created in process, are exploited by the enterprises emerging later on. These find their costs reduced due to the ready-built infrastructure. In this sense development is a chain of disequilibrium one following the other, which must keep alive rather than eliminate the disequilibrium. Tensions, disproportions and disequilibria are essential to maintain the tempo of development. Whenever an external regular contact and linkage is formed by weaving a transport network, the equilibrium already existent, is broken for a while making adjustments for the new situation. Contact, changes the demand, rivalry, competition, supply, and also the new cost-based price is established. This is what the trade does when transport is built. The labour market gets additional supply of labour or the labour migrants. Demand for factors like land the capital also changes. In this way, transport introduces a wave of change. When sizeable investments are already made on transport, new price and demand supply equations make opportunities for the new entrepreneurs to devote to easy money-making. Directly productive activities take birth by inducement of external economies. Thus, the role of education, electricity, transport, irrigation, etc., are the sectors which are of leading nature.

Trade, tourism, small industry and the improved agriculture do emerge which gets profitable due to the newly woven infrastructure in leading sector. Tourism becomes very lucrative activity once the transport and other social overheads are well built. There does exist a structural inter-dependence between the sectors. In the state of 'without transport linkage' there is only little incentive to invest capital in the introduction of modern efficient methods of catering tourist service and accommodation. Because not much of it is demanded. Market for the industry like tourism is too small and not much of the competitive spirit exists. But when the transport links are established, the equation of situations existing in earlier state gives way to the new equation which offers incentives for the potential enthusiastic entrepreneurs to emerge and feed the growing new stream of demand caused by tourism trade, and industrial manufacturing. New commercial vistas get confimed. Once the major costs of transport system building and information channels have appeared, running restaurants, hotels, travel agencies, guided tours, etc., become eminently profitable. As the trade, commerce, tourism, etc., grow, manufacturing gets geared up, it is natural that the demand for additional transport facility is created. Thus, the mutuality between tourism and transport is well settled.

Spatial Externalities and Variants

Transport investments are not similar in all cases. Some of them have tremendous impact on the route these pass through. Various forms have heterogeneous nature. Model distinctions, locations and routes, do vary so also the cost-distance relationships. These may be complementary as well as competitive. Canals, railways, roads, airways, pipeline, etc., have different impacts on the economies where they go and which they pass through. Roads are not ordinarily restricted to popular use, thus, these serve every location they run across but the pipelines of gas or oil do not make the same treatment. The bus transport affords lifting facility on way while the air services do not make the same facility.

Hodder and Lee have attempted the analytical presentation of the impacts and generated spatial externalities of such investments on transport. The noise of the movement of trains, planes, buses, trucks, etc., may not be as advantageous to the places from which these vehicles pass while canals inspite of doing nothing about the midway stations may add to the greenery as a side effect. There may also occur some marginal adjustments in locations of other amenities like market and places influenced by the transport networks. Hodder and Lee observed – "Transport induced reduction in time and money, costs of movement reduced the influence of distance upon the spatial distribution of economic activity and upon the interaction between and within the economies. They fuse market areas, reduce the spatial restrictions upon the location of production and bring additional buyers and sellers into contact with one another". (Hodder and Lee, 1974, 152) The locational specialisation and centering of activities in some areas with advantage is technically based upon the comparative advantage than upon market accessibility (Lloyd and Dicken, 1972, 89). Ohlin (Ohlin, 1935, 43) in his approach to trade supports the viewpoint and feels that regional specialisation can be attained by special free interaction and reduced costs of transportation round the globe. The specialisation intensifies the locational and spatial differentiation. Economically viable markets are created by transport links and the ever-widening number of goods get introduced in various competitive markets together due to the mastering of space by the transport system. Long ago it was held that the transport creates dependencies but the experience reveals that it is not always that. The self-sufficiencies are generated by the transport systems by import of techniques and inputs at the same time keeping the costs at the competitive level. Great geographer Lachene (Lachene, 1965, 183-96) rightly noted, "As a result of the externalities investment in transport performs a dual function. Transport provision serves both the short-term function of satisfying the demand for movement between areas and the long-term function of helping to shape the growth of places by inducing changes in accessibility and relative location". Gauthier (Gauthier, 1970, 612-19) identified three probable impacts of transport:

(a) Growth promoting impacts on local economy;
(b) Permissive growth inducements to other sectors; and
(c) Negative impact by deploying rare resources in the unwise investments.

These impacts may be supplemented by various other types of impacts which shall be covered in the next chapters.

Tourism and Transport Development: Indian Experience

It is known that Indian roads have been classified in two main categories: (a) surfaced, and (b) unsurfaced roads. Roads are well-developed and well-kept in some states. The trade, commerce, tourism and movement of people for occupation is met with in greater measure in such states where transport is developed. Uttar Pradesh is a populated state and a large-sized part of Indian Union. In terms of road development Uttar Pradesh (particularly the present Uttaranchal Himalaya) is one of the least developed areas in India (Pandey, 1989, 393-402) which has affected the overall growth of this state. Table 4.1 shows the road length in the states of India.

It is notable that Tamil Nadu, Maharashtra, Karnataka and

TABLE 4.1: Road Length in the States of India (in km.)

State	Road length		Total
	Surfaced	Unsurfaced	
Andhra Pradesh	1,08,739	69,273	1,78,012
Aurnachal Pradesh	3,991	10,101	14,092
Assam	11,590	56,828	68,418
Bihar	32,998	55,354	88,312
Goa	5,695	2,868	8,563
Gujarat	79,380	11,516	90,896
Haryana	25,538	2,626	28,164
Himachal Pradesh	15,143	15,050	30,193
Jammu & Kashmir	8,225	13,221	21,446
Karnataka	99,339	44,673	1,44,012
Kerala	45,249	1,00,455	1,45,704
Madhya Pradesh	88,620	1,11,517	2,00,137
Maharashtra	2,71,684	90,209	3,61,893
Manipur	3,598	7,343	10,941
Meghalaya	3,923	4,557	8,480
Nagaland	1,983	2,846	4,829
Orissa	86,929	1,75,774	2,62,703
Punjab	52,423	11,929	64,352
Rajasthan	76,813	52,861	1,29,674
Sikkim	1,527	307	1,834
Tamil Nadu	1,40,414	66,089	2,06,503
Tripura	4,577	10,152	14,729
Uttar Pradesh	1,48,303	1,07,164	2,55,467
West Bengal	42,558	32,877	75,435
Union Territories	29,581	3,111	32,692
Uttaranchal	15,090		15,090

Source: India, 1997.

Andhra Pradesh have greater length of surfaced roads which get the major part of tourist flows in the country. Uttar Pradesh has relatively lesser surfaced road length inspite of the fact that it has quite a big number of places of tourism importance. Regarding the other type of roads of unsurfaced nature, Orissa, Kerala and Andhra Pradesh have greater road length. Though this is too little in view of the transport needs and the area. Andhra Pradesh, Karnataka, Kerala, Maharashtra, Orissa, Tamil Nadu and even Uttar Pradesh

TABLE 4.2: Road Development in India

(in '000 km.)

Type of road	1951	1961	1971	1980	1985	1991	1992	1997
1. Surfaced	156.1	234.4	397.0	658.1	833.0	900.0	1,043.0	1,394.1
2. Unsurfaced	241.5	470.8	520.0	876.2	939.8	1,140.0	1,022.0	1,071.8
Surfaced highway	19.7	23.8	24.0	29.0	31.7	–	34.1	–
Total roads	397.6	705.0	917.0	1,534.3	1,772.8	2,040.0	2,065.0	2,465.9

Seventh Five Year Plan, Vol. II, and Ninth Five-Year Plan, Vol. II.

are better than rest of the states in respect of total road length (Table 4.1).

The growth of roads in India during the last 35 years of developmental activity has been quite assuring which indicates around a quadruple increase. Table 4.2 presents a short view of growth of road length in thousand kilometres.

The figures presented in Table 4.2 amply illustrate the rapid growth during 1961-85 and the programme of road building proposed in the Eighth Plan suggests that the priority is being given to the remoter and backward areas besides the congested metropolis and national highways. The objective of attaining increased mobility and tourism besides the growth of transport and trade shall have to be met by vigorous plan of road building and metalling the unsurfaced roads to turn them into all-weather roads by 2000 AD.

Tourism Gathers Momentum on Vehicular Growth

The number of motor vehicles on road is not only less per lakh of population but the distribution of vehicles over the states and localities within states is also extremely uneven. The rural areas

TABLE 4.3: Number of Motor Vehicles in India

(in '000)

Types	1951	1961	1971	1981	1985
1. Private vehicles					
(a) Two-wheelers	21	88	576	2,528	3,512
(b) Auto rickshaws	5	6	37	142	182
(c) Jeeps	24	32	83	119	154
(d) Cars	148	256	539	898	1,215
2. Public vehicles					
(a) Taxies	11	21	60	100	139
(b) Buses	34	57	94	154	206
(c) Goods vehicles	82	168	343	565	763
(d) Other vehicles	4	36	133	667	1,025
3. Total vehicles	329	664	1,865	5,173	7196

India Year Book, 1987-88, National Publishing House, 1988.

TABLE 4.4: National and International Aviation (1961-85)

	1961	1971	1981	1982	1983	1984	1985
(A) Domestic aviation							
(a) Total hours flown ('000)	94	90	93	95	99	107	118
(b) Kilometres flown (million)	28	33	44	45	48	52	58
(c) Passengers carried ('000)	745	2,056	5,560	6,151	6,822	7,908	8,616
(d) Seat km. available (million)	575	1,578	4,458	5,007	5,383	6,131	6,835
(e) Cargo carried ('000 tonnes)	804	2,282	6,460	6,933	7,605	8,172	9,097
(f) Tonne km. flown (crore)	08	16	44	48	54	61	67
(g) Capacity tonne km. (million)	100	222	686	745	819	873	960
(h) Operating revenue (million Rs.)	120	458	3,191	3,806	4,377	5,056	6,011
(B) International aviation							
(a) Total hours flown ('000)	35	40	64	69	72	74	69
(b) Kilometres flown (million)	17	26	44	46	49	50	48
(c) Passengers carried ('000)	229	491	1,938	2,140	2,228	2,220	2,208
(d) Passenger km. (million)	698	2031	7580	8257	8705	9384	7928
(e) Seat km. available (million)	1,495	4,173	11,370	12,387	13,614	13,060	11,594
(f) Cargo carried ('000 tonnes)	03	10	39	76	85	95	110
(g) Tonne km. flown (million)	95	290	1,078	1,176	1,221	1,314	1,153
(h) Capacity tonne km (million)	213	575	1,693	1,871	2,030	2,021	1,858
(i) Revenue earned (million Rs.)	193	701	5,420	6,560	7,371	7,753	7,985

Office of Director-General, Civil Aviation, Government of India, New Delhi/Bombay, 1985.

do not have vehicles in adequate number while the metropolitan towns have overcrowding of vehicles. In remote areas, vehicles are not available at all. Tourism growth is directly related with the vehicular transport (Table 4.3).

Indian aviation is not yet well-devloped to the purposes of development of tourism. Most of the tourist sites are not yet equipped with air services and aerodromes. The cost of air travel is also exhorbitant. The Himalaya ranges do not have the air services which could attract the foreign tourists in a large number (Table 4.4).

Trends of Investment on Transport

The percentage spending on transport fell with every succeeding Plan though the amount of actual spending has risen in every succeeding Plan as may be evinced from Table 4.5.

The Five Year Plans spent most of the funds on development of railways which developed tremendously during the period. The management of traffic, however, did not improve faster during the plans as rapidly so that the railway journey became more tedius and unmanageable for strangers to Indian situations. Percentage of outlay on road development did rise gradually to 34.1 per cent till Fourth Plan but it sharply declined later on. The actual amount

TABLE 4.5: Public Sector Outlay on Transport Sector

Period of Plans		Amount (crores Rs.)
1. First Five Year Plan	1951-56	434
2. Second Five Year Plan	1956-61	1,100
3. Third Five Year Plan	1961-66	1,983
4. Annual Plans	1966-69	1,032
5. Fourth Five Year Plan	1969-74	2,522
6. Fifth Five Year Plan	1974-79	4,078
7. Sixth Five Year Plan	1980-85	12,080
8. Seventh Five Year Plan	1985-90	22,596
9. Eighth Five Year Plan	1992-97	–
10. Ninth Five Year Plan	1997-2002	–

TABLE 4.6: Transport Mode-wise Allocation of Outlay During the Different Plans

(in per cent)

Sub-sectors of transport	First Plan	Second Plan	Third Plan	Annual Plan	Fourth Plan	Fifth Plan	Sixth Plan	Seventh Plan
1. Railways	50.0	65.7	66.9	49.3	37.0	37.4	42.2	54.6
2. Roads	7.0	8.0	22.1	30.0	34.1	29.4	28.5	23.0
3. Road transport	26.8	14.0	1.4	5.3	5.1	9.0	9.9	8.8
4. Shipping	10.9	7.8	6.9	8.4	16.4	18.7	11.7	9.2
5. Inland water	–	–	0.2	0.6	0.4	0.3	0.5	1.0
6. Civil aviation	5.3	4.5	2.5	6.4	7.0	5.2	7.2	3.4

Source: Report of National Transport Policy Committee, 1985, and Plan Draft Outline, VI and VII, Government of India, New Delhi.

spent was, however, rising quite consistently. Road transport developed in public and private sectors together and it made considerable progress over these years. Tourist traffic is handled by the bus transport in short distances. The development of roads and bus transport in Uttaranchal Himalayan tracts grew with rapid rate after Independence yet the coverage is not satisfactory till date. Plan-wise percentage allocations to different modes of transport in India are given in Table 4.6.

The economy has worked well to cater the growing needs of transport yet the growth of passenger traffic has been faster than the actual capacity growth in some sectors of transport. Domestic tourism has grown primarily as a result of improved transport links though the management dimension of transport is not well-attended which has ever resulted in passenger discomfort, unutilised capacity, revenue leakages as well as the huge losses to the public sector transport. The qualitative improvement in buses and railways has taken place in some states (Table 4.7). The gauge-wise route kilometrage of railways has been given in Table 4.8.

TABLE 4.7: Average Growth Rates Per Year for the Different Modes of Transport, 1951-85

Mode of transport	Average growth rate per year (in per cent)
1. Electrified railway route	8.6
2. Freight traffic in railway	4.3
3. Railway passenger traffic	3.7
4. Road length	4.5
5. Road transport – trucks	6.8
6. Road transport – buses	5.4
7. Major port traffic	5.2
8. Shipping traffic	10.0
9. Air traffic – domestic	10.5
10. Air traffic – foreign lines	11.9
11. Trend growth rate of transport	3.5

Figures drawn from Seventh Plan (Draft Outline)1985-90, Government of India, New Delhi.

TABLE 4.8: Gauge-wise Route Kilometrage, 1999

Gauge	Route (km.)	Running track (km.)	Total track (km.)
1. Broad gauge (1,676 mm.)	44,216	62,184	85,429
2. Metre gauge (1,000 mm.)	15,178	15,875	19,158
3. Narrow gauge (762 mm. and 610 mm.)	3,415	3,452	3,826
Total	62,809	81,511	1,08,413

Thus, the average highest growth rate per year during 1951-85 exhibits in air traffic (foreign lines) i.e., 11.9 per cent; while this rate of growth accounts for 10.0, 3.7 and 5.4 per cent for shipping traffic, railway passenger traffic and road transport (buses) traffic respectively.

5

Origin, Growth and Development of Tourism: Global and Regional Perspectives

The Phraseology

'Tour' (round) means a prolonged journey from place-to-place specially for pleasure or acting. In its common usage it covers a travel for pleasure trip or outing. In the ancient days a 'Grand Tour' meant a journey through Western Europe which was highly fashionable for completing the education of youth. 'Tourism' is the bent of mind in favour of globe-trotting, world travel peregrinations, roving, rambling, gadding, and even hoboism. It denotes an attitude of learning by travel and wandering. It is enjoying a trek, temporary migration of short stay for pleasure instead of settlement or occupation. It is jornada type trip and expedition. It may even be a hunting expedition, pilgrimage, hadj, a junket excursion, a self-sponsored outing. Tourism is often used for sight-seeing voyage, a package tour and rubber-neck tour. In fact, tourism is a thought, a state of mind of certain preferences as different from keeping static unchanged and isolated. It is a bent of mind for mixing with people of various places and lands with fauna, flora and nature of large number of areas. Tourism is often expressed to mean enjoyment – out station in the form of riding, driving, motoring, cycling, equitation, lift load trecking, gliding, sliding, slipping on snow, coasting, sailing, skating and gliding. Tourism, to youth, means pedestrianism, strolling, tramping, marching, hiking, parading for pleasure, and even a hippety-hop and going to new places in the mood of enjoyment and seeking pleasure. It is trotting and galloping on horse-ride in the untrodden path singing and competing with fellowmen. Globe-trotting is often the cherished dream of the youth. Nomadism for fun and not for making a living, also makes a closer meaning of the term 'tourism'. In colloquial meaning it is going on gad and haze around. It is a way of life to beat one's way. It is airing and joy-ride. The term is also used to connote mincing, meandering, strolling, land louping, errant, gallivanting, tiptoeing way-worn. It often gives an image of travel soiled and stained, sweated and fatigued. Tourism is traversing. All of the meanings where the term is used indicate the physical activity or state of body. Tourism includes it besides the fact that 'tourism' is a trend of thought, an attitude, a bent of mind, a line of thinking, a strategy and model of life. It marks a psychology and a network of motivations which form the attitude of tourism. Tourism is the outcome of a strange fascination of man for discovering the unknown and to quinch the thirst of curiosities. Man has from the earliest times carried the urge to explore and undergo new experiences. By its original meaning tourism is not ordinary holidaying, relaxation, outing or vagabound pleasure-seeking. It has a great meaning and objective in the enrichment of human life, knowledge, practice and overall social living.

Tourism Through Infancy and Youth

History illustrates the fascination of man for the observation of the beauty of nature, its topography, landscape, its plant growth, rivers, lakes and other water bodies. Human being has worked extensively for exploring nature and seeking aesthetic pleasure from the greeneries and waterfalls. In the ancient days the natural barriers to mobility checked the enthusiasm of great many people. The aspiration of travel did not fulfil for lack of easy transport. The information regarding varied sceneries was also unrevealed. The revolution in communication world has realised the aspiration left deserted so far. Now travel assumes a mass-character. Robinson (Robinson, 1976, i) treats modern tourism to have begun in the post-Second World War period. The institutional growth for the promotion of tourism, e.g. International Union of Official Travel Organisation (IUOTO) and World Travel Organisation (WTO) have led to the present phenomenal growth in travel across the national boundaries. In the '80s onwards the annual growth is said to have been growing at a pace of around 12 per cent.

Increased leisure of modern affluent societies, higher levels of living, rapid growth of disposable income, expanded horizon of knowledge, and comfortable and speedy transport has led to the fashionable tourism which enters the budget of every well to do relates to the science of geography in the sense that it relates to the environmental studies, it relates to spatial choice-making, it deals with specific types of human settlements and relates to spatial conditions. The rationality of human mobility over the space in tourism has some geographic determinants. Technically, as Robinson has found it, geography has a fundamental role to play in examining the spatial interplay of demand and satisfaction of the tourist (Robinson, 1976, xxiii). He claims that tourism is related to form, structure use and conservation of the landscape.

The consequences of tourism for the geographic field of study are very important specially the effacing and defacing of nature by human treading, transport and structures which are built by man on the surface for tourism. The created garbage and air, water and sound pollutions, are the impacts of the tourist pressure. The forests and natural fauna and flora get destroyed and peace gets eliminated. Heavy constructions and amenity structures practically change the physiognomy of landscape. Tourism industry may also at times lead to creation of reserved forests, decorated gardens, wild life parks and work towards preservation and conservation of natural environment. As an industry tourism affords livelihood and permanent occupation to a vast section of the labour force which settles in the so far neglected and isolated areas. Expert like Boesch (Boesch, 1964, 227-229) has illustrated how tourism brings about demographic changes as well. The uplands of hilly terrain round the globe lose population by out-migration for livelihood due to the failure of local feeble agriculture to feed the growing human heads. Local capital and skill finds escape to better developed areas. Tourism, when enters these areas, resettles the population in new occupations of catering and depopulation process is considerably checked. The ultimate impact is the scattering of population and discouraging the concentration in the central places and agglomerations of flourshing manufacturers. Such an impact has a geographic bearing as well as economic character. In its economic part of livelihood creation tourism enters the field of economic geography. The economic progress has the nature of concentrating in given highly favourable locations and localisation ultimately sets the background of spatial economic development differentials. The remoter areas, unfavourable for farming fertility-wise and unsuitable for industry cost-wise, keep relatively isolated and unattended by the entrepreneurs primarily for the cost considerations. Tourism offers the opportunities in such neglected locations and the wave of development covers them as well. As a commercial activity tourism promotes participation in trade even for the benefit of the areas which have nothing to share with others. It assumes the character of a trade when foreign tourist seeks a view by his personal visit to the scenic beauty-sites and areas of natural splendour. The areas which offer no agricultural prospects and industrial materials and yet earn foreign currency through the tourist traffic are the best contributors to prosperity. Very often the geographers treat tourism as that branch of study within this subject which relates more to the applied dimensions like physical and regional planning, weaving of infrastructure of transport, communication and spatial interlinks by railways and airways. Some specialists have classed tourism in branches like urban geography and urban planning.

Tourism is not the movement of people alone. The phenomena of travel is an essential ingredient of the wider process of tourism. "Globe-trotting" has been a particular way of life. The unsatiable hunt for a knowledge and new experience have brought human being to grasp the significance of this phenomena. In the early times the tribes lived only to defend themselves and kill the others. Those which knew more about the varied areas were more successful. Later winning tribes subjugated and put the conquered tribes as slaves at the bare minimum of meals. Such enslaved humanity technically termed as "living dead" were used as carriers of load and men to the distances. Brigands and dacoits obstructed the free travel. This problem disappeared with the emergence of the security and national states. Sixteenth century onwards travelling had become popular for education of youth. By the end of 18th century, travel was recognised as an appreciated cherished value everywhere. Gradually the social tradition evolved to favour outing on week-ends and holiday-weeks, specially in summer. Inter-space movement of the people for enjoyment, fun and entertainment came to be popular after the World War II, reconstructions.

Therapeutic values attached to mineralised water-bathing also encouraged people to go for long and distant water-bodies. Health resorts came to be developed in the model of asclepian sanctuaries of Greeks, and curative powers of these health resorts were highly claimed. "Bath in a fountain", swimming and off-shore sun bask gained popularity which encouraged outdoor travel for short intervals in Europe. Pilgrimage to take a bath in holy-waters of rivers have been popular in all cultures for several centuries. Gouty, dropsy, tummy ailments, sterility of women and hysterical fits are claimed to be cured by bath in mineralised waters. The water bodies specially those gushing out in cliffs became the great centres of amusement and diversion while musical instruments and recreational games when added to such camps, increased the attraction for out-door entertainment. Hydrotherapy has indeed been a big factor in bringing the old as well as women folk out of their daily routine to the water springs, fountains, sea beaches and rivers.

Coverage and Adaptations

It marks the spatial dimension of human mobility. The archaic concepts of 'Time' and 'Space' which restricted human mobility in the past have come to shrink to the confines of history. Revolutionary changes in transport, communication and inter-space movement has made human penetration possible even in inaccessible tracts over space and oceans. Space-tourism is the most modern concept. The future may even open avenues for tourism in galaxies. It expands the vistas of knowledge and thinking, makes life enjoyable and provides productive human service to millions of workmen round the globe. Tourism is a trade and benefits the traveller as well as his host. It is indeed a new mode of exploring as well as utilizing natural resources to the optimum human good. Beauty-resources of nature in the remotest untreatable parts of the globe are used by the industry of tourism without the course consuming them as inputs or raw-materials. Tourism has a very large number of fruits for economic and cultural interlinks are formed and fostered under the tourist activity. It is a great unifying force and integrating power which is unleashed by development of tourism. Tourism, indirectly weaves the network of intense human understanding and mutual respect among multilingual communities under various cultural settings and political regimes. Tourism affords a very good market for the products and services not actively demanded hitherto. Tourism is a truly cultural mission dressed with intense curiosities to know about others and to learn and share with others. It is not a cultural invasion campaign and a designed move to annihilate other ways of living, organisation and regimes. It tends to gain from experience of other cultures without any way tinkering or interfering with them. Tourism appreciates varieties and it is a drift from uniformity and symmetry. It gives the mankind a make of mind to appreciate other systems, accommodate and develop tolerance. It is against pollution and invasion. Tourism is a great education in itself for the person who undertakes the tour as well as for those who host him in their space and cultural landscape. The tourist spends to fetch the hospitality which promotes employment, industry and variety of production, primary as well as tertiary types. Tourism spreads tourism. When a tourist visits the other land he spends his currency and this earning of foreign exchange promotes tourism by the people of the other land. Economists claim that the multiplier effect of the spent income by tourism, in its cumulation, cause many times more income for various sections of the people. Thus, tourism is "development" in its true sense.

Development and enrichment of human life is the goal of tourism, therefore, it is much too sure that human being is the theme of this subject. In a long-chain effect of the movement of a tourist, starting from the emergence of his curiosities about nature, the people and their creations around him to physical shifting to other lands in satisfying his curiosities, gives birth to serveral tourist needs. The nature, intensity and effectiveness of the curiosities are inborn, persuaded and even generated in modern world. The root of the curiosities, their intensification and effectiveness (resosurcefulness to meet the curiosity) are not unoften been personal in history. There have been several instances when it was sponsored and patronised officially whether the state or vested power-groups or affluent status-based mercantile class. Single intellectual enrichment as sole objective of tourist movement has also been evidence in history. Such motivations were often inborn and inherent. Such tourists were by and large explorers and adventurists. Chinese travellers and saints undertook arduous journeys to acquire knowledge. The traders and merchants undertook tours along unknown and unbeaten paths to share their manufacturers or traded goods with people of other lands. This was motivated by the lust for profit and the metallic accumulations. The continued process of inter-continental commercial hunts for new countries from early decades of 15th-17th century in Europe were motivated by rooted lust for profit and margins of trade, finding suitable avenues and unrebuffed hospitality led to colonialism in later centuries. This aroused a great suspicion and doubt about the intentions of the new explorers hindering the path of tourism in modern sense of the term. Religious enthusiasm often motivated some of the explorers to search for new sets of populations to whom the religious messages of the ecclesiastical heads were to be reached. The hidden motives in such explorations were the uprooting of aboriginal cultures, forcing a cultural domination by establishing new faith and installing a political area of influence. Great many journeys were done even in the past to satisfy some religious faith commonly known as pilgrimage.

The modern connotation of the term 'tourist' is relatively different and is a recent origin. It is no more "time-killer", "spend thrift", one who devotes to "aimless loitering". It is not necessarily a "holiday maker" or a mere "pleasure tripper". While there may be these features and elements among tourists of the day, in its ingrained meaning tourism is not "time-killing". Ogilvie (Ogilvie, 1933) identified tourist by two main features: (a) being away from home for visiting other places frequently in breaks, for several months, and (b) visits are for non-earning purposes. This is quite a narrow meaning. The emphasis laid upon the non-earning character distinguishes tourism from the trade or profession-led temporary migration. Norval (Norval, 1936) similarly, hammered upon the feature of the tourist that he has no intentions of permanently residing in other land and does not enter-upon a business as his occupation. Tourist spends income earned elsewhere. Thus, employment seeker, when undertakes a journey with specific end of job-making is not a tourist. A tourist is a buyer but not producer. His purchase is intended for his daily living and comforts during his period of stay rather than piling of stocks for any commercial intentions. He may fetch a few specimen or goods for goodwill. Interests of the tourist are more towards sight-seeing, study of cultures, goodwill, appreciation of beauty of nature, seeing the manmade objects, monuments, buildings, enjoying music, arts and paintings, observing the wild life, enjoying the climate and seasons, literary sharing, vocationing and undertaking excursions. 'Pleasure' is certainly a primary feature of tourism. An 'overnighter' who happens to visit a friend for sympathy mission is also within the orbit of tourism. Given to the sole purpose of visiting new places for intellectual curiosities or pleasure, a tourist may also supplement his expenses by working temporarily for a day or two without, of course, having any intentions of settling in even a seasonal or long stay works. Tourist may be a social worker or educator without involving long stay and creation of any earning. The contact, effect, phenomenon, relationship developed in demanding and catering the material needs of tourists and goodwill developed between stranger and local inhabitants, caterers or similar minded people constitute the expanded texts in the subject of tourism. R de Meyer very aptly defined tourism as, "a collective term" used for human movement and its associated attendant activities caused by the exteriorisation and fulfilment of the desire to escape. The escape is find out to get a relief from repetitive monotonous routine at the homeland. This escape is for a short-duration to revitalise enthusiasm for dedication to routine.

Self-Propelled and Nurtured Tourism

Tourist activity is voluntary and choice of the person or group of persons undertaking travel. It is an outdoor recreation. Tourism may involve a particular type of mental attitude wherein a person seeks relaxation from routinized work and this is obtained by going out of the city, residential place, country, etc. This is purely for relaxation, recreation, enjoyment and sort of sporting. Tourist is even one who for a break of a week goes to the beaches towards a free sun-bask and to rivers for fishing as recreational avocation. If a person goes to stay for a weekend in an 'Ashram' and enriches his personality with preachings of saints and returns to his work with vigour and freshness of mind, he undertakes a tourist activity. A traveller with a mere wander lust is a tourist. Men and women move even across their country to see the athletic meets and matches. This is a fun and diversion from the routine of daily life. Love for travel is often evinced among families who want to train their children in more practical dimensions of life. 'Seeing' is 'knowing' quite apart from the routine textbook coaching in schools. This promotes tourism. The schools and colleges of the day take children for educational tours and nature study tours. Tourism, as it sounds today, was popular in the ancient civilisations of Greece. Olympic games and sports attracted huge traffic of participants and observers from great many neighbouring countries. Athens, the old city state in Greece had arrangements for stay of the visitors in the style of modern commercial hotels. Indian kings promoted movement of human traffic by officially constructing stay-in sites and by arranging to build roads as well as facilities of potable water closer to the roads. Courtesy and hospitality for visitors, strangers and travellers is engrained in Indian culture even today. Kings earned repute by great constructions and buildings including churches and temples so that people from remote lands visit and appreciate the art and skill of the land. Religious tourism had been popular everywhere even before Christ. Holidaying outside the homeland became popular when the political unification prowess ensued and smaller feudal entities merged into well-protected strong states. The security, justice and peace were guaranteed by these bigger strong states and free movement of human being became easier. The transport and communication revolution has rendered it possible for a layman with meagre resources to undertake tours and benefit by it.

Types and Style of Tourism

Precise distinction between tourism and non-tourism activity is indeed difficult to establish. The information regarding following may be needed to make a distinction:

(i) The purpose of the outstation stay,
(ii) Duration of the stay,
(iii) Distance crossed by the travel,
(iv) The activity of the traveller at the place of stay,
(v) The type of places visited by the traveller,
(vi) Expenditure incurred by the traveller and type of purchases affected,
(vii) Whether the travel was self-motivated or by any official activity.

Since such information is not always precisely known and, at times, the purposes are intermixed, therefore, precise demarcation is likely to be difficult.

Most common experience regarding the tourism shows that the purposes may be of the following main categories or these purposes may be found in an intermingled form.

(a) Change of climate and atmosphere for the purpose of health-protection and mental peace. This is generally defined as 'Relaxation Tours' usually practised by highly affluent classes. Physicians very often suggest, change of climate as the possible way of reducing tension and for improving health for the ailing. This results in movement to a new place for a short while. A great diversity is found in the human attitudes and reactions to new situations. A very big number of people shift to the hill stations during summer. Such tourism is also of the relaxation type.
(b) The other category belongs to the tourists basically interested in visiting the holy shrines, religious places and seeking blessings and sermons from the learned saints in the holy shrines and Ashrams. Millions of men, women and children go to remotely placed temples of Badrinath, Kedarnath, Jagannath Puri, Rameshwaram, Tirupati temple, Kushinagar, Vrindavan, etc., for a short stay or visit. Millions of Muslim travellers go for Mecca and Madina

> crossing the borders of their national frontiers moved by the religious sentiments. Visitors to papal city and Lourdes are in this category. This travel may be inside the country or outside the country. The tourists like to perform religious penances and make donations at these holy centres. The experience on way and teachings at these places enthuse new confidence and vigour in the life of the visitors. Some of these tourists are basically interested in making philosophical deliberations with the learned priests. The treasures of cultural heredity are explored by these pilgrims. Historical and anthropological curiositis are satisfied by the travellers by visiting ancient monuments and places.

Tourists like viewing the wonders of modern architecture, engineering, machines, factories, workshops, power houses, radio stations, river valley dams, observatories, airports and the huge installations related to a political regime like Parliament House or Rashtrapati Bhawan. Such tourists are generally students and teachers who undertake tours for studies with travel. Zoo has long been an attraction of the tourists everywhere.

Educational tours may be of several kinds. Sociologists and economists take the learners to the sites of identified cultural groups, economic strata of population, followers of specified occupations like crafts, dairy and agriculture. Tribal community life is an attraction for the sociologists. Botanists like taking students to site where a large variety of botanical life is identified. Some are interested in wild life and the forest-wealth, while very large number of students prefer visiting hills for mountaineering and rope climbing sports. The young tourists have preference for visiting snow-laden peaks and glaciers. The thrill and hypnotising beauty of greeneries and peaks constitutes a great interest of the young tourists. There has been a common tradition of arranging travel and learn programmes wherein the cadets of military science in the colleges choose organising camps in remote places. Social workers also arrange such camps. These activities are a part of 'Educational Tourism'. School teachers undertake such tours of students to coal mines, art galleries, historical sites and cultural centres.

Tourism is also motivated by officially sponsored activities where people like to participate. Independence Day parade in Delhi is an attraction of this type. Governments of various countries and local country councils very often organise such attractive meets where millions of the tourists flock-in, as participants or mere observers.

'Goodwill Tourism' is motivated by humanitarian love for the kith and kins, friends, neighbours, relatives, acquaintances, etc., as a mission to keep close relations. In such case also the outstation stay of the traveller is short and it is not intended for pecuniary gains. Such tourist movement adds to closer human understanding and building the social status and prestige. Besides the sight-seeing recreation and relaxation, such tourist movement helps the inter-personal relationships, sympathy as well as love. Millions of West Germans go to East Germany (presently one nation) on the Christmas week on the same mission of goodwill. They spend sometime there with their acquaintances and return. Similarly thousands of Pakistani nationals visit India and Bangladesh to meet their relatives on the social occasions.

'Business Tourism' has long been in practice among the Arabs who visited countries far and wide to seek business contacts and dispose goods or purchase goods. Nowadays, the government promotes such foreign visits of businessmen who prepare goodwill as well as market for the national manufacturers. They choose raw-materials as well as machines to build the domestic capacities. Business dealers, distributors, etc., are given some incentives as well as fiscal concessions for undertaking such foreign travel. This also helps the foreign country in terms of sales, orders for raw material, machinery or spares, etc., as well as the 'foreign exchange' which these travellers spend there. Since such travel is an 'Earning-based Tourism', it yields greater advantage to the country where such tourism occurs. Once it starts and some potentialities are found out by the businessmen, the flow grows in a competitive fashion. In fact, the fiscal concessions allow the gains of such travel to the businessmen.

Tourist activity is fostered by the 'Tourist Attractions' such as Taj Mahal, Egyptian Pyramids, Eiffel Tower, etc. Several governments intending to promote tourism build such attractions which would interest children, women and men. Their usefulness is universal and they offer the service of expanding horizon of knowledge and thrill. Some governments organize international or inter-regional conferences, meetings, sports, seminars, etc., so that the learned and experienced would find enough excuse to undertake the travel and both the nations reap the advantage of the deliberations. Most of the academic meets sponsored by the universities, research institutes and other public forums invite visitors from various nooks and corners of the globe. Official meetings of the state officials, public bodies, various sectors of worker's unions, business community itself and the lawyers, jurists, press and political organisations very often motivate large number of visitors of undertaking such tourist activity. The arrangements made for such visitors involve employment and sales in the locality.

Tourism Promotion Policy and Inducement

Since tourism is the habit-inculcation of going out of the usual place of working for a break in daily routine and seeking diversions temporarily in order to revitalise the working-vitality, it is of interest to know as to what intensifies human desire for outing. We know that modern way of life is extremely busy and occupied. It is indeed difficult to find time and resources for outings for sustained intervals in leisurely mood. While the tiresome routine of man in industrialised areas makes it a felt necessity to rest and relax yet the day-to-day preoccupations make it all the more difficult to abandon work for relaxing in remotely placed stations. Therefore, what is most essential towards promoting tourism is the provision of such vacations and job-free time interval. Some of the large establishments do have such policies wherein workers are allowed a tour-gap holidays. Some establishments arrange their meetings and get-together in hill stations or tourist sites so as to allow such opportunity of going out to the workers. Even the government departments try to hold annual review deliberations in places of tourist interest. 'Summer schools' are held in mountainous towns by the business training and research organisations.

Stronger stimulation is generated among people for going off-station tours and pulls of motivations are woven by deliberate policy. How such interests are promoted and generated and how such human attitudes are kept maintained and tourism-oriented behaviour is sustained needs to be investigated. This much is by far agreed that attaching a social status and prestige to tourism makes one of the strongest motivations. Fortunately the urban elites have come to join such a value system wherein out-going practices are the token of progressiveness and modernised outlook. Besides the status-oriented tourist activity, there is a type of value system which appreciates multi-dimensional personality growth. Everybody has a hidden lust for social appreciation and one likes to claim modernism in attitudes. If tourism is an indicator of modernism any resourceful person would prefer taking to tours to be bracketed among the modern gentry. A multi-dimensional personality is featured by development of skills, interests, arts and knowledge of even those spheres which are not directly linked to the daily routine. Dictated by the inherent hidden suppressed desires, choices, preferences and likes, a person chooses to pick-up one of the excuses which may enrich personality, for undertaking a tour postponing the routinised work for sometime. A businessman would pick-up the work, market-survey, sales-potential exploration or making business contacts and organise a tour. A student would go around to collect his study material. A minister would fix-up some meetings at the intended places where he wants to go for mere outing. The university teacher hunts for opportunities to deliver an extension lecture or attend a seminar. Special interests are attended by such tours which may relate to meeting people, having deliberations, discussions, having some photography of the beautiful sites, attending the cultural, political, educational, social or technological get-togethers. Some may honestly attend to the request of children to go to their places of choice while others go to attend at least social goodwill meets or attend marriages or other functions.

Tourism unites the separated and strengthens the ties of love and friendship. Occupation, residence and circumstances make people to depart and isolate. Tourism affords the opportunity to unite the separated friends and promotes human understanding as well as goodwill. Human being seeks freedom from the slavery of the routine. It is unattainable in the existing age of over-busy materialistic life. The aesthetic sense and higher values make a strong motivation in men to get relieved from the indulgence in money, bread-earning and fatiguing rivalries of materialistic life. A breath of peace, a moment of leisure and a state being away from the din and tourmoil is a cherished dream. The remote hill stations, mountain resorts and envigorating climate in lush green areas offer a captivating alternative specially when one feels like avoiding the inclement weather, sun lust, sea lust, scorching heat and unpleasant working conditions. Recreations, pursuit of absorbing hobbies, free swimming, trekking, hiking, leisurely participation in the likes and plays of children in holiday mood and long walks on hiss tracks with family and friends, etc., are quite powerful imaginations which stimulate even the busiest for tourism and when the hypnotic spell of the beautiful tourist resorts offer what they had imagined, they feel amply compensated for their expenditure on travel. If people do not go outing they adjust to the style of life for being quite ignorant of the other alternatives. Once tourism enters the habit it becomes rather very difficult for anybody to resist the temptation in future because tourism is more rewarding than being expensive.

Conditioning Growth of Tourism

The basic factors which lead to stimulate tourist activity and like mindedness may be many and may vary from country to country as well as from one cultural setting to the other. Yet some of them may be more prominent and applicable to all situations:

(i) Resourcefulness of the people;
(ii) An appropriate type of education and attitudinal growth;
(iii) Adequate development – transport and road development;
(iv) At least a certain minimum level of growth and efficient working of communications;
(v) Optimised levels of transport connectivity and "time saving" programming of tours;
(vi) Adequate information, data and inter-region contacts;
(vii) A minimum level of security, safety, peace, risk redistributing arrangements like travel-insurance, etc.

It is well-nigh known that unless the income levels, employment levels, and conditions of the employment are favourable, the tourism mindedness cannot be generated. Even if it is generated it takes the form of ancient nomadism. It is likely to defeat the very root of tourism. As a smokeless, unpolluting and uncongesting industry, tourism industry demands income-spending. Income generated in the home-occupations is spent for own comforts and enjoyment of services. It is spending for goodwill, knowledge, social contacts, honour and hospitality and courtesy given by the unknown hosts. This spending is the seed of sweet memories in future. One may have to spend for the travel, accommodation, beverages, food, other services, as well as the purchases out of the liberated fantacy. Unless the income and saving levels of the wanderers are adequate to meet these without offsetting the levels of living, efficiency and occupation at home, the tourist activity cannot be boosted with adequate margin. For a foreign tourist, the gains of exchange-rates in under valued currencies can be a big encouragement. For an illustration, a US citizen may be in position to make a gain by spending in India because the domestic purchasing power of dollar earned in US is far less than what US dollar would fetch in terms of Indian rupee and the command he exercises on goods and services in India with the same "dollar exchanged rupee" is likely to be far greater. This is a big advantage to the US tourist in India. Indian economy reaps advantage in the same measure because US tourist demands services which, otherwise, cannot be exported like scenic beauty, climate, seasons, trekking enjoyment, boating in lakes, accommodation and dining facilities. Thus, the gains of exports are attained and foreign rare currencies are earned without competing in world market and seeking favours in commercial treaties. With regard to inter-regional tourism, the gains of the activity do not occur in terms of foreign currency earning but it does transfer income from the well-off groups to the relatively lower socio-economic groups. The transfer of income is also from richer areas to the lagging mountainous tracts. If the overall levels of income are low, the development of tourism may be largely restricted for lack of traffic as well as the short duration of stay of the tourists who cannot afford spending more. The growth of income is the resultant effect of overall level of development which alone can assure self-propelled growth over a sustained range of time. Tourism is linked with developmental process both ways; it promotes the purchasing power and motivation for undertaking a travel for pleasure and the development alone can make the investments towards promotion of tourism, e.g. the hotels, transport network, guidance service, communication links, banks, railways, motor-service and so on. Tourism leads to development of tertiary sector faster than manufacturing as the investments tend to concentrate on creation of catering services. Most of the enjoyment which the tourist gets is the outcome of his own rhythm of heart and mental relief and raw materials used in this industry leave a large margin between total cost and price.

Tourism as a bent of mind comes from the education and attitudinal change among the clientele. The philosophy of hard and dedicated work, greater earning, lust for worldly pleasures, taste for learning, knowing, making acquaintances, seeing and observing a variety of people, various kinds of cultural experience, appreciation for historical places, literature, academic meets, arts and crafts, admiration of technological performance and developing a sense of participation are the results of good educational status. In an illiterate and ignorant society, the taste and liking for these higher values including higher aesthetics and love of nature cannot be easily generated. The role of education lies in higher development of human personality besides the addition to information. Greater the information higher is the curiosity. The educated societies have greater human mobility.

In its modern meaning, tourism covers out-station travel for enjoyment, fun, recreation and relaxation while it also covers the other types of travel for learning and wider participation in global activities. The spatial movements are, by far, restricted by the road-rail links, air travel facilities, sea transport, network of transport infrastructure and co-ordination. Efficient and well-woven transport facilities assure greater and convenient travel round a wider space within a stipulated time. Since time is the rarest resource in the busy life of man, better transport certainly helps in assuring punctuality. Greater the travel, more is the area covered, and higher is the number of places visited. This ensures greater satisfaction to the tourist. If the travel is uncomfortable, the tourist is unlikely to be accompanied by his children and the old members of the family. This discourages the number of tourists to grow. If the tourist can avoid discomfort and delay at every step, his total enjoyment of the tour is likely to be greater. Similarly if the tourist can fetch necessary information regarding the tour, places and advance booking of accommodation and onward journey bookings from the place of break, he is prompted to go for the tour programme. Keeping the tourist well-connected with the developments at home can make him more assured and contended. Tourists usually constitute a gentry of lavish spenders and keep satisfied if they are assured of a riskless travel and prompt service keeping with the scheduled programme. Tourists have always short of time and want to visit as many sites as they can within a short span. They always need somebody to help them in programming and arranging the tour. Thus, the role of tourism consultants and agencies emerges. Travel entails numerous technicalities for a single tourist to attempt but when these are handled by specialised travel agencies for groups of the people, it helps both, the agency as well as the tourist. Some of the tedius complications of travel are shared by these agencies. The system becomes less cumbersome. If the travel, risk-insurance, medical aid, accommodation, programming, journey to and fro and related problems are tackled all at a stretch, the tourists are easily motivated to seek a booking. In case the tourist agencies are able to meet all contingencies on way and bring the tourist back to his home safe, secure and satisfied, the visitor feels amply compensated even for the high rates of travel charges. Therefore, it is very much correct to claim that the role of transport, communication and tourist agencies is indeed high in promotion of tourism.

Visit to a new place involves a variety of worries for the stranger. A tourist requires a large number of helpers at various stages of his voyage (journey). It is more so if the travel is undertaken with family specially with the infants, infirms and women. The traveller is pleased if he gets such assistance as and when needed. Even the absence of load lifters and guides can put the stranger in trouble. A tourist need not carry big loads of bedding, heavy clothing and paraphernalia of kitchen if he is assured of these supplies at the place of his visit. The dak-bungalows, rest houses, hotels and such other arrangements of lodging and boarding help the tourists immensely. Similarly, the primary amenities at the station and around the place of visit facilitate him. Arrangements of potable water, sanitary fittings, etc., are essential parts of infrastructure to promote tourism. Accommodation for stay is important and it is more facilitating if such accommodation is booked in advance so that the tourist gets well-assured of the space facilities and services he will command at the place of his visit. Some regulatory controls on the hotel service and rescue aid services are also essential to ensure safety and protection to the visitors against indiscriminate fleecing in the hands of the hoteliers. This means some sort of legislative action is essential for promotion of tourism. The other dimension is the catering of the tourists and facility of restaurants, coffee or tea stalls, and a marketing place. The needs of the strangers depend on the cultural group to which they belong. This also depends on the age-group to which the tourists belong and the likes and dislikes of the visitors. It needs a great experience and unending patience to handle the tourist traffic specially because it consists of people belonging to a large number of language-groups and cultural settings.

Developing the Culture of Hospitality

Good tourist consultancy service helps promotion of tourist activity. This constitutes a basic infrastructure which relieves most of the worries of the strangers. These consultancies should be worth their name. These must create such useful literature as to guide the curious strangers in knowing more and more about the places, they visit. Pamphlets, guides, maps accommodation charts, rates, facility structure, time-table of bus services, organised tour services, availability in the places to be visited, details of helpout agencies, etc., should be made available to the tourists at reasonable prices. The motor-service stations need specially designed tourist assistance services. Physical infrastructure in this context includes, arrangement of amenities like urinals, sanitary fittings, rest houses and waiting rooms. Telephone facility and postal services should be placed closer to the stations. Medical aid arrangements and basic beverage services are necessary besides the security guards at the terminus. Luggage keeping service adds to the exercise of freedom by the tourists in choosing the hotel facilities. Good fancy-goods market is helpful in promoting tourist-based purchases. The tourists feel elevated if they are given opportunities of participating in literary meets, athletics, historical expeditions and art competitions. Such type of activities should be promoted in the places of tourist-liking. Climbing the tedius heights in mountains, tourist stations, specially with children and infirm, constitutes a big problem and it imposes a restriction on the exercise of freedom of the tourist. Rope-way services are of considerable help in promoting enjoyment of the visitors. Baby-sitting and child-care services in hotels enhance the freedom of tourists. Arts emporiums and facilities of photography add to the benefits of promoting interests of the tourists. Gardens, parks, exhibitions, zoo, play grounds, boating and swimming facilities constitute a part of the general fabric of tourism promotion. For foreign tourists, the port facilities should be well-designed so as to suit the needs. The exist and entry formalities at the airport should not be time-consuming and cause of harassment. Discourtesy in any form shown to the stranger is uncondonable sin. A close-knit co-ordination among the guidance bureau, transport agencies and hotel accommodation, is a precondition for a good tourist service. Every country aspiring for tourism developments has to work for preserving forest flora, wild life, land-forms and water-bodies like waterfalls, lakes, rivers, dams and beaches. Investments are essential towards beautification as well as the sanitation and hygiene. Historical buildings of archaeological significance need upkeep and adequate maintenance. All types of historical material evidence bearing testimony of the ancient life and culture need be collected in museums as an attraction for the tourists. In the similar way, craft goods, paintings and goods which constitute the representative of the past have to be preserved. The tourists demand a large number of facilities like clubs, dance halls, parks, theatres, entertainment centres, literary gatherings and science clubs and even reading rooms and libraries. Tourists appreciate joining talks and conferences. They like an appreciative reference to the culture of their belonging. Bars and entertainment centres are often treated essential for tourism development. Every tourist and visitor group has a different liking, therefore, it is impossible to enumerate what tourists may demand yet certain attractions are more important than the others. Peace, law and order, travel facilities, comfortable accommodation, attraction, beauty, and courtesy of people are more important.

Kaul (Kaul, 1985) has described tourism with greater eloquence. "Tourism invloves industry without smoke; education without class-room; integration without legislation and diplomacy without formality...." Kaul treats tourist, as a cultural and technological ambassador, an industry and an economic multiplier, an instrument of social progress, an expression of the right to leisure and promoter of international understanding, goodwill and peace. In a tour undertaken individually, personal choice of destination, amenities and sites is more predominant while the groups of tourists like organised school tours, picnic tours, etc., have special gains of overcoming the inconveniences and uncertainties of travel and loneliness in a strange place. Luxury and comforts do not carry as being an importance as the meaningfulness, love, sense of appreciation and behaviour. Good tourism organizers try to bring the tourists in touch of culture and establish cordiality between the stranger and the people. Over-selfishness, excess exploitation and pinching fleecing of the unaware stranger generates a sense of hatred for the place and people of the visited area. There is often an unpleasantness emerging between the hoteliers and the visitors due to excessiveness on the part of the hosts. There should be some rescue-office to protect the tourists against unpleasant behaviour. Tourism can prove to be highly damaging to the host land due to excessiveness on the part of tourists who lose decency and sincerity for the place they visit. Therefore, a due caution should also be taken against the visitor.

A Prudent Discrimination

Domestic tourism helps in redistribution of income and national integration but does not add to the productivity growth while it entails diversion of rare investible resources. It also increases import bill as the beverages and materials used in tourist stations are imported for the foreign tourists while domestic tourists also use them. It causes a sort of consumerism and conspicuous consumption. The rare investible funds are deployed for showy and luxury expenditure. It benefits the vested leisure class of the society at the cost of the hardworking masses. The vulgarity of moneyed class grows and is given status and hospitality. The luxury class gets the hospitality of the hoteliers greater than the foreign tourists. The foreigners are neglected to please the domestic spendthrifts. This discourages the flow of foreign exchange and cáuses damage to the nation. The pompous hotels spend the rare food and amenity availability and the administration attends to their needs at the cost of vast majority of actual working class. The backward countries are short of consumer goods and their supply is inelastic. When the luxurious vested classes of the country spend in vulgar way the prices of essentials go up and tourist stations face inflationary spiral causing hardships to the commoners. The generated income has only low income-multiplier. Diversion of investible surplus to non-essential and unproductive items is damaging for overall level of development and the direction of development. Foreign tourist, therefore, should be given special treatment so as to make tourism really effective for development. Any over-crowding worth the name on the excuse of tourism is not conducive to growth. Domestic tourists should be given secondary facilities and group-tourism in less cost should be arranged for them. Students, officials, academicians, artists, excursion parties, etc., should be accorded facilities at lower costs but these caterings should not entail imported goods. A prudent discrimination is by all means necessary in this regard.

Tourism Settles on the Bedrock of Infrastructure

Infrastructure means that set of external economies and amenity-cum-environmental situations which motivate the entrepreneurs to flock in for making investment in directly productive activities. In a technical sense irrigation, credit and marketing structures are infrastructure for agriculture. In the same way, tourism development as an industry and avocation of the visitors is strengthened to its stronger hold by few given amenities. Transport is foremost in these. The physical infrastructure includes roads, parks, cinemas, guest houses and hotels, travel agencies and host of guides in established stations, railways, airports etc. Sociospheric infrastructure is the amiable life-manners, administration of the people, behaviour of the staff serving tourists, etc. Aesthetic infrastructure includes the overall peace, tranquility, calm and quite greenery, scenic views and the atmosphere wherein the visitor forgets the worries coming from din and turmoil of busy stations.

There are several other dimensions of the facility structure, which help tourism in various ways. Banks, through-booking agencies, petrol pumps, vehicle repair houses, hospitals, tour monitoring offices, etc., have a tremendous role.

Promotional Forces in Demand for Tourism

It is well-nigh established in foregoing analysis of the potentialities of tourism development in Uttaranchal Himalaya that the region offers a very assuring avenue of extended tourism activity in this tract. The factors, mainly speaking in favour of this proposition are:

(a) Plentiful natural splendour and hypnotic spell of the scenery in Garhwal and Kumaun tracts.
(b) Rising levels of income and spendable income in European, American and middle-east countries.
(c) Growing popularity of tourism as a cultural phenomena among the economically well-off and new rich sections.
(d) Increased tourism infrastructure in the main nodal centres of India which afford an attraction and convenience for foreigners to undertake trips of remoter areas.
(e) Well-woven network of tourist accommodation as well as transport facilities in Uttaranchal Himalaya which allures the tourists to undertake trips of Himalayan tract.
(f) Promotion of a pro-tourism psycho-pathology of mind among the development enthusiasts at the official circles as well as among the inhabitants of the Himalayan tracts in Uttaranchal.
(g) The productive resources like land, forests and wild life have reached saturation or stage of exhaustion. The

manpower is growing unmatched by resources to feed upon. The hydel resources and mineral resources, which still leave adequate scope, entail technological strides and enormous investment on the capito-sphere. The political rivalries are by far deterrent in the course of economic growth in this direction. Exploitation of the scenic beauty, climate, unsatiable curiosity about Himalaya, and atmospheric peace and tranquility, remote from din and turmoil of rest of the world assure very promising scope of development ahead to ensure higher income employment and participative status to these far-flung isolated areas. This has far less capital requirement and it assures easy money-making as compared to farming and industry.

(h) Tourism, being a relatively new phenomena, assures gains to the vested classes who own properties and have greater grip over the ruling regime. Benefits filtering to the general masses, multiplier effect of income unfolding to other sectors, and overall linkages with other productive sectors of the local economy may not be as strong as the development of basic sectors, yet tourism has a great demonstrative advantage over the other sectors.

Development of tourism is by far a function of the following factors:

(a) Increased sensate culture among the prospective tourists – internal and foreign.
(b) The extent of curiosity and willingness among the visitors to personally visit the area and satisfy the curiosity.
(c) Pursue the tourist from the place of his landing or residence to the intended site so that other competing tourist sites do not exhaust him and his resources.
(d) Arrange for the tour programming, travel bookings, accommodation, midway catering and safe journey.
(e) Management of adequate living accommodation and boarding to the best satisfaction and bringing the tired tourist to the mental state of being at home.
(f) Devoting his every bit of time to the intended purpose of visit which covers enjoyment, site seeing, view of the

scenery, fun and frolic, cultural items like dances, singing, literary meetings, etc., with photography all along.

(g) Attending the visitor with utmost efficiency at every point so that the visitor feels like visiting the place again. Things of his need have to be catered and importance has to be given to his person and presence.

(h) Most of the tourists hold the trip with their friends and families including infirm, old, children and the females. Their convenience has to be carefully looked after.

The type of services involved in this extended chain are not catered by a single person. Several organisations have to be put to smart action in this context:

(i) Tourism promotion organisation which looks after the higher matters of policy involvement. These may cover, broadly, the publicity, advertisement, persuasion, and guidance.

(ii) Gearing up the organisation of transport network, road, rail, air and water transport, so that the journey is rendered convenient, less costly and within a very reasonable time-span. This requires the tourism planning.

(iii) The organisation of catering at various important locations which caters besides food, shelter, daily needs, affords proper informative literature.

(iv) The organisation of communication which inter-connects the tourist parties in outer stations and maintains the link-contact of the visitors with their home and activity world.

(v) The administrative structure which maintains endorsement of proper laws, regulations, safety, security, peace, etc.

Induced Curiosities: A Strong Motivation for Tourism

The term 'development' denotes series of changes brought in the existing state which mark a growth in terms of net efficiency leading to more production, a qualitative change in production, or change in institutional, structural pattern and organisational dimensions ensuring such growth of service or production over a long range of time ahead in a self-propelled form. The deliberate efforts to promote demand for tourist service and make arrangements to cater to the so promoted demand denote (De Kadt, 1979, 43). The tourism demand is promoted by deliberate publicity, advertisement and animating incentive structure. Thus, there are three main ingredients of this action:

(a) Expanded information and spread thereof in the curious human world.
(b) Animating and motivating tourist organisation and network of amenities and facilities like electricity power, banking, consultancy, tourist bungalows, etc.
(c) Policy-based incentives to the potential tourists in the form of holidays, advances and concessional freights and rates. Such incentives are offered to the tourists towards raising demand and to the caterers towards making satisfying supply of services. Concessional capital subsidies for building hotels and luxury buses constitute an example.

(a) *State Action*

Each state has its own arrangements of promotion of internal and external tourism in the state. To this effect official agencies have been created in every state. Uttaranchal Government has created a separate Directorate of Tourism. Besides there are separate independent corporate bodies working for development of tourism. Such bodies are working at both state and Central levels. Official levels also recognise tourism as an activity generating a number of social and economic benefits. It is generally held that tourism promotes not only income and employment but also understanding besides creating foreign exchange which is particularly rare in supply. Since tourists belong mostly to the dollar and pound regions, country is able to fetch the rare currencies.

(b) *Artefacts and Handiwork Marts*

Tourism as a market for the domestic handicrafts and art goods bear special significance. The marketing depends on the organisational build up to this end. Government in the Central as well as the state level is conscious of this fact. Tourists pay taxes on the commodities, services and at other levels which adds to the resources of the local bodies, state and Central Government. Government of India earned only Rs.32 crores of foreign exchange by tourism in 1971-72 which had risen to Rs.1,031 crores in terms of foreign exchange (Government of India, Seventh Five Year Plan, 1985-90, 314). By the year 1986-87 these earnings had multiplied to Rs.1,378 crores (Government of India, Mid-Year Appraisal, 1987-88, 27-28).

The activity has assured even greater pace in the later years of the Seventh Plan. Besides, the foreign exchange earned by foreign tourism, the domestic tourism is more useful in promotion of social and cultural cohesion and integration among the various regions of the Union. While the foreign tourism entails greater investment in creation of luxurious hotels and pompous arrangements, the domestic tourism feeds the handy-capital based retailers and restaurants. It encourages the middle class and lower class to participate in the enterprise. The students and lower middle class people are able to share the enjoyments so far confined to richer classes alone. Organisational dimensions are important in both the types of tourist movement. Domestic tourism serves greater mass of the people and a vast organisation of transport and tourist service becomes essential to cater the needs. Foreign tourist arrivals in 1951 were 16,823 excluding those from Bangladesh and Pakistan (Government of India, Seventh Five-Year Plan, 1985-90, 234). These rose to 8,84,731 in 1983. The tourism growth has been at a pace of 8.4 per cent per year during 1961-71 which rose to 8.86 per cent per year in the next decade. Indian domestic law and order conditions, relations outside and arrangements for tourists have a bearing on attracting the tourists to this side. A good organisation of tourist activity alone can assure prompt services at all levels. Recession in the homeland of tourists and exhorbitant rise in cost of air travel in later '70s have adversely affected the flow of foreign tourists, specially from United States, Canada, Western Europe, etc. Indian tourism agencies abroad do not work as efficiently as the agencies of the other nations so India is not able to participate very effectively and share the gains of growth in international tourism.

(c) *Modes of Advertisement and Styled Publicity*

Buoyant tourist activity round the prosperous world offers good potentialities of great advances in this field but for the effective organisation, India fails to make gains as significantly as it should. The tourism-organisation alone can weave appropriate package of publicity, persuasion, facilitation and marketing strategies. While the world tourism grows at the rate of ten per year, India shares hardly 0.3 per cent thereof.

Seventh Plan worked in the direction of structural changes in tourism promotion services and targeted annual growth of 7 per cent per year in foreign tourist arrivals. A certain degree of relaxation in policies and procedures of admitting foreign tourists to the land was also implemented. Tourism was recognised as an industry. In order to organise tourism effectively the private sector had been given a dominant role in investments on tourism accommodation and vehicular services. Private capital has indeed responded to the call. Public sector investments were to mainly focus on the development of supporting infrastructure.

(d) *Concentration on Tourist Activities*

Organisational strategy adopted in this context shows that a few tourist circuits and centres are being developed instead of spreading the activity over a wider space. This is wisely done to utilize the returns from a scanty investment immediately for ploughing back the returns. Some centres have greater influx and are manageable within the limited investment. The other thing noticed in recent past is that tourism is being diversified from the traditional site-seeing tour centres, primarily on places of cultural tourism; to the more rapidly growing holiday tourism within the framework of country's splendour dimensions. Diversification should be with a conscious attention to the aesthetic, environmental and socio-cultural implications of tourism projects. It is well-nigh known that tourists from affluent nations bring alcoholism, drugs of dangerous nature and have dangers of espionage, endangering the political stability. Demonstration effect of hippism has been rather to the disadvantage of the younger population of this country. Therefore, this new twist in organisational strategy is good.

(e) *Traditional to Non-traditional Lines: Activated Transition*

Tourism is being organised in India on the non-traditional lines such as trekking, winter sports, wild life tourism, beach resort tourism. These types of tourism are likely to exploit the abundant sunshine resources of sea-coast and sandy beaches, wild life resources and chaste Himalayan scenery. These types also lenthen the stay of the tourists resulting in greater spending here. Transport communication and amenities of life are essential for such tourism which is largely lacking in greater part of India (Owen, 1968, 12-20).

(f) *Focus on National Heritage Projects*

The recent strategy of organising tourism has assumed a new dimension. Restoration and balanced development of national heritage, projects of both cultural, historical and tourism importance to exploit advantage of India's unique place in cultural tourism and to utilize tourism as a major force in support of Indian prestigious heritage have been the major objectives of action in this context. Our cultural relations and affinity has been very close and of mutual gain with the great middle-east nations. south-eastern and east-asian nations have been in cultural fold of our systems where a due appreciation is received by Indian ways and etiquettes. These affinities offer plentiful avenues for development of 'ethno-cultural' tourism from these lands. Seventh Five-Year Plan aimed at launching a 'Discover Your Roots' programme in organising tourism for India (Government of India, Seventh Five Year Plan 1985-90, 235). Two new types: (a) conference and convention tourism, and (b) sports tourism, are being promoted.

(g) *Aroused Curiosities for Tourism Growth*

Organisation of tourism activity depends on two factors: (a) Making visitors India-oriented by vigorous publicity and affinities aroused and curiosities generated. (b) The effective organisation sound the prosperous world to reap the advantage at the same time building friendly relations abroad. This is a sound strategy not only for the tourism activity but is also essential for promoting export of fanciful art goods and services. This strategy of action is technically known as National Image Building and vigorous marketing strategy. Public and private sectors have to work together and abide by a common agreed code under this strategy. The participation of a vast majority of the upper middle and middle class gentry in tourism requires organisation of tourism in reasonable cost boundaries. The high class luxuries are not always essential. It is basically a high sanitation level which matters and not a pompous system. The service orientation has greater importance than an expensive feudalistic and luxurious tourist complex.

Pro-Tourism Development Strategy

The pattern of organisation of the activity in tourism development shows that most of the activities concerned with foreign tourism are handled in the central sector while internal tourism is managed, by and large, by the state agency. The state governments do not as a matter of fact allocate enough resources to the development of tourism which is mainly due to the rarity of resources. The central agency has relatively less constraint and has the proper wider perspective also. The building of accommodation, roads, rest houses, arranging transport services and encouragement of private initiative in this sphere has been a part of Indian Tourism Development Corporation. Bhartiya Yatri Avas Vikas Samiti has been in rapid action for last few years towards arranging inexpensive accommodation. The financial support is being given on this score. Sixth Five Year Plan 1980-85, spent Rs.187.46 crores on promotion of tourism as against Rs.326.16 crores in the Seventh Plan, 1985-90. This is the initial expenditure made by the public sector while the major part of the investments in this regard came from the private entrepreneurs.

Enchanting Vistas of Neo-Tourism

National heritage projects of tourist development include building of tourist complex and wider framework of facilities in the eminent centres like Fatehpur Sikri, Kushinagar, Brajbhoomi, Sravasti, etc. Mathura, Ajmer, Varanasi, Rajgir, etc., are being developed under an organised plan. Meditation Parks and Pavilions are being developed in the periphery of Buddhist Temples as the pilgrimage tourism is likely to promote the intended cause besides the goodwill. Wildlife tourism has gained momentum in the recent years and the number of wildlife National Parks have been dressed with all sorts of facilities and the sanctuaries have reached 211 in number. 15 National Parks have the status of reserved under Project Tiger. Similarly the reorganisation of tourism promotion effort includes adventure tourism and trekking activity. If all the hill states are brought in close contact by well-knit frame of air services such activities can be organised in global level tourism. There is a great demand of adventure tourism among the young tourists, sport-oriented visitors and the organised training parties. Indian Mountaineering Foundation and Youth Hostel Association are the pioneering organisations working in this direction. This needs the consultation groups, guidance centres, publicity agencies abroad. The infrastructure to this end covers the equipment catering shops, rescue patrol services and monitoring agencies. Tourism is being organised on these lines now and future growth may be largely guided by these outlines of strategy.

Giant Organisations and Promotional Super Structure

Social tourism is just another dimension where efforts are being diverted from general luxury-oriented tourism. Yatrika accommodation is being developed in large scale particularly for the benefit of the pilgrims. Chitrakoot, Amarkantak, Vrindavan, Kampil, Vidar, Karaikal, Puri, and Naina Devi projects are the schemes in progress. These projects in case successfully worked out and extended to other religious centres, are likely to promote internal tourism among the low and middle income groups. The organisational aspect has become more important particularly because the accommodation already created has to be dressed and managed. The flow of tourism has to be served adequately by co-ordinated efforts of all quarters together. Consolidation is essential before extension places are drawn. ITDC hotels today have accommodation of more than 4,039 rooms and State Tourism Departments have expanded the activity which needs a proper review and consolidation. Hotel Corporation of India (HCI), a subsidiary of Air India International has placed a prominent role in expansion of accommodation. The industry needs upgradation in service quality and management personnel. 25 institutes are working to this end besides 11 diploma level bodies of training, and 14 craft level institutions. Food-craft and nutrition centres are at work. 425 hotels of high standard are already at service with 31,000 furnished rooms and by 1990, the number of hotel rooms has risen to 43,663. The metropolitan areas have this facility in greater measure. The state of cheap rate hotels is embarrassingly bad which needs adequate regulation and control. In fact, the growth of international tourism depends much on the favours of friendly nations which divert the traffic and aid-up the building of infrastructure. Development of transport is primary to promote tourism (Hoyle, 1973, 73) which attracts the private capital to tourism.

The past decade in Uttar Pradesh was dedicated to step-up economic growth by efficient resource use and strengthening the impulses of modernisation by economic and technical self-reliance. Development of transport and tourism constituted a major area of emphasis in public and private sectors. Hill areas have chosen the strategy of reducing the isolation, poverty, unemployment, sluggishness of economic activity by rapidly utilizing the beauty resources of hill areas and the climatic resources to the wider benefit of the country at large and the tourist populace. This has consistently been woven in the development strategy for the region. Tourism development fits in the strategy of improving and developing ecological and environmental assets as put in contrast with the establishment of large and medium size industries which necessarily create pollution and damage. If adequate tourism education and regulations are brought the "keep the mountains unpolluted campaign" can be successful.

Organisation of tourism consistently fits in the other wings of hill development strategy like development of horticulture, building of power generating units, soil and water conservation, scientific management and development of forests and cottage works of bamboo, textile weaving, herbal development, etc. Dependence on primary occupations can be substantially reduced if tourism is organised in proper form and scale. Hardly 6 per cent output of the UP state is produced in the former hills of UP (presently Uttaranchal) while this per capita output grows at a very slow rate of 0.4 per cent per year. The growth of population in hills (Uttaranchal) is at rapid rate of around 2.1 per cent during 1961-74 and 2.2 during 1971-84.

Out-migration constraint of hill development may be checked if alternative employment is created in the hills by tourism activity.

Emergence of Income-Yielding Occupations along Tourism

Hill region of Uttaranchal is characterised by low income-yielding opportunities. The low income creates lesser demand and low level of commercial activity. When some demand is added by way of tourism growth the push to the commercial activity is likely to be effective. Tourism in its isolated form can boost-up activity in the periphery of tourism routes, centres and the visited sites. But the major problem is of raising rural income. Unless tourism becomes a base of the overall production and marketing, it will not add significantly to the benefit of the commoners. The large houses and hotels owned by Mumbai, Kolkata, Delhi, and Kanpur *Seths* will sieze most of the tourism income. Thus, the organisation pattern needs special attention and a design of tourism helping the local economy and inhabitants has to be chalked out. Local cultural pattern may have to be protected against consumeristic luxuries, which emerge from tourism. The places of tourist importance may require adequate sanitary and health cautions when they face influx of untreated visitors. Sunder Dhunga Glaciers, Gwaldam,

Tapowan, Kauripass, Roopkund, Nanda Devi, Pindari, Milam, Gangotri, Yamunotri, Badri-Kedar, Temples of Jageshwar, Baijnath, etc., may be dressed with adequate health, sanitation and hygiene education and amenities.

The thurst of tourism development has to focus on accommodation for low income groups, hotels owned by people of the area, transport services owned and managed by local people, development of satellite towns, sport fairs, literary and scientific gatherings in local institutions, regulation of wildlife use, etc. Development of tourism in hill areas should not mean establishing the luxury-clubs and enjoyment centres for the prosperity in the wider plains. It shoud be ensured that 80 per cent of generated income is reached to the poorest in this area. Assets should by and large be owned by the local people. Organisation of tourism has to see these aspects in depth. Construction of Dak Bungalows at important places of hills in the recent past has created work for the seasonally unemployed labour locally.* Table 5.1 shows the tourist accommodation created till the end of Fifth Five-Year Plan.

The products of daily needs of the tourists are not largely produced in this region. These are supplied from Delhi or Tarai areas. Thus actual income which filters to hill people by the tourist demand is negligible. The transport services are owned by capitalists of great urban centres, and accommodation is owned by tourism department. The inconvenience, constraints, insecurity, and insanitation has to be borne by the local people. This is important aspect which should be taken into consideration while proper organisation part of tourism is discussed. Local economy should be strengthened so that it is able to market its surplus production in tourist demand. It is clear, that tourism has to develop in proper coordination and linkage with other productive sectors. Unless the production is geared up, tourism will create stresses and strains

---

*Such bungalows were constructed in Chaukori, Pauri, Gangotri, Uttarkashi, Bhojwasa, Arakot, Bhimtal, Ghangaria, Pipalkoti, Rambara, Chopta, Jankichatti, Hanumanchatti, Ranikhet, Mussoorie, Kausani, Sat Tal, Kanwa Ashram, Khirsoo, Lansdowne, Dehradun, Gaurikund, Gwaldam, Mukteshwar, Yamunotri, Chakrata, Gauchar, Joshimath, Manila, Ukhimath, Ramgarh, Harsil, Ansuiya, Dunagiri, Laharkhet, Bharari, Gopeshwar, Poornagiri, Talwari, etc.

TABLE 5.1: Accommodation Facilities in Important Tourist Centres (till the end of Fifth Five-Year Plan)

Places of tourist interest	Total No. of beds
1. Nainital	138
2. Bhimtal	30
3. Sat Tal	10
4. Chaukori	8
5. Kanwa Ashram	8
6. Kausani	80
7. Rudraprayag	68
8. Uttarkashi	40
9. Aarakot	6
10. Bhojwasa	30
11. Dhanaulti	20

and diversion of resources to non-priority sectors. Roads and amenities will develop where these help the already prosperous tourism neglecting the isolated villagers of Himalayan ranges. The minimum needs and facilities of the local masses have to be attended in priority and they must be made to benefit by the tourist influx in their lonely abode.

Liaison with Global Structure

The tourism organisation, whether state agency or the private sector body started with the function of preservation of interests of the travellers. Touring clubs and automobile associations worked for the help of travellers. Later it was discovered that tourism embraces several types of interests concerning the state, i.e. trade, social, cultural and educational interests in the fold of tourism. United Nations under the declaration of human rights declared that the signatories would ensure to facilitate the entry, exit and stay of tourists, whether local or foreign, and would help creating conditions of goodwill, amicable treatment and comfort for them. The state as a protector and regulator of tourism would see that the cultural heritage and environment is preserved against the ill effects of tourism. State had a great role in weaving appropriate infrastructure and encouragement to this end. State creates such organisations, official bodies and agencies which co-ordinate with tourist affairs and acts as a catalyst between tourism and national economic and socio-cultural growth. The sponsored institutions technically work towards tourism promotion for overall promotion of human welfare preserving the national interests. They render informative, regulatory, legislative, executive, catalytic and supportive functions including the financial, technical and educational coverage. Organisations generally arrange for training and related supportive help in tourism promotion. Inter-linking is handled by such created organisation. The media promoted activity of tourism with the help of an organisation. The mid-agents in the process between the organisation and the travellers are travel agents, travel writers, tour organisers, bus operators and even those who organise conferences, seminars, plays, sports, trekking programmes and arrangement of pilgrimage. The advertisers, documentationists, brochure publishers, photo-producers, film-makers, craftsmen, etc., do constitute the links in between. Organisations usually keep the records and produce informative statistics in this regard which helps the planning of tourism in long run. Co-ordination of efforts at various levels and inter-linking fuction of domestic and foreign tourism is handled by the national tourism organisations. These also keep links and co-ordinate activities of foreign tourism organisations.

International Union of Hoteliers (1869), Alliance International De la Hotellerie (1921) and World Tourism Organisation are the pioneering organisations. Ho-Re-Ca (International Union of National Associations of Hotels, Restaurants and Café Keepers) (1949) played a great role in the universalisation of traveller service. Similarly, American Hotel and Motel Association (1910) which succeeded American Hotel Keepers Protection Association (1879), became a powerful organisation of this type. Inter-American Hotel Association of 32 member countries (1941) also exerted considerable impact on the overall promotion of tourism in Western Hemisphere. Federation Franco-hispano-Portugaise des Syndicate de tourism created in 1908 held its first conference in 1909 in Spain. International League of Tourist Associations was founded in the year 1898 which included various national organisations covering different tourist activities. This later changed into Alliance Internationale du Tourisme in 1919. In 1925, an International Travel Publicity Association had been formed which took various names later on. In 1946, it had been named as International Union of Official Tavel Organisations (IUOTO) with its head office in Geneva. The objective of the organisation was to encourage tourism, improve the conditions of travel and eliminate the obstacles. To this end this major organisation appointed six regional and purposive commissions. IUOTO was further styled as World Tourism Organisation (WTO) with Madrid as its headquarter in Spain.

United Nations (1945) inherited the covenants from League of Nations. Its designated organ, Economic and Social Council picked up the tourism promotion work. In 1963, it held a conference on tourism in Rome which suggested measures towards the rapid growth of activity in all member countries of United Nations.

The main regional Commissions which help IUOTO are as follows:

1. Tourism Commission for Europe,
2. Regional Commission for American Area,
3. African Travel Commission,
4. Middle-East Regional Travel Commission,
5. South Asian Travel Commission, and
6. Commission for Pacific and East Asia.

Tourism as an international phenomena and cherished activity has been encouraged by UNESCO and International Civil Aviation Organisation (ICAO) of Montreal. Similarly, International Air Transport Association (IATA) has been, together with IUOTO, in development of tourism. A similar organisation operating from London—IMCO (Inter-Governmental Maritime Consultative Organisation)—has put its efforts in encouraging tourism. International Recreation Association (IRA) New York and International Youth Hostel Association (IYHA) Copenhagen, have significantly worked in this direction.

There has been a very large number of organisations working in the sphere of co-ordination of activities regionally, nationally and internationally. Pacific Area Travel Association (PATA) started in Honolulu (1952) as Pacific Interim Travel Association was later renamed as PATA in 1953. It encourages the travel industry in various ways specially in providing links and liaison. It works over more than 35 countries. Confederation of Trourism Organisations of Latin Africa (COTAL) has played important role in holding conferences to inter-relate the activities and increase coordination. COTAL and CTA (Caribbean Travel Association, 1951) have worked together for Hotel-chains, transport links, restaurants and recreation activities in Caribbean countries.

The catalytic role of Arab Association of Tourism and Travel Agents (AATTA), East Asian Tourist Travel Association (EATTA) and Travel Agents Association of India (TAAI) in respective areas of solving regional coordination problems is so well-evident. These operate in the style of International Federation of Travel Agencies of Brussels 1919. In all the countries, such non-official agencies are exerting themselves to the promotion of tourism in their areas of operation. American Society of Travel Agents (ASTA) has been working from 1931 at New York and covers the areas of US and Canada under its fold of activities. Australia, Africa, Asia, Europe and USA have been covered by a major organisation WATA operating from Geneva since 1949. The role of these agencies is enormous in building atmosphere for the present day scale of tourism.

The Crucial Interlinks and Mid-Functionaries in Tourism

Tourism is the trend of human consumption and initiated production. These trends do constitute a mechanisam of international distribution of income and resource transfer. It operates via organisations, official as well as private. The official organisations may be state-owned, state-sponsored and state-financed. The private agencies may be general inter-group collaborations in discharge of certain animating functions. These may be the enterprises organised towards making profit by facilitating the production of some utilities to the benefit of the tourists who form the large-based clientele in the industry. The tourism product is disposed and marketed by a vast interwoven structure of independent tourist agencies. Travel agencies play a crucial role in organising the activity on behalf of the vast and multi-group clientele. Travel agency handles creation and delivery of package functions in the overall tourism process. Making the use of the principle of large-scale production, the agency renders a coordinated package travel service to each traveller individually and this, done in large-scale organised way, becomes a community service styled and forged as an economic enterprise. The idea was common among the migrant communities in the past everywhere. Since the seasonal purpose, the migrants to single direction distant land operated in guidance of experienced route-masters who arranged mid-way facilities for the migrant groups. Modern tourism assigns the credit to Thomas Cook (1841) who is believed to have arranged a tour of groups for a religious meeting. The process of colonisation opened new vistas for such large-scale movement of people by sea-route for new enterprises, jobs and trade. The route-masters rendered the service of guided travel in their own varying styles. The tripping for enjoyment came to be popular only in the later half of the nineteenth century. Invention and operation of modern modes of transport like railways have indeed made the business of the travel agent quite manageable. In the olden days, the caravans of traders moved to the non-traditional routes under guidance of route-masters who used their good offices on route to facilitate the caravans and accord the en route security. In modern connotation the travel agents have an entirely new field to plough. They pick-up tourist parties for holidaying, site seeing, trekking, outdoor photography, literary or sport gatherings, etc., and make them conveniently tour round and reach the parties back to their home as per assured schedule of the tour programme. Thus, the agency is an organising-cum-programming institution. Thomas Cook is the father of modern travel agency system in the sense that in modern form organised package tours for enjoyment were designed and implemented by him. He holds the credit of forging the idea of 'Universally Acceptable Standard Coupons' to the facility of travellers among a very widespread network of hotels (Bhatia, 1982, 256-57). Travel agency system got its present shape after Cook's London Agency (1865) later taken over by J.M. Cook, son of Thomas Cook. The office had established agencies all over Europe, America and India to arrange tours under a similar pattern. New entrepreneurial dash and drive emerged in tourism industry due to the completely fresh approach of getting in touch of passenger groups by personal attention to each individual and classifying the tour demand in sub-groups. Then, arranging the tours in co-ordination with rest of the travel agencies in such a way that the hazards of travel of individuals are tackled by scientific collaborated effort. The knitting of transport agencies of various modes of transport, accommodation agencies and service agencies in a common thread work led to superb organization of tourism fit enough to serve millions of tourists at a time with precisely personal attention to each individual. It covered under its fold banking, shipping and tour selling at the time of J.M. Cook.

US Express Company (1841), another travel agency had scientifically organised tour selling to various lands besides the work of financial intermediary to facilitate tourists. Wells Fargo Company had given birth to Express Company in United States. The emergence of credit cards, traveller cheques, exchange of currency, as well as travel insurance of person and goods are the novelties strictly to the credit of this pioneering travel agency.

Complementarily developed among the transport system and wide ramifications in the linkages have created a thriving atmosphere for entrepreneurship for tourism development. Innovations in transport modes, specially the air traffic growth has necessitated the emergence of inter-mode linkages where the travel agents play their major role. The collaboration between the governments alone can feed the growth of tourism without which the travel agents remain helpless. Beauty-lust tourism, sun-lust tourism and variety culture-lust tourism has been so rampant because governments agree to encourage and help in development of tourism in other countries. Travel agents operate only within the frame of law of various governments. Fiji's achievements in tourism depend on the cooperation of other countries and their airlines (Barke and O'Hare, 1982, 173). The smaller nations particularly the backward nations cannot afford an advance expenditure in mass scale on the internal transport links, accommodation, restaurants, general shopping and the arrangements of tourist convenience. Travel agents only coordinate and use the already available facilities but have no capacity to generate them unless the governments agree to provide the network of infrastructure. Tourism is likely to keep confined to localities within the continent in absence of world-over network of travel agencies.

Spread Effects of Tourism

Tourism is likely to be a highly concentrated activity confined to a few localities in few countries if the spread-over is not deliberately sponsored. The role here is of the government as well as the private agencies. Travel agents at this point bring the proper information to the proper people, at the proper time and fit in the information in the organised tours. The agencies directly influence the choice of the tourists and play a major role in determining the direction of tourism by designing a choice-structure. It is technically to the credit of the travel agent to advise the potential tourist on the various alternative tour circuits and their gains directly to the closer satisfaction of the lust of the party. The travel agent chooses the set of arrangements on way and at the destination. Travel agents have the greatest advantage of having inter-space contacts with all types of agencies so that they make the facilities available to the tourist to be free from the burdensome arrangement making at each point of the travel. By keeping a close touch with the transport agencies, programmes of trekking, conference organizers, auto-rental companies, hotels, equipment dressers and the various technical service agencies, the travel agents become a competent source of tourist assistance.

Consultancy Functions in Tourism Development

Technical consultancy and information dissemination constitutes the primary function of the travel agency. They keep the train timings, air service links, inter-agency phones, location maps and the up-to-date knowledge of the places of tourist interest on finger tips. Travel agent is a personal counsellor and commands the sole confidence as interest protector of the tourist. He advises not only on the matters regarding routes, modes of transport, systems and risks but also works to the aspects of cost minimisation on behalf of the tourist. The agents are, in fact, cultural coordinators, who use appropriate dialects and languages and win the inner-most favours of the tourist who depends and holds confidence on the chosen travel agency for anything he roughly thinks about. Travel agents are fantastic in their skills as itineraries who advise very forcefully bringing all the possibilities of utilising the leisure to this best enjoyment of the tourist depending on his own choice. Travel agents have the skills of a psychologist who reads the whims and aspirations of the travellers at the first sight. It is this psychic rescue offered by the agent which protects the traveller from his unknown terror of risks and difficulties involved in travel and prepares him to undertake a journey without a hitch. Successful travel agents are extremely courteous and friendly. They help the tourists even beyond their normal track of services.

Planning, programming and cost-analysis involved in tour agency operations is the most tricky affair. It involves the contacts with a very large number of agencies to fix-up an appropriate co-ordination. The traveller does not want to hold any responsibility for himself. He pays for every little greater relief. The job is uneasy and challenging to see everything done by pre-programming and monitoring from a remote distance. Initiative, drive, push and dash are the essential features of a travel agent. His approach is always personal with the clientele as well as the men he deals with in sorting out the uncertainties of travel. The job is not of an official or governmental approach where the ball is kicked to the party by state officials without a deeper sense of commitment. The helping tone and friendly behaviour of the travel agent wins a confidence on him which he discharges with utmost efficiency, sincerity and devotion. He at times crosses his limits and helps out of the way in order to keep the repute and rapport intact. The slogan of the agent is 'one man satisfied, wins ten more customers for the counter'. A travel agent is so conversant and talkative that the travellers disposed to a hundred destinations at a time are able to fetch accurate information regarding everything related to travel and contingencies. His knowledge is very up-to-date and precise without which the programme of the scheduled tour may be lost unattended earning disrepute and hatred of the people.

Travel agent makes provision of foreign currency for the travellers using his own arrangements with various concerned agencies.

This involves a very technical type of service and saves the tourists of the great inconvenience which might emerge on the bank counters in usual course. Similarly the avoidance of travel risks is also attempted on behalf of the traveller in the travel agency. The risks may relate to personal accident risk, risk of theft and fire, etc., to the luggage and belongings of the tourist. Agents not only arrange the transportation and refitting services but also ensure against the failures. They offer alternatives and minimise the uncertainties. The travel agent can get us booked a meeting and conference hall, arrange the lodging and boarding of delegates and also make arrangements of outdoor photography for the delegates sitting thousands of kilometres away. The arrangements are precise and time-bound.

Travel agent gets his finances from a large number of activities he undertakes on a commission. Sale of tickets, accommodation reservation, restaurant booking, travel insurance, traveller's cheques, exchange of currency arrangements and the charges on use of agency's assets yield his commission. The agent is usually a man of great organisational capacity, endurance and patience. He keeps several alternatives for each thing and works with sheer confidence. Group client bookings are of more interest to the travel agent while he continues making groups of the individual clients.

Travel agents round the globe are organised in Unions and Associations. There are national level and region level sub-organisations also. In advanced countries the agents are in close contact and are able to collaborate towards still better discharge of their functions. UFTAA (Universal Federation of Travel Agents Association) founded in Rome (1966) ensures the growth of tourism and co-ordinates the specialised organs of tourism growth and development. More than 74 national level associations of travel agents having greater than 18,000 small agencies within them, are covered by UFTAA.

Role of Petty Travel Agents

Travel agents in India are registered under law and their activities are regulated in the best interests of the tourists. The tourist guides employed by travel agents are approved by the department of tourism.

The agencies have authorised booking offices if these are so allowed by railways and can book foreign passengers on approval of Reserve Bank. These can handle the passort matters and other travel documents on approval of Ministry of External Affairs. The agents are registered under Shops and Establishments Act of the Government. In 1952 travel agents in India organised themselves in National Association AITAA. This has more than 300 member organisations but hardly a quarter of them have the approval of the department of tourism. The association operates in four major centres: Mumbai, Delhi, Chennai and Kolkata. The travel agencies have a mushroom growth in the recent decades specially in the context of internal tourism. The agents in India everywhere do not have an official recognition. This is very dangerous in the context of welfare of the tourists.

All travel agents do not have a wider grip of the travel affairs and they operate on some limited routes. A few of them in smaller localities are connected with the bigger agencies in major towns and work as sub-agencies. The agencies which organise tours in Himalayan ranges are indeed very lowly linked agencies. All major points of tourist interest have not yet been linked by air transport in Uttaranchal Himalaya. There are no air, bus or helicopter services for tourists in Himalayan tract. Motor and chartered bus services connect the major point of the region with the highways. Therefore, the travel agents operating in Delhi, Chandigarh, Bangalore, etc., are not able to reach the travellers in Himalayan tours unless they depend on the bus-services. Most of the agents conduct organised bus-tours. The regional development corporations in Uttaranchal Himalaya, e.g. Kumaun Mandal Vikas Nigam and Garhwal Mandal Vikas Nigam run the tourist buses and hired accommodation for tourists. The travel agents at a distance like Mumbai, Chennai, etc., cannot be much helpful in helping tourists towards travel in remoter Himalayan ranges. The communication linkages in these regions are indeed weak and rare. Travel agent of Delhi can get in touch with the local bus arrangers in Haridwar and Nainital and ensure some accommodation through the Vikas Nigam or other private hotels. The package of services rendered by travel agents in Europe to tourists is rarely available in India.

Organisation of tourism on large scale specially in the areas unconnected by airways and railways is a difficult task for anybody to attempt. Government of India has established tourist centres in USA and European nations so as to attract the affluent visitors to India. New Zealand, Australia and several other countries have Indian tourist centres. These are a sort of information offices handling publicity, public relations and co-ordination functions. In order to handle internal tourism efficiently, tourism development offices are working in Delhi, Mumbai, Chennai, Kolkata and several other major towns. They cater information to tourists specially the foreigners. A separate Ministry of Tourism and Civil Aviation has been created to organise tourism planning, publicity, travel, trade and hospitality. It also plans for tourist accommodation growth, growth of recreational and wildlife centres and also the market research for tourism. The overseas information offices in New York, Los Angeles, Chicago, Toronto, etc., see to our tourist promotion work in America, Canada and Latin America. Offices in London, Geneva, Paris, Frankfurt, Brussels, Stockholm, Vienna, Milan, Sydney, Melbourne, Perth, Tokyo, Philippines, Hongkong, Singapore, Kuala Lumpur, Colombo, Kuwait and several places in US have been able to give a good publicity to India's tourist attractions. Air India International has been helpful in rendering air transport service to foreign tourists coming to India. But all of them are not afforded the gain of visiting Uttaranchal Himalayas for dearth of air transport in this tract.

Development of the Hotel Concept and Hoteliering

Village dormitories or club-rooms had long been used in the past to accommodate stranger travellers and guests in Indian villages. Megasthenese (350 BC) had marked the system of treating the strangers in Indian way of life and he reported village common guest rooms of each community where the travellers could fetch adequate accommodation, water and cooking vessels. The passengers who stayed were carefully looked after by the village chief and movement of strangers was carefully observed and supervised.

Later on the monasteries, temples and Masjids came to become the stay houses for strangers. This gave birth to Dharmashalas around the temples. Still later the Panchayat Ghar and school buildings helped in accommodating guests. Even in 37 BC, Horace has reported a modest Inn on road to Brindisi from Rome (Kaul, 1985, 255). Britian had *Breighnibs*, house-keepers of open houses known for their hospitality on payment even before the Roman conquest. Romans encouraged *Diversoria*, posting houses and inns. The system of commercially operating *Hostellers* emerged in 14th century AD and by 1800 AD the word 'Hotel' had gained popularity.

A very large variety of hotels is traceable in the West today varying in their nature of service and the location of their service. Their qualities vary by size of their investment and mode of operation in business. These are designated as resort type hotels, transient and residential hotels. The hotels in mountains, sea side, river banks and related types are known as Resort Hotels. The passengers there usually come to seek, off-day pleasure, honeymoon celebrations, relaxation and retoning of health. Himalayan tracts have these types of hotels. In the known pilgrim centres like – Haridwar, Rishikesh, Deoprayag, Karnaprayag, etc., the tourists come to enjoy and meditate at the bank of holy Ganges. Similarly in Nainital, Bhimtal, Sat Tal, Naukuchiatal, etc., the tourists seek relaxation by getting lost in nature's scenic splendour. The Transient Hotels are patronised by the travellers who seek a business during their stay at the place. A traveller in Delhi goes to the capital for a business and likes to stay in railway rest house, road side hotel, airport hotel, suburban accommodation or a luxury-based public sector or private hotel. They use the telecommunications and transport vehicles to get in contact of the places or parties with whom they want to meet or talk for a business of their kind. The Residential Hotels are a type of guest houses extending the accommodation and routinised other associated services for extended periods of a month or so. Usually these offer all inclusive services and are demanded by the old, sanitoria seekers, ailing people or other parties for the seasons long. Such accommodation is only nominal in total hired accommodation. Passengers live like paying guests in these Holiday Homes. Hotels in modern concept are the chains of commercial accommodation at various places in different countries run under a common branch name, banner or identity. These are multinational commercial enterprises.

Paying guest accommodation is common in West and is

available on nominal charges. Similarly the guest houses are also a type of hotel. Campaigns, caravans, youth hostels, mountain huts and Dak Bungalows are the hotels identified by nature of use, brand name and facilities. The hotels in Himalaya are mainly of 3 categories:

1. Accommodation available in tourist centres, guest houses, etc.;
2. Privately owned and managed hotels; and
3. Dak Bungalows maintained and run by state departments mainly for the benefit of touring officers.

Besides these accommodation is available in Ashrams, cultural centres, temple complex and Dharmashalas at nominal charges. Then some low-charge motels are also available in chosen transport centres which also combine a restaurant along with the living accommodation.

Space-Demand in Tourism Industry: The Determinants

Demand for accommodation and hotel services is the outcome of the tourist influx. This depends on the propensity to undertake tours in domestic and external population. While this habit is, but far, a result of the affluence level, consciousness and alertness for tourism and the situational gain of locality, it thrives on the urge to enjoy nature's beauty, urge for gaining knowledge by seeing and physical observation, official work and organisation of work and the overall mobility level of population within and outside the country. How much of accommodation would be required depends on demand which is the function of: (1) number of tourists, (2) their length of stay, (3) space demanded by one tourist, (4) the number of days hotel offers the space in a month. This shows the relationship as:

(a) Whereas the 'space demanded' $= \dfrac{\text{No. of visitors}}{\text{No. of visitors per room}}$

$$= \frac{10}{2}$$

$$= 5$$

(b) Including the 'stay factor' = $\dfrac{\text{No. of visitors} \times \text{Stay span}}{\text{No. of visitors per room}}$

$$= \frac{10 \times 5}{2}$$

= 25 Night guests

(c) Including 'space-offer factor' = $\dfrac{\text{No. of visitors} \times \text{Stay span}}{\text{Per room guests} \times \text{Days rooms offered}}$

$$= \frac{10 \times 5}{2 \times 30}$$

$$= \frac{50}{60}$$

(d) Thus the 'potential occupancy' = 5/6

(e) Minimum rooms needed is known by Negi's (Negi, 1984, 225-28) method:

$$= \frac{\text{No. of tourists} \times \text{Span of stay}}{\text{Days for which hotel space is given} \times \dfrac{\text{Monthly guest nights}}{\text{Room nights}}}$$

$$= \frac{10 \times 5}{30 \times 50/2}$$

$$= \frac{50}{750}$$

= 15 rooms

The number of hotel rooms to accommodate 10 guests who stayed for five days and of whom 2 tourists lived in one room, is 15. The occupancy rate is the real determinant of the utilisation of the installed capacity of the hotel. Occupancy rate tends to vary widely during seasons, months, fortnights and weather conditions in hills of Kumaun and Garhwal. This rate can also be ensured smooth and fluctuations can be avoided in their wild form by wise management and booking pattern. The common method (James, 1969, 37-38) of ascertaining room demand is

$$= \frac{\text{Number of tourists} \times \text{Percentage of total tourists staying in hotel} \times \text{Span of stay per tourist}}{\text{Days of the year} \times \text{Persons per room}}$$

The planning design and methods are well-illustrated in the analysis to the credit of Roger Doswell (Doswell, 1970, 20-37), Doswell and Gamble (Doswell and Gamble, 1979, 1-78) and; John Lesure and Podd (Lesure and Podd, 1964, 40-64) presented very analytical scientific study of running a motel business.

Negi (Negi, 1964, 10-52) analysed the economics of tourism and hoteliering in global market of human mobility and Rogers and Phipps (Rogers and Phipps, 1977) presented the estimates and working procedure of economic management of hotels and related catering industry. Gray and Liguori (Gray and Liguori, 1980, 60-78) have discussed the operational techniques of management of hotels in the context of western world. The under-developed countries have some of their typical problems not experienced in the west, therefore, the management systems have to adjust to new situations in India.

It is more so in the context of hotel management and catering to the needs of tourism in hill regions specially in Uttaranchal Himalaya. The traffic flow is very much fluctuating in hills not experienced in the hotels of Agra, Mumbai, Chennai, Bangalore, Delhi or Kolkata.

Pushing up Tourism and Public Policy

The federal government or the local authorities have always shown interest in promotion of tourism in some form or the other. The political system, constitution, social development level and organisational capacity are the factors which show the extent of state participation in tourism growth. State itself may appear in entrepreneurship of running hotels to illustrate the private hoteliers. The tourist organisation in USSR, Cedock in Czechoslovakia, Interhotel in German Democratic Republic, Balkan Tourist of Bulgaria, Oris in Poland, ITDC in India are some of the burning examples. UK has national cooperatives. Tourism needs a good government and international cooperation, Peace, harmony, order, judicial system, standards of cleanliness, health measures, efficient transport and communication system, risk minimising mechanism, publicity media, non-discriminatory treatment of visitors, good standard of tourism personnel and institutions and efficient local governments interested in tourism.

State can operate by four instruments:

(a) Fiscal instruments – Incentives, loans, grants, aids, rebate.
(b) Infrastructural utilities – Railways, airways, roads, water sewage, power, phone, taxies, etc.
(c) Promotional techniques – Schooling, site development, organisation and skill development, advise foreign collaboration, beauty site development.
(d) Physical planning and designing – Legislative measures, regulation, model making, direction of the activities, feasibility, reporting.

Hotel industry is sensitive to culture and modes, ideas and fashions round the world. Space programme has encouraged to build hotels in sky. Automation, electronics, accounting, planning, designing, programming, packing, travel ways, inter-culture dishes, food-technology, computerisation, music patterns, dinner styles, servicing, etc., have brought tremendous change in hotel management and procedure everywhere. Field tourism is a branch in itself. International hotel corporations and global collaboration has pushed the frontiers of hoteliering far too ahead.

6

Optimum Resource Utilization by Development of Transport and Tourism

Economic Development and Spatial Spread

In the traditional development studies, it was confirmed that the economic, social or cultural waves of change engulf all the areas and aspects of human existence in their own process and adjustment with time. Any change introduced anywhere on the globe ultimately tries to make its place in the global system. In a long run the spread of activity and gains of development reach every nook and corner. It occurs under the influence of some automatic forces and reactions of the economies to a change. If there are no restrictions and policy bars imposed by the state the spread comes-up of its own, therefore, not much attention had been given to the deliberate uplifting of the spatial parts. In the same way, the theory of trick to down effects had suggested that if the markets are competitive and free mechanism of adjustments is allowed to operate in a capitalist system of organisation, the gains of development in terms of increased productivity income and employment filter down to each layer of society. Thus, there was no obvious need to interfere with the day-to-day working of the spread processes and distributional processes in reaching the development waves to the remoter, backward, disadvantaged, slow and lagging areas as also to the poorest of the poor strata of population. The underdevelopment of the areas or sub-regions had been often confused with low population. Jacob Viner (1953) found that the term of development is associated more with the people and less with the space. It is the use of the space for human good which brings the spatial dimension to the forefront (Viner, 1954, 34-52). Arctic and the Antarctic, Himalayan heights, Sahara desert and even the great tropical forests had no relevance in development process till these were used by mankind for their betterment. Even the sparsely populated areas or barren areas, if dressed with adequate resources to the benefit of man, these catch the sight of the investors, public or private, for these assure lucrative gains for human happiness. Unproven and guessed resource areas and inaccessible tracts are gradually coming under the fold of development investment.

Spreading the Waves of Development

When tourism is used as instrument, dispersal has to be ensured. Even the areas which have good potential prospects for using greater capital, labour and natural resources to support its modern population or population elsewhere at economically viable distances and which can afford to accommodate more people with increased income and employment levels at higher standards do get an opportunity of development under deliberate policies of regional development. Geographers have developed a very wide range of theoretical apparatus and techniques in regional development. The twist in strategy is remarkable. The emphasis in the traditional literature was on the natural resources and accessibilities, and now the emphasis is on the people, their working talents and technology. The crucial test of the realisation of development is the basic resource of man. Regions without adequate natural endowments have also been brought under the fold of brisk economic activities by transfer of resources with the help of transport technology. Things, which were never deemed as useful and worth in the remoter past, have now come to be a great potential, for growth due to advancement of technology and cultural transformation. The prospects of well-thriving agriculture alone is not the test of potentiality now. Tourism is one of the dimensions of economic development.

Impact Across the Borders

The spread effect of income augmented in one part of the globe or one region has a dimension bearing upon the overall upgraded demand for goods and services not in adequate demand so far. The deficiency of investment opportunities in some areas was a make of overall lack of effective demand. New income growth makes-up this deficiency. An American having attained high profits from business in New York finds himself uncomfortable in din and turmoil of busy urban complexes. He intends to seek peace and fun in remoter ridges of Himalaya and in untrodden snows. Thus, tourism is an international enterprise which makes the uncared beauty resources valuable at certain levels of income. At a given level of income and demand some regions are unviable while in risen levels of demand, shortage, upgraded technologies and greater knowledge, these become viable and pretty lucrative. Since the social and private rationalities in investment processes in the context of capitalist systems, are rather distantly different. Investments on the basic social overheads do not seem to appear easily unless something is done to build roads, railways, bridges, irrigation, housing amentities, power development, etc., on the state account. When these investments are made, the private investors find it profitable to workout their projects of production at low costs. This is the mechanism which works for development of the hitherto, neglected and remoter areas. Transport makes the exportable raw materials and usable idle labour force more attractive for supplies in other regions. Thus the inter-regional linkages get the stronger grip. The backward areas do not attract enough investors because there is neither enough purchasing power to sustain any enterprise nor any infrastructure which help reducing costs and making the exports from these areas. For dearth of this, these areas have unemployment among the workers. Without adequate technical improvement and new transport linkages enough effective demand cannot enter these areas. The fiscal measures to boost-up effective demand operate when the basic infrastructures are provided.

Market Perfection and Growth of Tourism Activity

Eckaus (Eckaus, 1955) opined that, "... unemployment difficulties of underdeveloped areas are not basically due to lack of effective demand but these stem from market imperfections, limited opportunities for technical substitution of factors and inappropriate factor endowments". Abraham Wald, Mrs. Joan Rabinson (Robinson, 1947, 42) and W.L. Valk have in separate studies illustrated the limitations of the technical substitution among factors in the reference of imperfect markets. The factor market imperfections lead to unemployment in the sense that for dearth of transport, knowledge of avenues elsewhere and effective mobility created by these keep the labour unused in a backward area. Transport and tourism releases this surplus either for use locally or through migration. Lewis long established that the idle labour used partially (Lewis, 1954, 22-34), unproductively or at leisure, gets released to the capitalist sectors of industrial or commercial lines in urban areas and is effectively used for higher wages because the marginal productivity of labour rises considerably by such a shift. Per capita capital used in capitalist sector is greater than the subsistence economy of the backward area. The shift of the labour is possible by network of roads and railways.

Geographers have concerned themselves with the relationship between demand and supply in transport networks and their interlinked localities. Experts like Taaffe, Morrill and Gould (Taaffe, Morrill and Gould, 1963, 240-254) developed a four stage idealised model consisting (a) development of scattered coastal ports, (b) selective growth of internal lines of penetration, (c) growth of interconnections between nodes in selected lines of penetration and (d) evolution of high priority links based on agglomeration economies at selected internal nodes and ports. In fact, the network expansion is a continuous process extending itself motivated by the supplies from the remoter areas. Studies by Bird and also a study by Hoyle explain the dimensions in different context. Economic development is considerably encouraged by the network of transport by (a) rising demand and products to be disposed outside, (b) reduction in costs of imported inputs, (c) emergence of new institutions, business establishments and (d) migration of surplus labour. The greatest advantage is in terms of entry of a new entrepreneurial group in the isolated localities to fillup the entrepreneurial vacuum. If the deliberate policy tools are applied to encourage economic activities and utilisation of resources after the networks are built, the process of spread is expedited.

Exploitation of Chaste Beauty Resource

Some of the regions keep undeveloped due to the neglect of the investors who are interested in immediate gains and not in long-term investments on the infrastructure for growth. The remoter hill areas, forest regions, sea coasts and river basins are beautiful for obvious paucity of arable land and accessibility. The only resource which is plentiful there, are the beauty spots and good climate. Both of the things cannot be exported. The system of exporting such resources to other areas is tourism development. Under this system such areas are woven with modern infrastructure, amenities and day-to-day life facilities of the great urban centres. The people from the prosperous part of the globe come to enjoy and stay there for sometime. In this process, they spend for their comforts which becomes a continuous source of income in such areas. The transport networks have the credit of reaching the affluent visitors to these remotely placed and less endowed areas. Mountainous regions are loved by the visitors for: (a) their envigorating cold climate specially during summers when scorching heat of the sun makes the life full of inconvenience in wider areas of the tropical world, (b) these areas have calm, peace, isolation, lack of pollution like noise, turmoil and the worries of excessively busy industrial and business centres, (c) the mountainous areas are full of greenery and forest cover, the lush green scenery is captivating for the people otherwise used to highly smoky, man-made factory and colonies of industrial world, (d) the areas are poor and simple in their cultural setting who can work to serve for the prosperous visitors within low costs without grudges, (e) the fast flowing rivers, waterfalls, serpentine roads, other attractive water bodies amidst the valley, etc., are utilised by the visitors and their stay yields income because this generates work of various categories for the unused labour force. Tourism creates some disturbance in the calm and quiet atmosphere and damage to the forests and water-bodies in some measure. But since the stay of the visitors is only short and unstable it is within the bearing capacity of the nature.

Tourism and Climatic Resource

Tourism industry in the remote hill areas thrives on the demand for the soothing climate for specific months in the year. The snow-clad high mountains make the air cool and the forests release the moisture in air so that the overall pleasure of living and trekking in the hill areas is enormous particularly when the other regions get affected adversely by the shooting temperature in summers. The climatic advantage in sea beaches, river banks and mountains makes the mobility of prosperous population in favour of these areas. For the dearth of transport networks, such fanciful mobility is restricted because the investment resources are indeed short to be spared for a luxury investment for remote areas. The road building, ropeway making, construction of bridges, penetration through hard rocks of mountains, managing water supply in upland areas, electrification and vast accommodation creation involves huge costs in bulk. The consumers of the climate-market are the only vested affluent groups for quite sometime till tourism enters into the habits of the general people. Foreign tourism in Fiji and some other countries makes a major part of the income of these countries. Himalayas have that potential yet the exploitation of this potential has not been possible for various reasons explained at length in the later chapters.

Initiation of Change in Lagging Regions by the Growth of Tourism

It has often been held that the tourism activity wherever develops has its own highly restricted circle and its benefits flow to a very limited circle or patches of areas. In fact, it was like this in the past. The tourism phenomena in Kashmir is traceable even in the remote history. The great pilgrim centres have attracted visitors from long distances even in the past. These do not have developed to the benefit of the local residents very extensively. Poverty of mountains is still phenomenal. The poverty-ridden beggars in all pilgrim centres are still as numerous as they were several decades ago. These things raise some fundamental questions about the impact on the local masses and their stability of livelihood, dexterity, skills and equipment. Experts argue that for the mutually accelerating interaction of these two parts, (a) tourism and (b) the local economy where tourism occurs, tourism could not have grown to the mass phenomenon today (Kaul, 1985, 253). But it is often found that tourism is taking different forms and shapes in different areas. It is not necessary that the overall impact of the tourist activity would go in favour of these regions because it is essentially an urban type service, creating, catering industry and does not create manufactured goods nor creates more agricultural commodities which would provide a permanent and sustained source of livelihood to the local inhabitants. It makes a hospitality industry depending on the number and spending habits of the visitors. If the visits get minimised the caterers may have to go starved and the accommodation may keep grossly unutilized.

Development of Market Structure

Tourism helps in development of market-structure in the areas where it penetrates. There occurs a large scale diversification of markets because in the changed situation under tourism predominance these are designed to cater to the extended needs of the tourist purchaser rather than the local purchaser having only low buying capacity. New investments on the fanciful goods and luxury-based goods come up in the market. The intensity of the business grows. Tourist being an affluent buyer is able to pay bountifully, therefore, the margins of the dealers go up and that maintains them in higher standards. Varieties and choice-structure gets widened in all spheres of life. The food habits, clothing patterns, living styles and the civic ways get more internationalised and leave the typical local patterns.

Tourism generates a new stream of income while in the same process it raises demand for the day-to-day consumer goods like eggs, milk, bread, vegetables, fruits, condiments, etc., these are supplied by the rural folk in the periphery of the tourist centres. This offers a higher price and a cash payment. Thus, a very wide range of goods are produced in the neighbouring areas to feed the tourist demand. The direct employment of the people in hotels, restaurants, guest houses, clubs, motor services, photography studios, entertainment houses and the like creates income to those who had nothing in hand to spend. Once they receive income, in turn, expand this in getting goods of their need. Thus, the demand wave gets still more strengthened for brisk commercial activity. Kaul

(Kaul, 1985, 90) feels that the key factor that determines the size of the multiplier, however, is the economic composition of the area. The greater the tourist spending and respending larger is the multiplier.

There is no relevance in the argument that any spending by the tourist leads to more production. The economists explain that demand is only one of the stimulators in this process. The supply constraints may be still enormous. In the highlands, there is not a big quantity of the grains, or other marketable surplus of the provisions. There are no industries nor any manufacturing activity. Therefore, a activated demand in 'Badrinath' or 'Deoprayag' for instance, cannot generate factories there. Where we can't trace land for any agricultural activity, large scale supply of vegetables is practically impossible. What would happen in such cases. The goods are imported from other regions at enormous transport costs and served to the tourists. Such imports are sizeable leakages in the multiplier effect of the tourist income. For the international tourism, the case may not be the same as for internal tourism. The foreign tourist, so served, is also helping in raising output in the country visited, irrespective of the places visited. But if the foreign tourists are served with imported wines and foreign make commodities, the gain again slips to the other lands. The margins earned by the caterers are for a shortwhile and net impact on the economy may be negative as the foreign liabilities grow and dependence increases. Therefore, it may be inferred that domestic tourist service with foreign imported goods is not a positive contribution either to the country or to the region. If the goods purchased and consumed in the process are the domestic makes, preferably the local-makes, the gain is indeed enormous for the local industry, agriculture, horticulture and the labour employment.

There cannot be an unqualified support for tourism promotion in each case. Tourism is a luxury-based industry which may not be within the worthwhile priorities of a poor land. The municipal bodies have to twist their expenditure pattern in order to accommodate the tourist activity. It involves diversion from priority to the luxury-based expenditure from the standpoint of the less developed areas. For instance, the expenditure on accommodation which is occupied for only three months in the year, pompous decorations, luxury clubs, very high sanitation and catering standards, etc., are not within immediate priorities of development unless tourism constitutes a very large part of the total economic activity in the locality. Foreign tourism is not the basic support to the total process. Domestic tourism keeps the industry sustaining and the layout of the incurred investments utilized. A domestically fostering travel industry attracts the greater measure of the foreign tourists. Thus, there is a complementarily between these two.

Household Manufacturing Boosted by Tourism

Kashmir crafts and cottage industries, sarees of Varanasi, beeds and coral garlands at sea beaches are the illustrations of tourism-promoted activities. Tourism income is a big allurement for the government specially the foreign tourism. That yields foreign exchange. In this process the infrastructural expenditure involved is met at priority in state sector. This opens avenues for private entrepreneurs to flock-in to make a hay by reduced costs and external economies generated. If tourist income promotes local industries, the activity is worth encouraging. Thus, adequate efforts should be laid to promote them wherever these have not found a base yet. The official position should be exploited to see that the areas in the grip of brisk tourist activity and its neighbouring areas share the gains adequately. Monopolised tourist income of few business magnets in backward areas is more damaging for local development than promoting.

Tourism has demonstrative effect on the general consumption pattern and thereby a twist in investments occurs. More showy, pompous and expenditure unrelated to productivity can emerge damaging the dexterity and simple ways of living. Alcoholism is a curse that is often associated with tourism in coral islands. But these demerits can emerge even without tourism. The educational infrastructure and general alertness on this score can safeguard the distortions in local culture.

The religious and cultural tourism has greater depth and impact on the visitor but does not leave much to the people of the place visited. The objective here is to visit not the people or the area but the shrines, temples, mosques and churches which have certain religious impact. In the recent years these pilgrim centres have emerged as cottage craft producers and good lot of sales are encouraged by pilgrim traffic in some centres. But in local areas of Garhwal, Kumaun and other undeveloped areas, this traffic does not lead to encouragement of crafts because these areas do not have much of this activity. Some woollen textile cottage works are met with in the areas like Joshimath but the marketable surplus is not much and products are useful for cold climate while the visitors choose goods to the requirement of their own regions. Visitors in Ajmer Sharif are able to get some handicrafts of Rajasthan.

Aesthetic Diversion and Preservation of Human Values

The luxury tourism in hill stations is of the nature of customers in restaurant. The purposiveness and sense of sincerity to the cause gets reduced to purely material enjoyments in this. A tourist hardly cares to know the problem and life patterns of the people who serve him. The values of sophistication should never be forgotten in process of blind enjoyments. These should lead to definite welfare orientation benefiting the visitor as well as the visited. The creativity part of life is maintained when tourism promotes marketing of local products. Therefore, manufacturing activities should always follow the tourism promotion. In some tourism predominated areas there is seasonal activity for summers but in rest of the seasons, the labour force as well as the accommodation, roads, infrastructure, keep under-utilised. The solution of this also lies in the local industrial development. The products of these may be marketed during the activity of the busy season.

Personality Enrichment by Tourism

Aesthetic and spiritual tourism had advantages of a total fulfilment and satisfaction of being revitalised by divine touch. This is more useful to the young and growing than the old. This rebuilds the values and understanding of nature. The infrastructure constructs in this context are the great parks, wildlife centres, dense forests, waterfalls and great greeneries. The Himalayan forests, which have been in growing grip of tourism now, are fast eroding in these tracts. It is much for sure that tourism does not necessarily invest on development of local resources unless a policy corrective makes these preconditions imposed on the commercial beneficiaries. This brings to the inference that tourism has to be organised in such a pattern that its impacts on the local economy are to the betterment of environmental economic and socio-spheric dimensions. The tourism adds to network of transport in its own furtherance. It creates demand and cultural mixing. New cultural currents lead to enrichment of local culture if tourists do not confine within the courtyard of hotels.

Tourism Optimises the Factor Mobility

Tourism interferes with the local occupations and income creation activities in various ways. It has adverse effect in some cases and advantageous in other cases. M. Barke and Greg O'Hare (Barke and O'Hare, 1984, 176) reported that while tourism is a very predominant occupation in Fiji yet the dispersal of the activity is highly concentrated in few eminent locations. There are two important pillars on which the entire national industry operates, e.g. (a) the luxury hotels and (b) the airport. When more than 90 per cent of the tourist arrive by air, the other transport networks do not find much support. The tourists are guided and taken to trips by the hotel agent who monopolise every activity by themselves. Very few of the tourists try to explore the markets by themselves or visit any of the places of their own choice. The hotels are mostly concentrated in areas near the airport. The hotel groups employ nearly 3,000 people and not more than double of it are in tourism-related indirect employment. This is very much evinced that tourism of this type is not a labour intensive enterprise. The gains of the tourism are largely concentrated in these busy hotels. The industry is certainly more lucrative, stylish and remunerative. Labour from farming and local agriculture specialised in cash crop of sugar tends to migrate to tourism or its related activities. The land market is also facing a bid from tourism as against agriculture. Tourism has created inflationary conditions and booming price spiral due to tourism while large part of the local people have to bear the brunt.

On the Art of Hospitality

The material used in the Fijian Hotels for catering adequately illustrates that the gains of multiplier effect expected from tourism leak-out of the economy. Fiji has nearly 6.4 lakh people. 58.4 per cent of meat and poultry, 54 per cent of fish, 54 per cent of fruits and vegetables, 82 per cent of other food, 58 per cent of beverages and nearly 52.7 per cent of total purchase are imported from other countries (Varley, 1978, 27-35). Similarly the hotels operating in Himalayan range (especially Uttaranchal) produce too little supplies to cater the demand of tourists who flock-in as the summer begins in April. These supplies are transported in small bits on trucks to the remote areas. The net gain to the local producers thus, does not emerge. Fruits, vegetables and even the corn is imported from remoter plains or Dun areas to meet the tourist demand in Garhwal. The payments made to bus transport, or to railways till the foothills, are pocketed by the government or bus owners while the other arrangements are done by the tourist agencies from Haridwar, Dehradun or Rishikesh. People of Garhwal are the spectators of the buses and are marginally benefited somewhere in petty services of serving tea at few places if the large corporation shops do not lick-up that business too. Similar experiences are reported in other studies elsewhere. E. de Kadt (de Kadt, 1979, 172) has also raised some basic doubts about the impact of tourism on local development. Kosinski and Prothero (Kosinski and Prothero, 1974, 67-77) had analysed the dimensions of the tourist movements on the development indicating how it pushes-up the demand as well as incomes. It was in the style of Leeming (Leeming, 1977, 58) who devoted to studies in Hong Kong reporting the gains to the local system. Gilbert (Gilbert, 1976, 85-87) in the context of Latin American economies also found similar gains and lapses in the context of tourism while casting influence on these economies. There are great gains of the tourism bred income if it spreads and trickles down to the lowest rungs of society. If it does not, the policy measures should act to make it that way. The effects depend on the elasticity of factor market and supplies in the consumer market. When supplies cannot grow and the constraints and imperfections are informidable, new incomes can create inflationary trends over straining even those groups of society who do not share the gains from the tourist traffic. In either case, the role of the state becomes important to see that the local interests are not neglected by the tourism

Tourism and Modernisation

It is not unoften that the entrance of any new order, neo system, novel ways and cultural innovation is possible by the development of tourism. It has happened so in the context of underdeveloped areas. After Second World War, the posting of war personnel of great powers in some countries introduced new angles of approach in respect of life styles and redefinition of enjoyment of life. The colonial and missionary experience in developing areas introduced some changes identical as pro-Europeanisation. Some of these changes were unhappy and unforeseen consequences for the guideless innocent cultures of superb values. Even the technological change as the experience has not always been to the human gain in the sense of long run peace. George M. Foster (Foster, 1962) reported on the acceptance of the change in a cultural system. Similarly Edward Spicer (Spicer, 1952) explained the chain of cultural currents of change and consequent losses of humanity in the sense of sabotage in the aborigin systems. A similar attempt was made by Eisenstadt (1966) to understand the net impact of grafting in the pretext of modernisation. While inter-appreciation, inter-adaptation and intermixing leads to new values and growth, conquering super imposition of values on innocent cultures is more in tone of imperialism.

It so happens in the process of reckless development of tourism and spoils the variety composition of human cultures. Treating the rich and dominant as an ideal type is sinful and a dangerous infectious disease. At times ethnocentric narrowness is enforced by the tourism development. Pollution, alienation, audacity, etc., being the main disenchanting trends of pseudo-Western style, these become burdensome when these are planted in remote Himalayan petty townships while the traiditionally more congenial ways are forgotten to achieve modernisation. A due caution to safeguard against this change is to the gain of the local traditional cultures. Rationalisation of authority and functional specialisation growth is to the gain of productivity.

The changes introduced by alien cultures in Lebanon were analysed by various scholars. Lincoln Armstrong and Rashid Bashshur (1958) complained about a sort of cultural disaster. While some change was analysed as modernisation by Elie Abib Salem (1973). Tourism brings new style, showy and attractive but are these always more producutive? Do these promote dexterity, honesty, sincerity, skills, sympathy, love, affection and welfare for all? It is well-nigh established that tourism pushes-up income and easy money-making in a system where hard labour alone could eke-out a loaf of bread. The deforestation, land erosion, increasing pollution, increased risks to life, property, dignity and existence of the guideless high landers do emerge from unrestricted and unguarded tourism. All that glitters is not gold but the properly managed tourism animates the developmental waves.

7

Structural Design of Transportation Network and Emerging Pattern of Tourism

Spatial Interaction

The analysis of spatial distribution invariably emphasize the interactions. Such interactions, as described earlier, are in a sence flow of goods services, ideas, or men. Some of the non-parametric techniques of this kind are well-illustrated in works of Kendall (Kendall, 1955, 20-82) and Siegal (Siegal, 1956, 117-35) published in the mid '50s. Gravity model and transportation problem model are more prominently discussed as related to linear programmes. Operational optimalities can be drawn with the help of these models. The models try to measure the operation interaction between the places or areas. Isard (Isard, 1960, 493-568) in 1960, presented a probablistic approach to the derivation of a gravity model affording a simple analytical tool in the hands of geographers in this regard. In this context Carrothers had deeply analysed the concepts of human interaction between spaces at length (Carrothers, 1956, 94-102). Similarly, Ficken, Dorfman, Samuelson, Solow and Henderson have made use of the linear programming techniques for finding the values where a given linear function of the several variables takes on an extreme value. The aim is to maximise or to minimise a linear function containing several variables subject to a number of constraints.

Since the development in economic, social and political fields emerges from the specialisation, the grater specialised transportation denotes more development. The mode of transport shows the level of development of the regions. Transport connectivity is the useful concept pertaining to network systems and exhibits greatest number of possible interconnections. Very often graph theories have been used to illustrate the connectivity of networks. Number of routes and modes of system are often used to express the ratios. Kansky in 1963 explained the methods of graph theory (Kansky, 1963). Gould (Gould, 1960, 59-69) used the methods in respect of Ghana networks of transportation. Abler, Adams and Gould (Abler, Adams and Gould, 1971) in their wider analysis of the spatial geography explained that movements or flows on the earth space begin with a static distribution at an instant in time and end with a static distribution at a later point in time. The distribution may be similar and different at points. Spatial distribution patterns are very often described as population dot-maps, isopleth maps, of consumer's buying power. The mapping of flows and determining the trends of flows, portraited in maps, is indeed difficult. The flows belong to different categories like goods, men, ideas, etc. In fact for geographers, point-to-point movement and their channels are important, therefore, transportation becomes the basic theme in Geography. The origin and destination may vary extensively and may even be the same. Group movements from several points to one point and even several points together at the same time, make an interesting area of study to explore possibilities of manipulations for optimalisation. Catering and distribution of services to any universe is possible by understanding the patterns of transport networks. For economic and other societal interactions a centre's range of influence is often described as 'Meanfield', the area nearest the centre accounting for most of the interactions. It explains the range of spread and coverage with reference to distance orbit. Abler et al. explain that networks are structures designed to tie together various points which are located in one, two and three dimensional space. They produce regional geographical systems by carrying flows of people, goods, messages, and anything else that is moved from one place to another (Abler, Adams and Gould, 1971, 238-39).

In the context of hill areas of the northern Uttar Pradesh in India the transport network systems can be immensely useful in suggesting the future models of tourism planning and strategy of catering the tourists with optimal gains to the local economy, low costs, less constraints and to the people undertaking the tourist activity.

Topography and Transport System

The Himalayan tract as a whole, has poor accessibility due to the typical topographical constraints (Pandey, 1989, 393-402). The foothills and Duns have relatively a greater accessibility if the networks are developed. These tracts are well-woven with road/rail transport and interconnections between the habitations in this tract are intercepted by frequent rivers and rivulets flowing down from upper hill ranges. It is this region which has the main gateway for entrance into the hill region from all angles when approached from south, south-east and south-west. The hills are intercepted by deep ravines in between and roads have to be carved across the hills with moderate height and slopes befitting the needs of vehicular movement. This makes the distances to dreary and tiresome for the tourists for travelling across by motor. Ropeway facilities are yet to emerge which make the journey more close and convenient. Map 7.1 shows the pattern of the hills and their frequent interception by the ravines. The transport road-routes indicated herein, indicate the long distances which have to be crossed by the tourists in order to pass from one small habitation to the other petty settlement. Till the modes of transport are confined to motor vehicles there is no way out to do away with these awesome distances. The hill-based settlements are guided by the nature of the earth's surface, availability of water and arable land. If the habitations are seen in single landscape, it may be made out that these constitute points of a wider network of roads which suggest the inter-spatial interactions by movement of goods, men and ideas. How best these points can be interlinked and how the cost of the inter-spatial movement can be reduced in terms of time, money and labour are the challenges of the transport system.

The transport system suggests an entirely new meaning when studied in the context of the ropeways and air-services. These avoid the entire burdensome cross-encircled road structures and the costs and human labour. In the context of the tourism development what

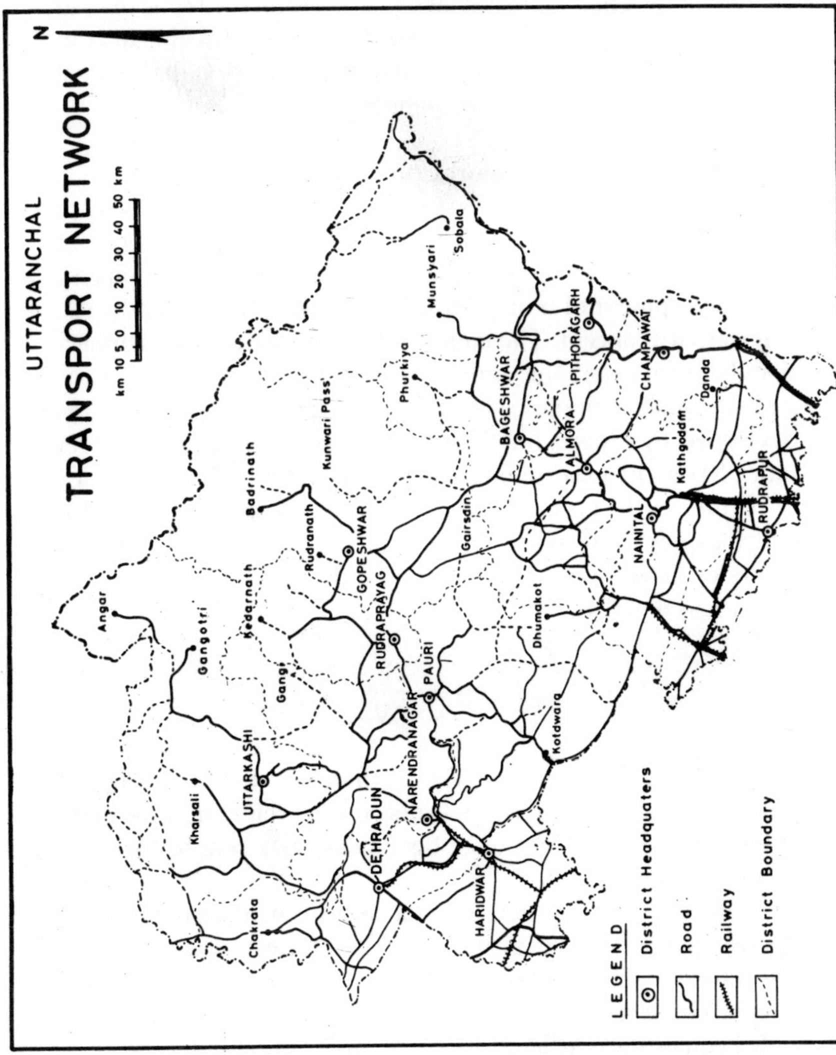
UTTARANCHAL
TRANSPORT NETWORK
N
km 10 5 0 10 20 30 40 50 km
Angar
Gangotri
Kedarnath
Badrinath
Rudranath
Kunwari Pass
Phurkiya
Munsyari
Sobala
GOPESHWAR
RUDRAPRAYAG
PAURI
NARENDRANAGAR
UTTARKASHI
Kharsali
Chakrata
DEHRADUN
HARIDWAR
Kotdwara
Dhumakot
Gairsain
BAGESHWAR
ALMORA
PITHORAGARH
CHAMPAWAT
Danda
Kathgodam
NAINITAL
RUDRAPUR
Gangi
LEGEND
District Headquaters
Road
Railway
District Boundary

FIG. 7·1

matters more is the time factor. In a given time space the tourists would like to cover the entire hill range till lofty Himalayas in a single or few breaks. But since the amenities are not yet developed and the probable costs are also enormous in view of the dearth of oil, the tourism development has to work within the frame of road transport. Bulk goods vaulages are otherwise infeasible also in present cost structure, technology and the resources at the disposal of the planners of tourism development.

Transport Connectivity

Yeates (Yeates, 1968) very aptly indicated that the network of transport is an index of the higher level of economic development. The development of transport network is often measured by the connectivity concept. The larger and greater are the interconnections between geographic entities, better is the level of development and smoother is the price level over the space. Graph theory, as developed by experts like Kansky (Kansky, 1963), applies Beta index (β) to the measurement of connectivity. In fact, Beta index (β) expresses the ratio between the number of edges shown by ΣE which expresses the routes in a transport system and the number of nodes or vertices in that system indicated by ΣV. thus, the measure is noted as:

$$\beta = \frac{\Sigma E}{\Sigma V}$$

In case of a particular node $V = 1$, therefore, Beta index for an individual node equals the number of edges or routes incident upon that particular vertex. Value of Beta index is the number of intersections at a vertex.

The degree of connectivity at a vertex is marked by the local degree. Network of veins and arteries in human body is a good illustration to show the transport network system. In fact, the edges may be connected by several vertices to different directions. The index equals unity when the vertices are connected by the same number of edges. It may be greater than unity when the edges are in greater number as compared to vertices. The illustration given above assumes the vertices in the opposite directions. Vertice means the point opposite the base. It is the meeting point of the lines bounding an angle. The interesection of the curve with its axis is vertice.

In any angle, there are two edges E_1 and E_2 and there are three vertices, V_1, V_2 and V_3. Thus:

$$\beta = \frac{2}{3}$$

$$\beta = 0.66$$

If the vertices are interconnected all routes we have 3 edges and 3 vertices as well. Thus, the index would be:

$$\beta = \frac{3}{3}$$

$$\beta = 1.00$$

In case the edges interconnected are greater than the vertices, the index would be greater than unity. Kansky draws a graph bearing six deges and four vertices. The index thus would be:

$$\beta = \frac{6}{4}$$

$$\beta = 1.50$$

The Beta index offers a measure of connectivity irrespective of the size of the involved area. It serves as the indicator of the connectivity between different geographical units and countries. If the measure shows the connectivity index as less than unity, this means that the areas are only partially interconnected. When the Beta index is 0, this shows that there is an absolute absence of transport network. If it ranges between zero and unity of the network of transport is believed to be only little entailing only handful of routes on which the flow of goods, resources and men is possible. At the point of unity, the index marks a state when all vertices are joined in connected graph and a complete network connection is formed by joining the minimum number of edges. When the Beta index exceeds unity, it expresses a state of higher degree of interconnection between the edges (Yeates, 1968) marked the third world countries like Ghana, Bolivia, Iran, Ceylon, etc., as only partially connected networks of transport and Beta index of these tends to stay around 0.90 which is less than unity. Similarly the other group of nations among those the Third World like Turkey, Algeria, Iraq, Sudan, Thailand, Nigeria, have been found holding a Beta index of 1.0 which makes a complete simple interconnection of transport. Bulgaria of socialist wing, obtains an index of 1.10 which means the interconnection is of better level as compared to simple complete interconnection. Nations like Romania, Mexico, Yugoslavia, etc., are at still higher level of transport connectivity, the index being 1.20. Chile is placed at still higher degree of connectivity. Advanced and high status transport connectivity, however, is evinced in France, Hungary and Czechoslovakia where the indices are placed nearing 1.40. Experts have very explicitly proved that connectivity index is a reliable indication of operational value when seen in reference of other indicators like per capita income and living standards. The usefulness of transport connectivity index is in the proved merit of its being linked as average linear positive relationship between per capita income as an indicator. A correlation coefficient also verifies the relationship. The experts have established that if transport connectivity is raised in the Third World countries only moderate rise in per capita income is evinced whereas the same increase in the context of an advanced economy marks greater strides in per capita income. Greater level of connectivity is met with an advanced level of economic development insofar as the rail-road transport connectivity is concerned. The adequately reliable measure of economic development is the per capita income index. This implies that a boost-up incurred in investment on rail-road transport network in a backward economy is likely to raise income level but in a small measure as compared to the economy which has higher level of economic development. This occurs in the initial stages of the transport development. If the basic stage of complete simple connectivity is established the pace of change in per capita income may catch speed. Discussing the theme in the phraseology of economists, it may mean that transport connectivity promotes the flow of goods and unless the surplus output of disposable and marketable nature is generated the transport network may take its own time in promoting output and gearing up the commodity flows. The transport of goods depends on roads and network of roads depends on the established links between human habitations. The main roads interconnect the main habitations and centres of civilization and these are connected by the feeder roads. Peter Gould (Gould, 1960, 30-40) tried to draw an inter-temporal development map of the growing road network in the context of Ghana and illustrated that in natural course of development short distance roads emerge at the first instance, which get linked to a major highway in due course. The outlet by highway encourage the smaller locations to be linked to highway. Gould identified five principal stages of development of roads in both contexts of primary and secondary or feeder roads. A sequential pattern of road development, in course of evolution, was identified by Taaffe et al. (Taaffe, Morrill and Gould, 1963, 503-29) and at least six identifiable stages are separted by them:

I Stage = Commercial nodes and shipping ports are interlinked.
II Stage = Interconnecting links between ports and closer hinterland.
III Stage = Emergence of feeder links connected with the penetration route hinterland.
IV Stage = Sub-feeder links interlink the penetration line and feeder roads.
V Stage = Complete multi-angular interconnection bounding the human-habitations.
VI Stage = Development of National Trunk Line routes interconnected left and right with inter-regional and regional trunk routes.

Since vertices in the Beta index mark the 'nodes' and the edges indicate the 'routes' the nodes tend to vary in size and composition while the flow of the traffic, goods and men, tend to vary in magnitude. The interrelationship between network pattern and flows make the interrelationship between these elements: (a) flow along the edges and (b) size of the node. Beta index actually shows the connectivity of a 'node' as amply illustrated in the classic works of Kansky (Kansky, 1963). The interrelationships had been well proved in the context of Southern Illinois and North-Eastern Carolina, road network of transport system. UN Economic Commission for Europe in 1962 accumulated large scale penetrative data on location of international routes, traffic flows and population clusters. This study adequately guided the mapping of transport network round the globe (United Nations, Economic Commission for Europe, 1962). The size of the 'node' suggests the measure of the traffic flows. Flows at a node are settled by the passenger and goods traffic by the motor vehicles on roads. Yeates (Yeates, 1968) rightly points out that, "... local degree measuring the connectivity of a 'node' and motor vehicle traffic to measure the flow at that 'node' are the two basic variables. Motor vehicle traffic at a node is defined as the sum total of the average daily motor traffic along all edges incident upon that node". The size of the node has greater significance in this reference. The generated local income, area and population make the easiest measures of the size of the 'node'. In fact, population represents many variables together. It speaks of consumption demand, income generated, output flows, movement of labour force to work sites as well as the demand for factors of production. Investment decisions are also some way related to the population. Therefore, large towns usually attract greater flows and these also generate flows by the disposable output and factor supplies. The degree of sub-system connectivity has also to be high in this reference due to greater population and size of the town. The size of the node has a bearing on the flows emerging and those being attracted from the sub-systems. There have been several studies in the past to empirically verify the relationship between connectivity flows and the size of the node. The international highways are used in greater measure for movement of people as compared to that of goods. Therefore, rail-road connectivity has the supreme role in the tourist movement. "... Maps can conveniently represent sources, destinations and directions of flows. But three-dimensional systems are exceptionally hard to describe satisfactorily on a single map ..." (Abler, Adams and Gould, 1971, 255). We often use graphs and associated matrices to look at entire transport network at a glance. A graph is made-up of edges representing routes and vertices representing nodes or places. It is easy to make-out that each network has a finite number of places and each route definitely joins to two places. No two places are generally joined by more than one route and routes have the nature of allowing two way movement of traffic. Graphs only mark the topographical position of nodes.

Pandey (Pandey, 1989, 399) in his work on 'Transport Network Connectivity and Economic Development of UP Himalaya' concluded that on the basis of the Beta index maximum and minimum connectivity was found in district Nainital (2.24) and Uttarkashi (0.83) respectively. The findings suggest that Nainital, Almora and Tehri are highly connected districts of the region, Pauri-Garhwal, Dehradun, Pithoragarh and Chamoli districts are moderately connected and Uttarkashi is poorly connected (Table 7.1). In the foothill regions of the former UP Himalaya transportation network is efficient in comparison to the hills (Pandey, 1983, 8-11). Besides Beta index other topological measures like alpha and gamma indices, cyclomatic numbers, accessibility index and average path length, etc., are also of worth importance. In a micro level study of district Nainital Beta, Alpha, Gamma indices and Cyclomatic numbers are calculated 1.68, 34.38, 56.28 and 99 respectively (Pandey and Tiwari, 1983, 212-23).

TABLE 7.1: Transport Connectivity in the former UP Himalayas

Name of the district	No. of vertices	No. of edges	Connectivity (by Beta index)
Nainital	17	38	2.24
Almora	10	22	2.20
Pithoragarh	14	18	1.28
Chamoli	7	9	1.28
Pauri-Garhwal	9	15	1.67
Dehradun	7	10	1.42
Tehri-Garhwal	3	6	2.00
Uttarkashi	6	5	0.83
Uttaranchal Himalaya	73	123	1.67

Source: Pandey, D.C. (1989), 'Transport Network Connectivity and Economic Development', op. cit., p. 400.

Traffic Management and Road Development

Hill areas have greater need of the vehicular services as the region suffers from the dearth of other modes of transport as contrasted with the areas in plain topography where the bullock-carts, horse-carts and vehicular transport helps the transport needs. Trucks, buses and mini-trucks cater to the entire need of movement inter-spatially whether for men or goods. The increasing labour mobility and the tourism has increased the need of transport very rapidly over the last thirty years in Kumaun and Garhwal. These areas are food deficit areas, therefore, the required transport between wider plains and remote hills is all the more. The forest, agricultural, horticultural products are sent to other areas in plains from hills which also raise the need of the vehicular transport.

Field survey* in the context of this study revealed that in the single entrance gate of Rishikesh en-route to Garhwal, there were 545 vehicles registered for tripping into the deeper rims of the Garhwal hills in the year 1987-88. These grew to 4,740 in 1988-89 and 2,143 out of them were scooters and motorcycles. 826 were heavy and medium load carriers—trucks and lorries, 612 were commercial passenger vehicles of light weight 531 buses were operating while nearly 274 private cars were on road. The number of jeeps, tractors, trailers, etc., was 345 in Rishikesh (Table 7.2).

The abnormal growth of vehicles is due to the tourist-service vehicles and the two wheelers like scooters, motorcycles, etc., which have grown by leaps and bounds due to increased value of land as well as due to compensation paid for land under Tehri Dam Project. The number of buses has increased from 25 in 1987-88 to a staggering figure of 580 in 1990-91, due to new routes operating from Rishikesh to other parts of the country for the promotion of tourism in the area.

The movement of goods from the foothill stations of Haridwar, Rishikesh to entire Garhwal sector of hills may be evidenced from the nominal goods tax revenue and their growing amount (Table 7.3).

---

*Data obtained from RTO, Rishikesh.

TABLE 7.2: Number of Vehicles Registered at Rishikesh for Routes to Garhwal Hills

Type of vehicle	Number of vehicles			
	1987-88	1988-89	1989-90	1990-91
Heavy goods carriers	4	2	10	12
Medium load carriers	40	70	816	710
Buses	25	41	531	580
Mini-buses	2	2	9	3
Taxies	36	47	307	NA
Auto-rickshaws	12	29	305	313
Two-wheelers	370	381	2,143	2,478
Private cars	30	39	274	608
Jeeps	8	11	199	215
Tractors	9	4	44	49
Miscellaneous	9	NA	102	104
Total	545	626	4,740	5,072

TABLE 7.3: Road Tax, Goods Tax and Vehicle Tax Revenue in Rishikesh over the Years 1988

Taxes and Revenues	Collection (Rs.)	
	1988-89	1989-90
1. Motor vehicle tax	7,29,295	48,28,180
2. Commercial vehicle fees	10,34,149	12,37,688
3. Goods tax	30,21,997	40,83,047
4. Passenger tax	79,16,348	83,33,035
5. Road tax	15,840	24,860
Total	1,27,17,629	1,85,06,810

Source: RTO, Rishikesh.

The revenue collection indicates a rapidly rising trend even without any rise in the rates. This is due to the increase in the number of vehicles on road.

Uttaranchal has 9,805 km. metalled roads and the average per thousand square kilometre area is 192 km. This is more than the average for the state of UP but this is not a correct indicator insofar as there is no comparison of the topography and terrain in the two regions. The hill areas have a thin population due to the nature of the tract. The average length of roads per lakh population is 188.7 km. as compared to 44.94 km. for the UP as a whole. In Garhwal division the road length is 5,296 km. as compared to 4,509 km. in Kumaun. Metalled roads per thousand square kilometre area in Garhwal division is around 176 km. while in Kumaun it is 214 km. Roads per lakh population are 204.8 km. in Garhwal which compares favourably with 178 km. in Kumaun. The state and status of road development in the hill areas may be studied from Table 7.4.

Studies on movement of traffic, its emergence and belonging undertaken in course of this study suggest that most of the traffic in Garhwal emerges from the western and south-western parts of the country. Hardly one-sixth belongs to the eastern part and most of this traffic is of Bengalis and this occurs in the autumn season specially on Durga Pooja festival (Table 7.5).

Roads constructed in Uttaranchal state by various departments, e.g. PWD, local government, irrigation, forest, DGBR, canal and others. It is exhibited in Table 7.5(a) and 7.5(b) that district Nainital (including Udham Singh Nagar) has the highest length of pucca roads, i.e. 3,341 km. following by district Pauri-Garhwal with 2,486 km. District Uttarkashi has a very poor road

TABLE 7.4: Road Development in Constituent Regions of UP, 1984-85

Regions of UP	Surfaced road length (km.)	Road length per 1,000 sq. km.	Road length per lakh population (km.)	Villages connected by road
1. UP Himalayan region (presently Uttaranchal)	9,805	191.78	188.70	2,488
2. Western region	16,137	196.34	38.27	5,897
3. Central region	7,539	164.49	36.01	2,427
4. Eastern region	15,747	183.44	35.29	9,047
5. Bundelkhand region	4,142	140.78	71.00	897
Total Uttar Pradesh	53,370	181.28	44.94	20,756

Source: UP Statistical Abstract 1984-85, Dept. of Eco. and Stat., Lucknow.

TABLE 7.5: Emergence of Sample Tourist Visitors by Directions and Places of Belongings, 1998-99

Direction to which parties belong	Garhwal		Kumaun		Total
	Summer	Autumn	Summer	Autumn	
1. Eastern India	10	12	20	18	60
2. Eastern UP	2	3	5	6	16
3. Southeren and central UP	5	12	11	8	36
4. Southern India	10	8	15	16	49
5. West India	26	35	42	15	118
6. Europe	6	5	10	9	30
7. US and Canada	4	8	10	13	35
8. Japan, Korea, Singapore, Australia	7	4	7	3	21
9. Middle-East and Africa	3	1	50	1	10
10. Other foreign lands	6	8	9	12	35
Total	79	96	134	101	410

connectivity and the lowest length of pucca roads in Uttaranchal, i.e. 856 km.

Growth of Tourism

Tourism has made great strides round the globe. In some countries it constitutes a very big source of national income. India does not receive a substantial part of global tourism traffic. The principal reasons for this deficiency are as below:

(a) Indian tourism potentialities are not publicized.
(b) The motivation mechanism is poor in India.
(c) Indian infrastructure for tourism is not appropriate.
(d) Indian procedures at entry and exit of foreign tourists are cumbersome and discourteous.

Though the growth of tourism in India in recent decades has been quite encouraging yet the coverage of world flow of tourists is quite meagre while the situation is much more favourable for Pakistan and other neighbouring nations. The major part of tourists visit the Pacific areas, European and Latin American areas. US

TABLE 7.5(a): Road Transport in Uttaranchal Himalaya, 1991-92

(Road length in km.)

District	Pucca road under PWD (in km.)				Pucca road under local Govt. (in km.)		
	State highway	Main distt. road	Other distt. rural road	Total	Zila Parishad	Town area, Nagar Palika	Total
1. Nainital	356	256	1,803	2,415	258	167	425
2. Udham Singh Nagar*	–	–	–	–	–	–	–
3. Almora	243	380	1,270	1,893	0	48	48
4. Bageshwar*	–	–	–	–	–	–	–
5. Pithoragarh	98	78	812	988	0	0	0
6. Champawat*	–	–	–	–	–	–	–
7. Tehri	70	116	947	1,183	0	45	45
8. Uttarkashi	90	51	558	699	0	9	9
9. Chamoli	64	62	980	1,106	0	0	0
10. Pauri	310	117	1,649	2,076	01	32	33
11. Rudraprayag*	–	–	–	–	–	–	–
12. Dehradun	146	241	942	1,329	71	416	487
13. Haridwar*	–	–	–	–	–	–	–

*Data not available.

Source: *Sankhikiya Patrika* of the respective districts, 1991-92.

attracts a very good number of tourists from Europe every year. In India foreign tourists have grown from 74,000 in 1952 to 1,23,050 in 1960, 1,48,000 in 1965, 2,80,820 in 1970, 4,65,275 in 1975 and nearly 8,10,001 in 1980. The figure had risen to 8,30,001 in 1986 to 24,81,928 in 1999. The income in terms of foreign exchange specially dollars, had been more than Rs.564 crores in 1980 to Rs.13,042 crores in 1999. Tourism led to exports of handloom, art goods and handicrafts. The service of tourists at their places of visit, stay and purchases entails demand for several types of goods. This encourages these industries.

The Himalayan region of India offers the best sites for relaxation but these tracts have not been linked by air fitted and knitted in amenities for tourists. The internal tourism in Himalayan ranges has increased by leaps and bounds in recent years but such

TABLE 7.5(b): Road Transport in Uttaranchal Himalaya 1991-92

(Road length in km.)

	District pucca road under other departments						
	Irriga-tion Deptt.	Forest Deptt.	DGBR	Canal	Others	Total	Grand total
1. Nainital	92	70	0	339	0	501	3,341
2. Udham Singh Nagar*	–	–	–	–	–	–	–
3. Almora	0	184	71	0	0	255	2,196
4. Bageshwar*	–	–	–	–	–	–	–
5. Pithoragarh	0	0	341	0	0	341	1,329
6. Champawat*	–	–	–	–	–	–	–
7. Tehri	31	24	260	0	0	148	856
8. Uttarkashi	0	0	148	0	0	148	856
9. Chamoli	0	0	228	0	13	241	1,347
10. Pauri	0	323	54	0	0	377	2,486
11. Rudraprayag*	–	–	–	–	–	–	–
12. Dehradun	71	180	0	0	71	322	2,138
13. Haridwar*	–	–	–	–	–	–	–

*Data not available.
Source: *Sankhikiya Patrika* of the respective districts, 1991-92.

tourism causes transfer of resources from other regions of India to these tracts. These areas are not the producers of goods demanded by the tourists and are imported from other regions of the country, therefore, income again flows back to other regions. Foreign tourists definitely add to the national resources. Visitors to Taj Mahal, Ajanta, Ellora, Khajuraho, major cities and sea beaches are growing every year. But the hills of Uttaranchal are not able to attract as big rush of foreign tourists as these areas can attract. Indians have not created proper publicity and have not shown efficiency in the art of motivation and persuasion. The official ways of Indian airport personnel and the public services, etc. are very clumsy and troublesome.

An effective tourism sector is supposed to be efficient in pleasing the tourists. The travel agents get frustrated if the tourists are harassed every nook and corner for little bit of service by corrupt bureaucracy and workmen. The information channels and transport communication links have to be quite satisfactory for foreign tourists. Sanitary conditions and hygienic state of the places of visit have to be of international standard where Indian tourist services fail. Himalayan tourism has a better point on this score. The infrastructure like air services to the remote hills can help tourism here. Tourism Development Council and Tourism Development Corporation of India have neglected the primary needs of efficient air services for remote Himalayas. The hotel accommodation has been increased in recent years in public and private sectors. The information and guidance services are at their infancy in India. The Committee (1963) on tourism felt that official role in development of tourism has to be greater specially in providing infrastructure. Earlier Hotel Corporation of India (1965), Indian Tourism Corporation and Tourism Transport Undertaking Ltd. were the major corporate bodies meant for the development of amenities and accommodation in India. These private bodies were merged into one big body in 1966. The Indian Tourism Development Corporation (ITDC) was formed in its existing form in 1970. This has helped in making suitable accommodation available for tourists but the costs are still enormous. Uttaranchal Himalayas have not been favoured by ITDC in terms of good vehicular and air transport facilities which could connect the passenger landing in Delhi with the captivating scenic beauty of Himalayas. The government of Uttar Pradesh has provided funds for road building and building of rest houses in selected sites but the management-personnel in these has been by far wanting. Development of tourism in Himalayan ranges should be linked with the routine developmental action for economic growth in this region. Unless supportive production structure is geared up in fruit culture, art goods, handicrafts, vegetable growing, mushroom, local transport, owned and managed by the hill men, tourism is not likely to help the inhabitants of the area.

Reorganisation of Publicity and Public Relations

Indian cultural and political missions abroad and tourism information services have been inert and passive in arousing a curiosity and building strong will of the fanciful tourists to see and appreciate Indian scenery and heritage. The strong selling campaigns and vigorous publicity by other country missions have made tremendous gains for their countries. The technique of presenting Indian case for tourism have been by far wanting and highly bureaucratic. A better mutual understanding and friendly relations are prepared by good public relations and a highly constructive publicity helping the true cause of the clientele as well as the host nation. Organising societies, social groups, associations, forums and stages by which the true information about the tourism potential of the country is highlighted, have to be nurtured and supported where Indian missions have miserably failed. Indian nationals abroad also afford the same gains of tourism if persuaded and managed by the tourism information services. The cultural societies sponsored officially and in private initiative can successfully create orientation for tourism in India specially regarding the rarest Himalayan landscape. The western tourist agencies can be brought in the close touch of the information regarding India by efforts of the dedicated missions abroad.

Mutuality of the interests is invoked by public relations and appropriate publicity through literature, films, group-discussions and radio. The dissemination of information and volunteered assistance to the potential tourists can help a long way in raising the levels of appreciation of Himalayan landscape, scenic grandeur and cultural heritage of India. Keeping links with authors, journalists, poets and great admirers of beauty and culture abroad can bring the merit of Indian case to light. Great men may even be invited and hosted in the country and persuaded to bring the Indian beauty resources to the knowledge of the consumerist society. Expert advertisement agencies render useful services in raising the image among the affluent sections. The film-makers of the great western society may be given proper amicable treatment and may be persuaded to make films on Indian scenery, specially the Himalayan natural beauty. Considerable goodwill and pro-India consciousness can be generated with the cooperation of the Indians in the foreign lands. The misconceptions and misgivings about India and Indian society need be removed by appropriate level of touch and relations with the foreigners. The internal tourism organisation must be efficient and should keep the goodwill intact. This requires considerable element of dedication to the national cause. The hotel personnel and transport operators have to work in tune with the overall frame of policies to encourage tourism and build amicable relations with foreign countries. Indian approach to the problem has been of quick money-making and fleecing the visitors. The behaviour which the tourists receive is either the over-idealisation or a perfect cynical behaviour. The working of day-to-day service in communications, transport, banking, hotel service, power supply, etc., in India is not as pleasing as required to benefit from tourism. The social role of the travel agents in India has not yet assumed the importance it deserves. The feed of the customer information, process of customer creation and retention of clientele are also arranged by the travel agents. The advertisements, publicity and public relations help the agents in fetching the customers who can be served with efficiency. In a busy world of the day, a tourist hardly finds enough time and preparedness to handle uncertainties of travel and he shuns expressing his incompetance, inadequacies and forgetfulness before everybody. This situation makes a good offer or surrender before a travel agent who shoulders most of these worries on behalf of the traveller. Travel agents, if well-versed in their art, can persuade tourists to undertake the right type of trips which satisfy the urge and lust of the tourist. Indian travel agents are not as rich and resourceful as US and Canadian travel agents but can fetch remunerative business by netting greater number of affluent tourists by cooperation of eminent travel agents of the west. Experience and information of Indian travel agents is far too low as compared with those operating successfully in the west.

Package Tour Planning from Nodal Centres to Himalayas

The tourists seek site seeing tours from the specialised agencies in the central localities like Delhi, Mumbai, Chennai and Kolkata. The air services can be helpful in keeping touch with the tourist and tourism information centres. The travel agents can offer their bit of service to the visitors at convenience of the tourists. They can exert their persuasion power to motivate tourists for visit to Himalayas. In absence of air services, the package tours can be arranged by the travel agencies. They can co-ordinate the priorities of the travellers and group them such as skiing enthusiasts, art lovers, culture appreciators, visitors of monuments and those moved by the lust of nature's beauty. The tour brochures issue the information about the package tours. Tour manager takes up the burden of catering to all needs of the travellers having convinced the travellers regarding cost, duration, direction and other involvements of the planned package tour (Kaul, 1985, 639-681). The travel agents keeping touch with tourism development officials in Himalayan stations, can book appropriate accommodation and other requisites before hand. Tour agents can give cameras on hire, hill station baggage kits and medicinal aids to the benefit of the tourists. The travel agents, air services, hotels and information centres have to develop an interlink in order to serve the tourists better. Tourism in Himalayas can be raised very significantly if the centres in nodal places divert the traffic to these beautiful mountainous scenery.

Himalayan Potentialities and Development

Uttaranchal with its abundant cultural heritage, historical monuments, relics, shrines, holy places, snow capped mountainous scenery, lush green forests and tribal variety of culture patterns offers great tourist potential. The region is surplus in labour resources and utilisation thereof can be done by development of tourism, external and domestic. In UP, Agra, Kushinagar, Varanasi, Allahabad, Sravasti, etc., are the places of tourist interest. Alluvial plains of Ganges and Yamuna basin present lush green crop fields sheltering a large variety of cultures and living styles. UP being at a low level of economic and social development has not developed very efficient modes of transport and communications. The state's attention to the sphere of tourism has not been much due to the inappropriate strategy of development. The role and potentialities of private initiative in this regard has also not been exploited so far. The department of tourism could play a catalytic role in stimulating the development of tourism. A proper strategy, definite priorities and linkage building in development schemes could help this state a long way. Since UP is the parent state of

TABLE 7.6: Expenditure on Tourism during Five Year Plans in UP

Plans	Expenditure (Rs. in lakh)
First Five Year	1.00
Second Five Year	19.00
Third Five Year	12.00
Annual Plans	15.17
Fourth Five Year	50.50
Fifth Five Year	378.16
Spending by Centre	63.00
Total	538.83

Uttaranchal, therefore the development pattern in Uttaranchal moved towards the same pattern of UP.

UP spent Rs.538.85 lakh on tourism from First to the Fifth Five-Year Plans. It created a capacity of nearly 2,000 beds for tourists and tourism complexes were built. Most of them (1414) are located in the Hill areas of former UP. The expenditure incurred during plans has been shown in Table 7.6.

Actual growth of tourism has been faster than the growth of accommodation and amenities in hill stations of former UP. The government has neither interest nor resources for such backward areas like hills. The loss in terms of foreign exchange by lost business affects the region state and the national government. The pattern of the state expenditure (1978-1982) shows that infrastructure building for tourism has starved for funds and planning (Table 7.7).

It may be noted from Table 7.7 that the expenditure on survey of potentialities and development is the lowest and is in only 1981-82. The financial outlay earmarked has tended to fluctuate up and down over the years. The expenditure on tourist centres had dwindled in the years 1979-81. The state government has shown no inclination for tourism development because the significance has not been appreciated here for its being a backward state and planning authority had no long-term perspective of the state while making the Plan. The Sixth Plan (1980-85) document of UP spelled

TABLE 7.7: Outlay to Tourism in Uttar Pradesh from 1978-79 to 1981-82

(Rs. in lakh)

Major heads	1978-79	1979-80	1980-81	1981-82
1. Administration	8.00	8.32	6.77	8.66
2. Accommodation	219.00	207.00	181.84	236.16
3. Survey and Statistics	–	–	–	1.62
4. Tourist Centres	9.00	16.11	12.71	16.57
5. Information and Publicity	15.00	14.17	19.87	24.00
6. Other Items	2.74	3.90	2.65	2.86

Source: Sixth Five Year Plan 1980-85, UP, pp. 454-55.

out the strategy of tourism development in the following words (Sixth Five Year Plan, Government of UP, 454):

1. More emphasis will be laid on the development of international tourist centres to earn more and more foreign exchange.... It is hoped that about 5.3 lakh of the 17.0 lakh international tourists in India would come to Agra by the end of the Plan.
2. To encourage domestic tourists for visiting places of religious and cultural importance in the state by providing, cheaper accommodation facilities at these places;
3. To develop historical and archaeological places for attracting tourists and to preserve cultural heritage of the state;
4. To develop cultural tourism by organising autumn festivals at various places in the hills and festival melas in the plains;
5. To remove regional imbalances by developing tourist places in backward areas;
6. To encourage youth tourism by providing facilities at chapter rates for trekking etc.,
7. To encourage private entrepreneurs to build star-category hotels for benefit of high spending variety of tourists.

An outlay of Rs.20 crore had been proposed in the Sixth Plan in Uttar Pradesh. Only 6.5 crore had been fixed for the hill areas whereas 13.5 crore had been fixed for plains of wider UP.

Towards acceleration of pace of tourism growth in Uttar Pradesh a corporate body was created under the title of 'State Tourism Development Corporation' in 1974. The main objectives of the corporation are to: (a) promote, take over, develop and establish hotels, restaurants, traveller's lodge, recreational places and handicraft centres; (b) to establish new transport units for smooth running of tourism and; (c) to provide conducted tours for tourists visiting Uttar Pradesh STDC of UP has taken over the charge of managing the accommodation and commercial units. Tourist bungalows at Varanasi, Lucknow, Haridwar, Allahabad, Agra, Sarnath, Ayodhya, Mahoba etc., Overall management efficiency in UP Corporation is very low so that tourists shun the use of such accommodation as compared to private hotels. The corporation taxies are run by STDC at Agra. Some telex services for reservation are provided for tourists at tourist offices of Calcutta, Delhi and Ahmedabad. Conducted tours are organised from Lucknow and Varanasi centres of STDC Corporation inspite of its heavy charges for accommodation makes only nominal profit per year.

Two other major public corporate bodies manage tourist activities in Uttaranchal: (a) Kumaun Mandal Vikas Nigam and (b) Garhwal Mandal Vikas Nigam. These bodies are expected to dash ahead with development of tourism growth in respective areas. These are developing new tourist complexes for the purpose.

Development of Yatri Niwas

Construction of Yatri Niwas* in places of pligrimage like Varanasi, Allahabad, Chitrakoot, Badri-Kedar, Rishikesh, Haridwar, Deva Shareef, under the Sixth Plan and by the Seventh Plan most of the projects had been implemented. Improved Tourist Reception Centres have been established in chosen centres of Uttar Pradesh to facilitate tourists. These are equipped with transport, accommodation, food, reservation and onward journey programming facilities, also cater representative souvenirs containing essential information. The centres proposed in Sixth Plan are given in Table 7.8.

*Each Yatri Niwas has one four bedded room, one six bedded room and one eight bedded room each with attached bath room. These are cheaper than tourist bungalow accommodation.

TABLE 7.8: Proposed Centres of Pilgrimage Under Sixth Five Year Plan in UP

Pilgrimage Centre	Proposed capacity of centre (beds)
1. Agra	40
2. Haridwar	40
3. Varanasi	40
4. Ranikhet	40
5. Mussoorie	40
Total	200

Development of Youth Tourism

Development of youth tourism is relatively a new dimension in Uttar Pradesh. The young are interested in thrill, physical exercise, some personal performance credit, wildlife, scenic beauty, trekking and mountaineering. The tourists aging 17-24 years are in greater proportion. In 1979, 62.3 per cent of them belonged to this category. To meet their demand considerable reorganisation is necessary in the structure, allocations and attitudes of the personnel. Sluggish luxurious bureaucracy is unfit for planning such tourism. Greater inter-departmental coordination is essential between forest, irrigation, transport, horticulture and education department, etc., for tourism development in hills. Government of Uttar Pradesh established youth hostels with cheaper accommodation for the youth. Varanasi, Agra and Lucknow youth hostels were added to the existing ones with 20 beds each during 1985-86. Holiday homes in the hill areas emerged during Sixth Plan. Rest Houses and Conference Complexes were developed at Agra and other tourist stations. New sanctuaries have been developed in recent years to the purpose of youth tourism. Money intended for tourism has been diverted to plain areas during the Plan and Parikrama routes of ghats in Varanasi, Ayodhya, Mathura, Chitrakoot and Vithoor have been improved. The plan investment during Sixth Plan has created man-day employment of 34,98,200 labourers directly while indirect employment was several times greater.

Tourism development is somehow linked with development of transport and road development. During 1980-85, UP plains spent Rs.9,609 crore on roads and their maintenance. Rs.2,481 crore had been spent on UP hill areas. Thus, nearly Rs.1,209.3 crore had been spent on the transport development. Several other projects had been undertaken during Sixth and Seventh Plans for promoting tourism in religious centres and beauty spots in hill areas of Uttar Pradesh.

Capacity Saturation in Tourism

The tourism development has important considerations of some basic facts which relate to:

- (a) Assessment of potentials and capacity of development at known levels of technology and without clinging to higher scales of social costs;
- (b) Making assessment of options in strategy and utilisation of potentials;
- (c) Choosing the pace of expansion and resource allocations in localities optimally;
- (d) Determining the symptoms of capacity-strain, the appearance of which indicates the vertical trend of costs and declining marginal return on investments;
- (e) Allocation of investments in the directly quick yielding projects as distinguished from the investments on animating infrastructure;
- (f) Trickle-down effects of the tourism growth to the welfare of the people of the region chosen for tourist activity and strains for the local masses due to tourism and pressure on scarce resources.

It is well-known that in a federal system there is acute rivalry among regions and alternative uses of scarce capital resources for a grip on investments. How and where should these investments be optimally useful has to be carefully analysed by the planner. Somewhere the tourist activity assumes so much of the importance and emphasis that other sectors have to starve for dearth of investment resources. In other situations, the tourism is a centre of vested prosperous sections of society, therefore the development of tourism is a political issue. In still other situations, the investments continue concentrating in few given localities while rest of the claimant regions act in semi-colonial relationship with the dominating tourist centres. Kaur identified the situation of tourist towns in symptoms like stagnation in spite of increasing investments because the cost of accommodating still greater activity rises vertically while yields are only minimal (Kaur, 1989, 239-245). The tourism investments continue in spite of this because the infrastructural and social costs are shifted on to society in general while economic gains are monopolised by the vested classes. The ecological hazards grow in the state of capacity saturation. These hazards by the large become a social liability as distinct from a private burden. The vested classes are able to immunise themselves against the ill effects of overgrowth and saturated capacity growth. The returns in terms of satisfaction reaped by tourists in these locations go on decreasing and costs of accommodation, risk coverage, health cover, etc., multiply fast which is met by the enhancement of rates. The tourism development is so designed that the much more captivating, envigorating and beautiful tourist attractions are not brought in touch or contact of the tourists because this may severely damage the vested interests of already developed saturated stations. Still another style noticed recently in the development of tourism is that the saturated stations by their political influence monopolise the amenity-dressings in a backward region. This puts the tourists under no-option state but to go to the saturated stations inspite of their monopoly rates. The travel agents and hoteliers run their own package tours to rest of the localities and take the tourists back to the saturated station. In this state, the neighbouring localities inspite of having better potentialities of development as tourist station do not get their due recognition, opportunity and flow of income. While such localities share the disadvantages emanating from tourist traffic they fail to reap economic gains. At this point, state's deliberate interference is necessary to diversify the tourism flows. Another symptom of saturation is the abnormal rise in land-values and increased cost of living. The congestion of facilities and crowding results in disutilities to the tourists as well as the local non-tourist industry population.

Cultural shocks of unredeemable nature emerge in highly saturated locations. Further expansion of tourism in such places though politically often suggested, yet causes more damage than a gain.

Good Image of the Country Promotes Foreign Tourism

The tourist activity in India, specially from the foreign lands needs special attention for its gains in terms of 'Exchange Earning' as well as the amicability developed with the foreign lands. The image of the country in the affluent West is not high. India is treated insanitary, unhygienic and highly backward in social traditions and faith. India represents illiteracy and ignorance. Visit to this land is appreciated for a new experience of tribal communities and for social work on humanitarian grounds. Researchers prefer coming to India for a trip. Advanced countries have a higher technological scale, therefore there is nothing in techniques which can be learnt by them here. There are some development enthusiasts who cherish the news of economic development and modernisation in this country of which the past was known mainly as a land of snake-charmers, puppet shows and magicians. They are interested in seeing India's growth over the last few decades. Some of the journalists, news reporters and feature writers come to India for recording strange states of tranditional poverty, chronic backwardness and deity-worships. Few of the visitors have a high image about the relics of Indian heritage and historical monuments. The historical monuments, towns, temples, churches, holy places, Moghul architecture, historical Monasteries, paintings do constitute an attraction. Few of the visitors are aware of the nature's beauty in Himalaya, which is imparelleled exciting experience to anybody who happens to visit these mountains. United Kingdom and United States contribute nearly 15 and 12 per cent tourists respectively (Table 7.9).

International tourism in India has grown substantially over the last three decades. The foreign exchange earnings during 1992-93 were estimated at Rs.3,989 crore and for the year 1994-95 at Rs.7,449 crore which were increased almost double in a period of two years. Foreign tourist arrivals during 1998-99 were 24,81,928 and foreign exchange earnings from tourism were estimated at

TABLE 7.9: Foreign Tourists in India

(Number in '000)

Country	1951	1971	1981	1984	1984 (No.)	1984 (per cent)	1995 (per cent)
1. United Kingdom	6	40	116	124	120	14.3	15.0
2. United States	4	55	82	96	96	11.5	12.7
3. Sri Lanka	1	17	76	75	69	8.3	07.5
4. Federal Republic of Germany	3	18	54	48	45	5.4	05.5
5. France	1	17	57	47	44	5.3	05.4
6. Japan	2	12	29	30	31	3.7	03.9
7. Canada	–	07	25	25	29	3.5	04.5
8. Australia	–	11	21	25	22	2.6	03.0
9. Italy	–	06	28	24	23	2.7	03.9
10. Malaysia	–	18	26	23	23	2.7	03.1
11. Others	5	100	339	319	335	40.0	35.5
Total	22	301	853	836	837	100.0	100.0

(The visitors of Pakistan and Bangladesh are excluded.)

Source: Data supplied by Ministry of Civil Aviation and Tourism, Government of India, New Delhi.

TABLE 7.10: Foreign Tourists and Earning from Foreign Travel in India

Year	Tourist arrivals	Earning (Rs. in crore)
1950-51	16,829	NA
1960-61	13,984	NA
1965-66	1,59,603	NA
1976-77	5,33,951	284
1977-78	6,40,442	530
1978-79	6,65,332	564
1979-80	7,65,000	919
1980-81	8,00,150	1,165
1991-92	16,77,508	3,318
1992-93	18,67,651	3,989
1993-94	17,64,830	6,509
1994-95	18,86,433	7,449
1998-99	24,81,928	13,042

Rs.13,042 crore. Hence tourism has become one of the most foreign exchange earning sectors in India (Table 7.10).

Himalayas Need Air Links for Tourism

Most of the tourists come to this country by air. They engage Air India planes from their homeland. Thus, the gain is doublefold. The facilities of sea travel are not yet well developed to cater to the needs of tourism, therefore the passengers reaching India by sea route are hardly 1 or 2 per cent. 70-75 per cent tourists reach India by air routes. It is, therefore more prudent to develop air strips in deep-central Himalaya specially in Uttaranchal state to attract more tourists. The tourists coming by land constitute nearly 29 per cent and these belong to the neighbouring lands. It is well observed that the share of the tourists coming by land is increasing over the years. The prohibitive costs of travel by air has discouraged the visitors from relatively less affluent nations. Travel by sea is falling very rapidly in the recent few decades. Tourist parties of the young can be more conveniently served in the sea route. This is also economical (Table 7.11).

TABLE 7.11: Foreign Tourist Arrivals in India by Mode of Transport

(Number in '000)

Mode of transport	Number of tourists			Percentage to total		
	1981	1983	1985	1981	1983	1985
1. Airways	767	848	897	89.9	71.0	71.2
(a) Domestic	167	448	397	–	–	–
(b) Foreign	600	400	500	–	–	–
2. Sea Route	48	33	1	5.6	2.8	0.1
3. Land Route	38	313	362	4.5	26.2	28.7
Total	1,620	2,042	2,157	100.0	100.0	100.0

Source: Statistical Abstract, Ministry of Tourism and Civil Aviation, Government of India, T. 12, 13, 14.

In spite of the enormous expenditure incurred by central and state governments on development of transport, the general-state of transport and travel in India is not satisfactory. This puts the unaccustomed foreign tourists in undue strains at every point. Percentages of total outlay on transport development during Plans were as shown in Table 7.12.

Economic Investments in Hotel Industry

The hotel industry displays an ideal model of economic enterprise organisation. It has greater return on invested capital as compared

TABLE 7.12: Total Outlay on Transport during Five Year Plans

Five-Year Plans	Allocation on transport (in per cent)
First Five-Year Plan	22.1
Second Five-Year Plan	23.5
Third Five-Year Plan	23.1
Annual Plans	15.6
Fourth Five-Year Plan	16.0
Fifth Five-Year Plan	14.1
Sixth Five-Year Plan	12.4
Seventh Five-Year Plan	12.6

to other investments. It is a capital intensive type investment. Land, building, furniture, furnishing and equipment form the capital expenditure. Fixed assets are major part, making 90 per cent. Site cost is enormous. In variable cost, the return and turnover is fast. The stocks constitute relatively very low (3 to 4%) cost. The gestation period of investment is extended over a long period. It involves long-term finance. Building, civil work, electric fitting, sanitary fitting, carpets, air-conditioning, boilers, water treatment plant, filteration plant, pumps, drainage, swimming pool, land scaping, shopping arcade, crockery, glassworks, cutlery, wares, linen, uniform, utensils, liquor, drinks, architecture, etc., have enormous financial involvement. Emergency costs, risk insurance, fire, oil crisis, strike, lockout, war, peace disturbance, power failure, etc., create problems leading to collapse. Building cost is around 52-55 per cent, equipment costs are 37 to 40 per cent and furniture cost is around 7 to 10 per cent.

Risks arise not only in fire, war, lockouts etc., but also arise in failure of management and leakages, wrong forecast of hotel demand, state policy and taxation, wear and tear, recession, wars, obsolescence, etc., are main problems. Profitability ratio is higher when the total actually keeps operating and it is around 25 to 32 per cent of the occupancy multiplied by rates. Usually the rates are determined 0.1 per cent of cost of room. More than 50 per cent space has to be commercial bed area. 8 : 10 ratio is between employees and rooms. Cost of land is 10 per cent of the building cost.

The building costs vary extensively between areas. The cost of construction of two bed-rooms at 1990 prices may be around:

Rs.30,000 to 35,000 – luxury grade
Rs.19,000 to 24,000 – conventional hotel
Rs.8,000 to 12,000 – motel grade
Rs.6,000 to 8,000 – economy hotel
Rs.4,000 to 6,000 – road side Inn

The costs tend to vary with the topography and the place. Hill areas are very unfavourable for building purposes specially modern amenity hotels. An ordinary guest house in mountainous terrain involves a cost of Rs.45,000 to 52,000 for 4 bed-rooms.

The fittings and other costs put the figure to 73,000 in an average class of hotel. The rates as standardised 0.1 per cent night come to Rs.73 to which flat charges for costs of electricity, water, etc., Rs.15 + 12 are added making Rs.100 per room. These charges are then made to vary by seasons and rush of tourists over time. Rs.170 for summer, Rs.100 for moderate autumn and Rs.70 for slack season. The average thus, reached is Rs.113.

The greater the dressing and fitting costs in an accommodation, the charges grow vertically adding Rs.50 on each.

Electric geyser – Rs.50
Television – Rs.50
Telephone – Rs.50

The costs tend to rise when the service is catered in remoter parts yet the room construction cost is less as upper storey is built. Thus the upper storey rooms have lesser charges. The cost of room in various types of hotels may be shown in Table 7.13 at 1990 prices in mountainous terrain. The added costs vary extensively due to the surcharge which owners add in situations of lesser occupancy and fluctuating rush. Additional costs are met by adding these to rates.

The average occupancy in the sample accommodation monthwise as tabulated in the tourist survey came to be 50.61 per cent (Table 7.14). Table 7.15 indicates the mean average occupancy rates over the months during 1986-1987-1988.

TABLE 7.13: Construction Cost and Per Day Room Rent in Various Types of Hotel in Mountain Terrain at Current Prices (1990)

Type of Hotel	Construction cost per room (Rs.)	Per day per room rent rate
One Star	Rs.1,39,800	Rs.140 + 10 = 150
Two Star	Rs.1,54,650	Rs.155 + 15 = 175
Three Star	Rs.1,72,900	Rs.173 + 27 = 200
Four Star	Rs.2,15,000	Rs.215 + 35 = 250
Five Star	Rs.2,80,000	Rs.280 + 120 = 400

TABLE 7.14 : Place-wise Space Occupancy in Hotels, Guest Houses and Rest Houses of Kumaun and Garhwal (1996)

Sampling round	Place in sample	Percentage occupancy during month												Total
		Jan.	Feb.	Mar.	Apr.	May	June	July	Aug.	Sept.	Oct.	Nov.	Dec.	
1. First	1. Haridwar	40	20	50	42	35	48	30	50	60	60	70	30	39.58
round	2. Gwaldam	30	20	15	25	40	60	70	30	38	13	42	36	34.92
Units–4	3. Haldwani	45	57	39	54	62	71	68	43	53	41	55	66	54.50
	4. Ranikhet	60	34	48	72	80	94	39	64	69	74	34	37	58.75
2. Second	1. Bhimtal	30	28	17	56	76	84	48	56	70	76	64	72	56.42
round	2. Nainital	22	28	48	68	94	90	78	62	71	72	33	22	57.33
Units–5	3. Rudraprayag	28	23	52	48	63	72	56	42	62	58	35	17	46.33
	4. Srinagar	64	58	64	88	82	87	52	35	42	60	70	68	64.16
	5. Sattal	13	17	22	28	17	58	48	31	42	36	32	16	27.66
3. Final	1. Nainital	28	66	70	68	84	87	83	88	84	97	96	34	73.75
round	2. Almora	54	70	38	35	42	42	68	28	32	42	66	30	45.58
Units–6	3. Joshimath	27	30	34	48	69	89	89	60	70	68	38	23	53.75
	4. Rishikesh	32	58	36	58	70	96	80	56	72	52	34	27	55.90
	5. Pithoragarh	6	12	22	38	66	66	.48	35	27	60	28	15	35.25
	6. Ramnagar	38	34	52	56	78	97	84	89	78	62	53	34	62.91

Tabulated figures from the three round survey, 1996. Monthly figures have been rounded in Table 7.15.

TABLE 7.15: Mean Monthly Average Occupancy in Hotels (1995-97) in Uttaranchal

(in per cent)

Months	Average of 1st sample	Average of 2nd sample	Average of 3rd sample	Total average
1. January	34	27	34	32
2. February	18	31	24	24
3. March	52	44	45	47
4. April	92	65	72	76
5. May	94	87	83	88
6. June	96	98	94	96
7. July	67	84	78	76
8. August	62	73	69	68
9. September	76	84	81	80
10. October	73	84	76	78
11. November	68	76	70	71
12. December	22	33	23	26
Total Average	62.83	65.50	62.41	63.50

A Case for Coordinated Capacity Expansion

The overall rate of utilisation of space depends on the flow of the tourists and their length of stay. In case the length is prolonged by new programmes of entertainments and site seeing added to the hotel service, the utilisation rate can improve. Proper publicity in prosperous areas in the country and abroad can help the flow of tourists considerably which can utilize this built-in capacity (Table 7.16).

There is a coordination system between the hotels to accommodate the passengers and utilize every bit, but the traffic occurs suddenly in summer and autumn while there is only slow flow of the traffic in other seasons. While drawing the expected revenue the hoteliers have counted only the period when the pace is ready and hotel operates (Table 7.17).

The utilisation rate, if raised, raises revenue and the addition to operational service cost and materials is hardly 20 per cent. The net profit per room, adjusting all running, fixed costs, the net

TABLE 7.16: Excess Unutilized Capacity and Loss of Revenue

(in Rs.)

Sample	Expected full capacity revenue	Revenue from used capacity	Per cent	Actual revenue lost
First	52,26,750	41,00,170	78.45	11,26,580
Second	28,07,900	19,88,800	70.83	8,19,100
Third	17,28,550	11,52,360	66.67	5,76,190
Average	32,54,400	24,13,776	72.00	8,40,624

revenue per room is Rs.1,203.00. The accommodations in mountainous areas have only marginal utilisation and these rates are considerably high in Haridwar, Rishikesh and Haldwani. A policy of co-ordinated expansion in the capacity of the tourist houses would prove to be gainful for greater revenue. Tour planning and concession-schemes of planned tours can help, both the organisation and the tourists in the region.

TABLE 7.17: Cost of the Sample Hotel Services in Uttaranchal Himalaya

Samples of study	Const. including all costs of operation (Rs.)	Cost per room occupied (Rs.)	Recovery Revenue (Rs.)	Per room gain (Rs.)
First	85 × 246 = 20,910.00	246	1,487	1,241.00
Second	112 × 238 = 26,656.00	238	1,393	1,155.00
Third	128 × 254 = 32,512.00	254	1,468	1,214.00
Average	325 R cost = 26,693.00	246	1,449	1,203.00
Of I, II and III samples	Annual fixed cost = 13,346.00 Rs.40,039.00	123 369	Deducting = Fixed cost	1,080.00

APPENDIX 7.1: Main Types of Catering Establishments in Tourist Industry

1. Hotels
2. Motels
3. Restaurants
4. Push Table Service
5. Ethnic Restaurants
6. Speciality Houses
7. Coffee Shops
8. Walk-up Service
9. Fast Foods
10. Luncheonette
11. Grill Room
12. Hospital Catering
13. Bed and Breakfast Stairs
14. Hotel Garnis
15. Snack Bar
16. Transport Catering
17. Railway Caters
18. Air Catering
19. Ship Café
20. Drive Inn and Automats
21. Disco Theques
22. Clubs
23. Labour Catering
24. Canteens
25. Rest Houses
26. Dak Bungalows
27. Cafetaria
28. Line Cafetaria
29. Scrample-up Café
30. Counter Service
31. Rotels Vending Machine
32. Baker's Bench
33. Camps

8

Development of Tourist Complexes and Morphological Analysis of Tourist Sites and Resort Centres of the Uttaranchal Himalaya

It is known that Himalaya has long been a centre of attraction for all those who have heard about it. The curiosity is promoted by the writings of the geographers, journalists and the visitors to the Himalayas. Religious importance attached to the region by great pilgrim attractions has also been a very significant factor in making Himalayas popular among the visitors. Beauty of Kashmir has long carried a repute for the ruling masters. The English had the great curiosity to cross over to Tibet from Himalayan route. Pande reported that out of the two distinct sub-zones of Uttaranchal Himalaya, the Garhwal region is somewhat newer and lower than Kumaun in the context of socio-economic development (Pande, 1989). The seedlings of religious tourism first germinated in Garhwal Himalaya.

Sites and Centres of Tourist Attraction in Garhwal

Garhwal is truly the abode of Gods and the people in Garhwal have the privilege of being the most deligent of God's sons. The Hindu philosophy and religious works were deeply understood and followed to the word in this area. The great force of inspiration and impetus built and pervasive culture for the entire country. 'Shivism' had an influence in the area and the temples in this region represent Lord Shiva in his various mighty forms. Entire Garhwal is the host of temple culture, dedication, devotion and worship. British gazetteer of Garhwal mentions that there are more than 5.5 hundred temples in Garhwal and nearly 3.5 hundred of them relate to Lord Shiva (Atkinson 1886, 701). Lord Shiva settled in the mighty mountain as Parvati, the daughter of Himalaya, was married to him. Holy Ganga emerged from the 'Shikha' of Lord Shiva. Garhwal has 'Panch Prayags' i.e., five great confluences. Any body entering Garhwal from any side has the feeling of entering the abode of Gods, by the very rhythm of its environment and scenic splendour, so rich and varied. Garhwal has an ever virgin beauty and a calm and quiet atmosphere wherein the great thinkers and eminent philosophers have sat for their erudation and 'Tapa'. Kayastha et al. wrote, "In fact, Hindu Sages and Sanyasis had identified sites of exceptional physical attractions through their keen land scape perception which are unrivalled even today in their beautiful setting" (Kayastha et al., 1983, 206). In fact, the flows of Holy Ganges and tributaries woven round Garhwal have drained and purified every bit of this abode of Gods.

There are several petty townships and urban localities in Garhwal. Thirtyone towns have been identified as the eminent centres of tourism. Some of the localities though important for religious tourism are less known due to their being remotely placed. A few tourist sites are being described here as an introduction to the tract.

Dehradun

Situated in 31° 19' N latitude and 78° 2' E longitude, is the extended town of Dehradun. It is abound by gorgeous ranges from the northern and southern sides. To the eastern side the town has holy Ganges and to the western side of Dehradun has Yamuna river. Both of them flow across the plains by different routes to unite at Allahabad. Dehradun has a height of 640 m. above mean sea level and the town covers around 90 sq. kms. As per the census of 1991, this town had a population of 3,68,053, perhaps the largest in the Himalayan tract in one town. The records of ancient history indicate that Dehradun has its existence even in remoter times back. This was a part of the Kedar Khand and it sheltered the Rishies, Saints, and Devotees of Lord Shiva to perform their penances and offer prayers in isolation. Even today a casual visitor may feel to himself that the environment all around in this town brings the peace and blessings of the sacred souls who protect the area against sin and turmoil. Dehradun has the smell of Great Guru Ram Rai of Sikhism in 17th century who had come to settle here and inspired the humanity by his erudation.

Dun valley is a town that bustles with life, cinema theaters, restaurants and shopping complex. Dun valley had been ruled by the Raja of Garhwal for several centuries. Later the Gorkhas captured Dehradun valley but they have not left much of their influence there. In 1814, it was taken-up from Gorkhas by the British. It became a centre of military education and cultural growth. Indian Forest Research Institute of Dehradun has earned a great name. Similarly the Survey of India is eminently known establishment of the town. Several public schools train the young children for future India in Dehradun. The town permits a free and close access to places of great interest. Malsi Deer Park makes a very favourite tourist attraction for the addicts of wildlife and aesthetics. Sahastradhara Sulphur Spring, at a distance of 14 kms. from there, is an ideal location for a picnic. The green surroundings, calm and quiet makes a wonderful site for relaxation. The town has a pro-British garb of culture. The surroundings well compare with England's Sandhurst and the U.S. West Point. Judged from the angle of urbanisation features, Dehradun offers the features of a model town while it retains the cultural admixture of Garhwal guilelessness and British modernisation.

The town is taking its physical shape parallel to the shape of the valley. It is around a 12 kms. long strip in a triangle shape. The base is in the south and east while the apex lends to north-west parallel to infantry bazar. The marketing areas meet at Ghanta Ghar (clock tower). There are several neat and clean Dharmshalas and hotels, dressed restaurants and cinema houses to the centre.

Social complex of the town has some speciality. The literacy and education is greater than any town in Himalaya. There are posh localities where retired personnel of defence forces and central government organisations have settled. Immigrants from upper Himalayan ridges have settled in Dehradun for its gain of educational and medical facilities. Culturally the western immigrants from Sindh, Punjab and Gujarat area have a dent over the lifestyles. The town has cosmopolitan tone. Settlers from south India and Rajasthan dress the town with cultural solidarity and variety. Historically, Dehradun grew in its modern form only after British penetration in this beautiful valley. Captain Raper (1810) had reported this locality as an extensive village. Due to the military influence and settlement of selected gentry, its cleanliness surpasses the hill station of the north.

Dehradun is the centre of researches, thinkers, artists, teachers, students and the top layer intellectuals, journalists and writers. This weaves a very rich cultural variety. Geological Survey of India, Oil and Natural Gas Commission, Indian Military Academy, Survey of India, Forest Research Institute, Doon Public School, University, Colleges, etc. have sheltered selected brains of the country in Dehradun. Tapkeshwar temple and 'Robber's Cave' at short distance from the town are places worth visiting. Tapovan is also close to Dehradun where 'Dronacharya' and 'Kuru Princes' had performed their penances.

Bus services connect Dehradun from all sides. The known travel agencies like Chugh Travels, Lopan Travels, Nijhawan Travels, Trans World Tours and Kumar Travels have well woven network of services to facilitate the passengers in planning, arranging and conducting tours. Dehradun is the end point of Northern Railway inter-linking Dehradun with Delhi, Lucknow, Varanasi, Calcutta, Amritsar, Bombay etc., 'Vayudoot' air services are also available in Dehradun. Air service is at 27 kms. from Dehradun and is situated at Jeolly Grant. Accommodation-wise, the town has well equipped facilities. As the pressure of demand grows tremendously in summer, the rates shoot-up. The dharmshalas are also well dressed and known for its prompt services. Guest houses have been built by various official agencies. But these are usually retained to the luxury of government employees. Kumaun and Garhwal Vikas Mandals of the region have made good arrangements of travel in this area.

Scholars of chronicles search for the clues to know the history. At Kalsi, nearly 51 kms. from Dehradun, they fondly read the engraved boulder to understand Ashoka's decrees in originals.

Jagatgram Aswamedh ritual centre is also very close to Kalsi, where 'Shalivahan' had this done in the third century A.D. Rajaji Wildlife Sanctuary is 20 kms. from Dehradun.

Dehradun is situated at 640 m. (about 2,100 ft.) from mean sea level. The maximum temperature in summer is 36.6°C. In winters the maximum temperature recorded is 23.4°C and minimum is 5.2°C. Snowfall is rarely experienced even in extreme winter. The number of tourists visiting Dehradun every year is around more than one lac and most of them are men of academic interest and young mass of recreation interest.

Mussoorie

The town has reputation as a queen of hill stations in India and is noted for the scenic beauty and a highly palpitating social life. It is situated at 30° 27' N latitude and 78° 06' E longitude bearing an elevation of 2,005 m. above the mean sea level. The town extends over 68 sq km and had a population of 18,233 in 1981. Tourist Guide mentions the town as, '... rising as a horse foot shoe shaped foothill that overlooks on the one side, the great plains sweltering in their pestilential heat with Holy Ganga, oiling its way through slowly sluggishly across them on the other, the vibrant, magnetic silhousette of the Himalaya is Mussoorie....' (Tourist Guide to Garhwal Region, 1989, 8).

It is only one and half century ago that the town took birth. British had a hunt for luxury stations where the rulers could enjoy the abundant loots undisturbed and unnoticed. The labour was cheap and practically free in slave India. Captain Young had spotted the Landaur bazar site ideal to the purpose to military isolation. Salubrious climate bracing weather, scenic splendour and remoteness from din and turmoil of wider plains of slave India, favoured the site for developing into a summer sojourn. Soon in 1827, Elizabethan structures of Hotels came into being. British aristocracy had developed a fancy for the place where guileless simpleton hardworking boys could be fetched for no costs and could be used as cooks, coolies and faithful guards. The feudals of wider plains joined the British in building the luxurious buildings at the hill top. It represents the tastes of the leisure class and devotes to every source of entertainment off feeds on 'Holiday' spirit of spend thrifts and pleasure seekers. Known for dancing, riding, theatre, skating, sporting, painting, flower show, dog show, library, beauty contests, trekking bids, etc., mark the cultural part of the town's life. Local people are poor and prepared to serve the vested luxury class of Indian society and foreigners to their likes. A few years ago they served as coolies, dandiwalas carrying 'human loads' on palanquins and hand-pulled rickshaws. Local sharing to tourists wealth is negligible as most part of tourist income goes to the pockets of the hotel owners, businessmen and the vested classes who belong to regions outside the hills. Poverty is still the preserved fate of hill people. A large measure of ease, rivalry and leisure still lingers here from the long British past. The names of buildings, routes, hotels and institutions still remind us of the British rulers in India. The rhythm of the nature remains unspoilt in winter when it snows in Mussoorie. The town has most fashionable Mall Road. The Happy valley, Tibetan town, Chortans and temple clinge to precarious perch on cliffs. The exotic Tibetan ware and prayer systems make something a new experience to the visitors. The rope-way trolleys wait on the passengers from Jhula Ghar to the historic Gun Hill. The views from the moving trolley are picturesque affording summary trial of snow clad mountains, Badrinath, Kedarnath, Nanda Devi and Bander Poonchh. The parks and roads are neat and clean, smiling with glowing flowers and lights all around. There are beautiful day and night. What does the tourist like depends on his taste and choice. Mossy Falls, 6 kms. from the town, is a pleasing and captivating scene. No body affords missing a view from Benong Hill at a distance of 10 kms. from the town. Pony ride is a great enjoyment. A visitor in Mussoorie feels amply rewarded and costs well recovered when goes to Kempty Fall. The tourists whether moved by any religious thrust or not, never miss a view of Surkanda Devi temple, it is at 3,048 m. Nearly 45 kms. from the town by car and 3 kms. straight height walk leads to the site. This point places before the visitor the entire glorious view of Great Snowclad Himalayan peaks. It is so wonderful indeed to be there. Mussoorie offers the best hill trekking scope and experience is thrilling to any body who undertakes it. Nagtibba trekking, Mussoorie-Dun trekking, Didital trekking, etc., are worth excursions to enjoy. Mussoorie-Chakrata road is ideal for the addicts of aesthetic values in nature.

To the inner zone of the town we get the tourist service complex dressed with hotels, cinemas, rinks, restaurants, cafeteria and clubs for recreations, dances, boosing and drinks. Library bazar in the Mall road shows the attractive shopping complex. To the eastern part Kulri Bazar is situated on the Mall which also leads to side of camel's back. Area offers golf rinks, banks, restaurants and phone exchange. In the middle zone of Mussoorie, we find the educational centres, state offices and shops of various descriptions. To this side the parks and playgrounds are situated. The trekkers, riders picnickers, photo-addicts and painters go to the outer zone of the town wherein garden, happy valley, camel's back, falls etc. are attractions of great interest. LBS academy, modern schools and other offices are situated to this side. Mussoorie is hardly 35 kms. from Dehradun and 60 kms. for the air service at Jeolly Grant. There are more than 78 hotels, 8 dharamshalas, 7 guest houses and other 6 tourist bungalows. The rents in luxury-based western hotels are exhorbitant for ordinary people but in low-rated residential hotels rooms are available in less than Rs.300 per day. There is no rental regulation in the town. The town is visited by more than one lakh people during the summer and the traffic is on an increase. Richer peasantry and the new rich business-class of the plains visit the place now who lack in fine taste for an excursion. Educational institutions sponsor students tours to Mussoorie but their stay is only little due to the exhorbitant charges. Hardly 15 per cent people revisit the town and among those who do so are mostly officers of the government or companies who spend nothing from own pocket. The foreign tourists are around 7 per cent and the average stay is 3 or 4 days. There are not much of local craftgoods to be purchased from Mussoorie. Money poured by the tourists does not trickle down to the local inhabitants in Mussoorie while the soaring prices squeeze their already low purchasing power. Vested landed interests and hoteliers retain most of the income received from the visitors.

Haridwar

It is believed that the locality i.e., Haridwar is the gateway of all

Himalayan Shrines of Uttarakhand viz. Badrinath, Kedarnath, Gangotri, Yamunotri etc. It is the beginning of the abode of Gods. On the right bank of holy Ganges, at the foot of Siwalik mountains lies the beautiful small township of Haridwar. In the great ancient days the town was known as Maya Puri for its abundance of water which washes the veil of Maya. It is in the foothills and looking to the north from Haridwar, are the gorgeous mountains where settles Lord Shiva and is the plentiful beauty and scenic splendour available to human beings also if they go there. Haridwar is the beginning of Teerthas in Garhwal. The town was surrounded by very dense forests in the past where Saints and Rishies used to perform their penances to seek the super gifts from God. Still, there are several such centres of meditation and religious preaching. Though, the genuine part of the ashrams, once, is now usually unreal yet the name, Maya Puri, is still appropriate in this sense. Austerities and penances are still performed. Kumbha Mela is still held every twelfth year in Haridwar. One who takes a holy dip in Ganges at this place, gets rid of his worldly sins and attains purity of heart and soul. The 'Amrit Kalas' elixir of eternity won in Samudravimanthan by Devas in collaboration of Asuras, was hidden in Haridwar, Prayag, Ujjain and Nasik. The rivalry between the two, Devas and Asuras, for the 'Amrit Kalas' full of nectar led to spills at these four sites. Therefore, Hindus take bath at these places to take advantage of the spilled nectar.

Haridwar is known, among the visitors, for Brahmakund, where the nectar pitcher had been placed by Devas. Haricharan temple shows the footprints of Lord Vishnu. Ganga temple and Birla tower are the places of interest. The pleasure of worship Aarati at these is indeed great for the devotees. Beautiful terraced gardens of Ganga canal are centres of attraction even for non-Hindus.

'Sapt Sarovar' and Rishi Ashram in close proximity of Haridwar make a very delightful place to visit. Kankhal Asharm of Ram Krishna Mission has the galaxy of great learned Sadhus having European blend of rationality with Indian depth of philosophy. At 3 km from Haridwar, there is Gurukul Kangari University, red mandir and a museum. Kangri pharmacy has specialisation in Himalayan herbs. The other great attraction is the rope way linking Haridwar with Mansa Devi Temple at steep heights of Bilwar

Parvat. There are large number of temples in Haridwar like Gorakhnath Ayyapa, Vilwakeswar, Kaal Vairav temple, Geeta Bhawan, Maya Devi temple, Shrawan Nath, Manokamna Sidhi Temple, Manav Kalyan Ashram, Vishnu Bhavan and Narayani Shila are visited by millions of visitors with tremendous enthusiasm. The town has several tourist agencies and a big bus station connecting to all important places of India. It has a Railway Station of broad guage of Northern Railway. The old and retired persons have a real peace in Haridwar. The town is known for 'Vaidyas' of great eminence for curing the most incurable diseases. It is a great loss to miss a visit to Haridwar in lifetime. Haridwar is at 292.7 m. above the mean sea level and extends over 45 sq. kms. area. It has a population of 1,87,392 persons as per 1991 census.

Rishikesh

It is celestial abode for all those who had enough of worldly life and want to lead a peaceful, pias and a life devoid of turmoil and disturbances. It is at the bank of Ganges at a distance of 12 kms. from Haridwar. The site is surrounded from all the three sides by mountains and makes a pilgrimage centre for the largest community in India. In the ancient days when the Shastras and Puranas were written, this area was a dense forest. The place was a centre of 'Yoga' and performances of penances and Tapasya. The kings used to come to the place for their retirement days. Yogis were practising their religious practices under the trees at the bank of river Ganga. It is still a centre of yoga ashrams.

Satya Narain temple, Bharat temple, Puskar temple, Rishi Kund, Raghunath temple, Laxman Jhoola, Shatrugna temple, Triveni ghat, Swargashram, Gita Bhavan, Kali Kamli Ashram, Parmarth Niketan, Shiva Nand Ashram, Kanwa Rishi Ashram and Neelkanth Mahadev Temple are the main attractions around the city of Rishikesh. There are several other institutions known round the globe i.e. Academy of Transcendental Meditation, Shankaracharya Nagar and Kailsh Ashram. Rishikesh has a very rich cultural and environmental impact on the visitors of all beliefs and sects. Jeolly Grant airport is closest which receives Vayudoot services from Delhi twice a day. Taxies, rickshaws and three wheeler services are readily available in Haridwar and Rishikesh. The town of Rishikesh is like a strip at the right bank of Ganga, 356 m. above the sea level. In 1981 it had a population of 29,145.

There are package tours being organised by agencies for Badrinath, Kedarnath, Yamunotri, Gomukh, Hemkund and Valley of Flowers. GMOU Ltd. runs vehicles allround the Garhwal region and GMVN organises package tours from Muni Ki Reti, close by Rishikesh.

Trekking tours are organised by the young enthusiasts for Panch Kedar, Rup Kund, Khatling glaciers, Hari Ki Doon, Nanda Devi Sanctuary, Tapovan, Kauripass, Dotital, Nag Tibba and Chardham. There are very experienced guides and arrangements are appreciable. These trekking tours are for 3 to 17 days long. Hotel accommodation and other stay arrangements are quite in plenty. Rates are relatively cheaper in this town as compared to Haridwar. The high class hotels are very well kept and services are really pleasing.

Badrinath Shrine and the Peripheries

At an elevation of 3,122 m. above mean sea level, 32° 44' N latitude and 79° 30' E longitude, there is Badrinath on the confluence of Rishi Ganga and Alaknanda. It falls in Chamoli district of Garhwal division. It is a very small township having a population of 2,576 in 1981. The temple of Badrinath represents the Lord Vishnu, who looks after the upkeep of the world and welfare of the creation. The Shrine relects the peace and serenity. Badrinath is one of the four Dhams, other being the Dwarika dham, Rameshwaram and Jagannath Puri. Pilgrimage of the four completes the minimum expected by a pious Hindu. At the bank of Alaknanda there is the temple in front of which pilgrims are wonder struck by a hot spring. From Badrinath, the Tibetan border is very close. Mana is the last village of India at a distance of 4 kms. from Badrinath. Sacred Hindu Vedas and Puranas were written sitting in Vyas Gupha close by Badrinath, is connected by the bus transport from stations in foothills. The distance from Rishikesh to Badrinath is 295 kms.

After November the area gets too much cold and becomes rather difficult for the visitors. The doors of the temples are closed in the end of November and reopened only in the first week of May.

It is indeed of great interest to note that Badrinath temple has always a Head Priest of Namboodiri origin in Kerala. Narada Kund and Surya Kund are hot springs where the devotees take bath. At Mata Murti (at a distance 3.5 kms. from Badrinath), the Tapta Kund is of major interest. The beautiful magnificent Vasudhara falls at 5.5 kms. from Badrinath, make a very captivating scenery. Nearly 400 ft. (122 m.) water fall in Alaknanda stream is another beautiful scene where the tourists get lost in nature's beauty. Bhim Shila is another beauty place where tourists enjoy the scenery of nature near Mana village. It is a confluence of Saraswati and Alaknanda. These are the areas of perpetual snow.

Enroute to Badrinath shrine various tourist sites of religious importance are crossed. Deo Prayag, at a distance of 71 kms. from Rishikesh, is one of these places. Its elevation is only 518 m. from mean sea level. It is a confluence of two important rivers, Bhagirathi and Alaknanda. There is a temple of Sri Raghunathji and Lord Shiva. It is a very exciting view.

At 38 kms. from Deo Prayag there is a big township of Srinagar. The town is reached after crossing 107 kms. from Rishikesh. It is at 610 m. height from mean sea level. The devotees visit the temples of Kamleshwar Mahadev and Lord Vishnu on the bank of fast flowing Alaknanda river. It is picturesque view to see the flowing waters at Srinagar. The township is a well-planned and adorned city.

It has the centre of H.N. Bahuguna University of Garhwal. Its tourist complex is quite spaceous and dressed with modern facilities. There are quite a large number of hotels and restaurants. It is a very good place to stay if the tourists are plying on cars. Srinagar is quite calm and quiet. At a small distance of 20 kms. from Srinagar, we have the district headquarters of the Pauri Garhwal. The township of Pauri, perhaps, the most beautiful town. It opens a single sight view of the great gorgeous snowclad Himalayas. The view is wonderful and captivating to any body who gets a change to visit pauri. If one proceeds to Badrinath route, he can escape from going to Pauri and can stop at Rudra Prayag. It is at

34 kms. from Srinagar town and attains a height of 609 m. from mean sea level. The town is marked for the great confluence of Mandakini and Alaknanda. There are temples of Sri Rudranath and Chaumundi in Rudra Prayag. Rudra Prayag is the place where road bifurcates to Kedarnath route.

Badrinath Shrine

The temple dedicated to Lord Vishnu is 15 m. tall built in the form of a cone with small cupola of a gilt ball and spire and perched at an altitude of 3,110 m. in the middle of the valley. It is believed that the image of Badrinath had been thrown into the river, Alaknanda, by antagonism, in hands of Buddhists. Later on the image of Badrinath had been retrieved and again stalled at the place by Guru Shukracharya. But there are no clear evidences to prove this. The place is known for its scenic beauty. It gives an imposing view of Nilkanth Peak at the height of 6,600 m. in western side. The place keeps snow bound for several months in winters when the chief priest of Badrinath temples come to Joshimath. Badrinath temple has mainly 3 wings; (a) the sanctum or sanctorium (Garbh Grih), (b) worship place (Darshan Mandap), and (c) assembly hall (Sabha Mandap). There are 15 seizeable idols sculpted in black stone. Lord Visnu's idol is 1 m. high. Other idols are also finely sculpted with image of Lord Visnu's consort, Goddess Lakshmi, Vishnu's mount Garurh, Shiva-Parvati, Ganesh, etc.

Allround Badrinath there are a large number of recreational spots. Besides the religious interests there is much to gain for visitors of all kinds and tastes. Panch Dharas are known places for religious visitors. These are: (a) Prahlad Dhara, (b) Kurma Dhara, (c) Urbasi Dhara, (d) Bhrigu Dhara, (e) Indra Dhara. Similarly, the Panch Shila are the centres of attraction for devotees who assign great significance to Narad Shila, Varah Shila, Garur Shila, Markendey Shila and Narshing Shila. Hot water spring is used by all visitors for a dip before worship and darshan. Brahma Kapal is a place fixed for Shraddha purposes where propitiation of rites is done for deceased ancestors. 'Sheshnetra' is a big size boulder looks like snake's eye. It is said to be the eye of Sheshnag.

Similarly, a beautiful meadow at a distance of 3 kms. from Badrinath temple marks the foot prints of Lord Vishnu. The imprint is on a boulder. The place is known as 'Charan Paduka'.

On the long route to Badrinath the visitors stop at one of the Panch Badri. The place is Pandukeshwar at a height of 1,920 m., nearly 24 kms. short of Badrinath. Yogdhyan Badri temple has a very interesting idol of Badrinath in meditative posture. It is said that when Pandavas in Mahabharat age, handed over Hastinapur to King Parikshit, they retired to this place for their penances. Pandu, father of Pandvas, had performed penances here for Nirvana, emancipation of his soul.

Yogadhyan Badri, is a place of historical interest. Copper plate, showing old inscriptions of Katyuri period, constitutes an attraction for the visitors. It gives clues of the history of Katyuri Kings.

On way to Badrinath, Narshing Badri is the seat of his holiness, the priest Rawal of Badrinath, for winter-meditation. Here an image of Vishnu with Lakshmi, is carved in with great craftsmanship on a black rock. Joshimath is the seat of Briddha Badri. At a distance of 17 kms. from Joshi-Math to the eastern direction there is an old temple of Bhabishya Badri, Badrinath of future. It is along the Dhauli Ganga river beyond Tapovan and needs some trekking of 3 kms. from the main vehicular road. The place is at 2,744 m. from the mean sea level surrounded by dense forests. It is indeed a very stimulating scenic view. "The approach along the Dhauli river is stimulating. The name Dhauliganga means 'White River' and truly it is a roaring torrent almost everywhere upstream from Tapovan and passes through almost perpendicular cliffs on either side, several hundred metres high and wild in the extreme" (Annonymous, 1985, 12-13).

Tapovan has hot springs of sulphur and the view of Tapovan valley towards north exceptionally heart-winnings. The lovers of nature and scenic beauty stop at Briddha Badri, 7 kms. short of Joshimath. Its temple is believed to be the ancient seat of worship of Vishnu even before the enshrinement of Badrinath temple by Guru Shankaracharya. Along the Pinder River in Gwaldam route shifting southward towards Gairsen near Atagad is Adi Badri, centre of 16 temples. It is 17 kms. from Karn Prayag. These temples are small in size and belong to Gupta period of Indian history. Narain temple is the main among these having a statue of Lord Vishnu nearly 1 m. high and sculpted in balck stone.

Badrinath road terminus has a lead to Mana where Vyas Gufa and Keshav Prayag are the places of attraction approached by trekking. Bhimpul, bridge built by Bhim, one of the Pandavas of Mahabharat age, is very interesting to view. Vasudhara water-falls are captivating in this route beyond Badrinath. It is near Mana, at a distance of 5 kms. from Mana village. It is 145 m. fall of water in a beautiful background of snowy peaks, glaciers and steep rocks of terrifying view. Satopanth lake is also in the same direction. A triangular lake of serene water, crustal clear, with a circumference of about a kilometre lies at a distance of 25 kms. from Badrinath. The height of the place is 4,402 m. from mean sea level. The trekking along this place is very interesting and full of enjoyment for the young enthusiasts. The parties rest inside the great caves which sheltered great saints, rishies, in the past. Saints used to perform penances here and some used to jot-down the philosophical ideas triggered in their mind by the benevolence of nature.

Valley of Flowers

Great geographers and experts of recreational resource development like Archer (Archer, 1983, 137), Blache, (Blache, 1952, 1-24), S.C. Bose, (Bose, 1976, 78-108), Berry R. (Berry, 1979, 27-52), have marked natural scenery as a most potential source of tourism development. Valley of Flowers in Garhwal Himalaya affords great avenues of development of tourism in this tract. It is very captivating area for any body to visit and appreciate. Valley of flowers is situated to the east of Badrinath at an altitude of 3,658 m. from mean sea level. It needs a trekking of 5-6 kms. The valley is 10 kms. long and 2 kms. wide in conical shape. It is along Puspavati river. On the Badrinath highway, one gets down at Govindghat and takes to 15 kms. trekking to reach Ghangharia. From this place the valley is approachable at 5 kms. trekking. Ghangharia is a place where boarding and lodging facilities are well-woven.

Valley of Flowers has been described as Nandan Kanan in Sastras. Hanuman visited the place in search of booti or herb to cure Laxman. July, August and first week of September are the appropriate days for a visit to the place. Innumerable kinds of small but exceptionally bright and beautiful blooming flowers are seen spreading like a carpet. It is a rare spectacular scene. The valley ranges between 3,362 and 3,658 m. in altitude. For those addicts of trekking, there is a very adventurous route to reach Ghaursali and Niti via Bhyunder pass above 5,000 m. in height. This route presents very rare view of a dozen snow peaks like Rataban, Mana, Mukut Parvat, Kamet, Lampak, Hathi Parvat etc. There are beautiful snow clad peaks having a picturesque view.

Hemkund

There is still another route from Ghangharia to the slopes leading to Lokpal lake or Hemkund. It is at 4,329 m. high from mean sea level. It is encircled by seven snowclad peaks and dressed by glaciers around. Fed by the crystal clear serene water from the snow around, Hemkund, is the source of Him Ganga. Sapt Shring and Hati Parvat glaciers provide water flows to the kund. Sikh Saint, Guru Govind Singh, had performed penances and meditation near it in his earlier births as believed and mentioned in Granth Saheb as well. There is a Gurudwara built there and a temple, as well, at the bank. Hemkund can also be approached from Vishnu Prayag directly along the ridges but it involves great climbs.

Nanda Devi Sanctuary

At a height of nearly 4,500 m., Nanda Devi Sanctuary is indeed of a great interest to botanists, nature lovers and trekkers. More than seventy lofty peaks surround the sanctuary. All of these Nanda Devi Peak is the highest (7,819 m.). The area is known for its lush green meadows, chuting white water falls and rich fauna and flora allaround. The entire range is fit for trekking with proper preparation and in adequate expert guidance (Table 8.1).

Yamunotri

Uttaranchal Himalaya is proud of this pilgrim centre in Kedarnath,

TABLE 8.1: Altitude and Distances of Localities in Nanda Devi Range from Rishikesh

Places	Distance from Rishikesh (km.)	Altitude (m.)
Joshimath	250	1,890
Lata	275	2,317
Lata Kharak	285	3,689
Dharansi	292	4,250
Debrugheta	300	3,500
Deodi	306	3,364
Ramni	313	3,520
Bhoj Ghera	318	4,060
Tilchunni	323	4,200
Inner Sanctuary	331	4,500

Badrinath and Gangotri axis. The location of this centre is towards the western part of Bander Punch at 6,315 m. height. Yamunotri temple is at a height of 3,322 m. which is dedicated to Yamuna. The area has the speciality of having hot water springs and boiling hot water gushing out of the rock-gaps. A bath in Surya Kund prepares the devotees for worship at Yamunotri temple. Divya-shila near the Surya Kund is typical rock at a height of 4,421 m.

Auli Bugyal

It is a beautiful skiing place where such facilities are provided by Garhwal Mandal Vikas Nigam. Moving towards Auli from Joshimath, tourists are captivated by excellent panoramic view of the giant mountain peaks, Kamet, Dunagiri and Nanda Devi. The area is covered with deep snow during winters till the late March. The Bugyal has a 3 kms. breadth and at places there is low elevation. Skiing is organised by trained people and the young tourists have a great fun and adventure. The equipment gears, boarding and lodging facilities are available. There are good arrangements of medical facilities also in this place. The place has great potentialities of being developed as winter sports centre.

Kauri Pass through Curzon Road

One goes to Kauri Pass from Tapovan via Khulara or also through Joshimath-Auli, Gorson, Chitrakantha. Still another route is Joshimath-Mrig, Tugasi to Khulara. Gailgarh is the common meeting place for all these trekking routes. Closely at 5 kms. from the place is Kuari Khal pass. Usually the trekkers take to Tapovan route as it is shortest, nearly 21 kms. Very charming meadows are there. Delisera range is closer from Kauri Pass and presents world's most picturesque view. Standing at the Kauri Pass, the vision sweeps from the gorges of Trisul in the east to the great peaks of Kedarnath in the west. The peaks are Chaukhamba, Neelkantha, Kamet, Gauri Parvat, Hathi Parvat, Nanda Devi, Dunagiri, Bethartoli etc., Lord Curzon managed visiting Kauri Pass in 1905 by trekking, therefore, the trek is named as Curzon road.

Kedarnath Shrine

It is at an altitude of 3,583 m. built on a morainic ridge jutting out at right angles from snowy range below the Mahapanth peak and flanked by alpine meadows. Mandakini river emerges from snout of Chorabari glacier at a short distance from Kedarnath temple. The temple is built by large and evenly cut slabs of grey stone. It presents rare craftsmanship. The temple is spacious having two parts: (a) sanctum sanctorium known as garbh grih, the worship place, (b) assembly hall or mandap. Kedarnath is approached by trekking 15 kms. from Gauri Kund. Vaisukital (4,150 m.) is at 6 kms. from the place from where we go to Paintal, 2 kms. still further northward. The lake is beautiful. The view of the lakes, Chorabari, Vaisukital and Paintal, are very fascinating to the visitors (Table 8.2).

From Guptakashi one can proceed to Madh Maheswar via Kalimath, Ransi, Ganndar route. Rishikesh to Guptakashi is around 178 kms. and a trekking of 6 kms. ahead reaches the traveller to Kalimath. A further march onwards of 7 kms. leads to Ransi, Ganndar is hardly 6 kms. from here. This leads to Madh Maheswar at a distance of 11 kms. ahead. This temple is at a height of 3,289 m. Shiva temples of Rudranath, Tungnath, Kalpeshwar etc. are in

TABLE 8.2: The Distances Place to Place en route to Kedarnath from Rishikesh

Places	Distances from Rishikesh (km.)	Altitude (metres)
Rudraprayag	139	610
August Muni	158	762
Guptakashi	178	1,479
Sonprayag	204	1,829
Gauri Kund	209	1,982
Kedarnath	223	3,583

this periphery and these offer something rare for a human being to see. The region is the best area for trekking (Table 8.3).

Sites and Centres of Tourist Attraction in Kumaun

Kumaun is a land of fairies. Its lush green meadows, mountain peaks and glacial valleys have hypnotized the visitors for several centuries. Ramnagar, Haldwani, Lalkuan, Tanakpur, are the railway stations leading to an access to Kumaun Himalaya. Ramnagar connects with Garhwal routes as well as Kumaun routes upward. Very close to Haldwani there is Kathgodam station of North Eastern Railways which provides all services of tourist convenience. The main places in Kumaun are Jim Corbett Park, Nainital, Bhowali, Almora, Ranikhet, Dwarahat, Gwaldam, Kausani, Baijnath, Bageshwar, Berinag, Bharari, Dhakuri, Pindari Glacier, Rupkund, Milam Glacier, Lipu Pass, Pithoragarh, Ghat, Lohaghat, Champawat and Banbassa. There are various other small places of great beauty. Bhimtal, Naukuchiatal, Sattal, Khurpatal and various other lakes are of superb natural beauty in Kumaun. For Savite Hindus the temples are of great religious importance. Baijnath and Jageshwar temples are of great historical value. Manila is a unique locality of natural splendour. Dunagiri temple of Durga attracts thousands of tourists every year. Beauty spots like Binsar, Dhwaj, Chandak, Abott mount, Chaukuri, Sukidang and Punyagiri are the rarest of the nature's presents on earth. Kumaun has an eternal calling for all. Persons of all walks of life tastes and fantacies

TABLE 8.3: Accommodation for Tourists in Garhwal Scenic-Sports (1985)

Routes	Stations	No. of beds available	
		1985	1997
Badrinath Route	(i) Gaucher	4	18
	(ii) Karn Prayag	90	140
	(iii) Nand Prayag	30	60
	(iv) Chamoli	10	40
	(v) Pipal Koti	44	79
	(vi) Joshimath	126	202
	(vii) Govindghat	4	12
	(viii) Pandukeshwar	4	10
	(ix) Badrinath	84	148
Kedarnath Route	(i) August Muni	4	10
	(ii) Chandra Puri	4	8
	(iii) Guptakashi	20	38
	(iv) Phata	4	8
	(v) Rampur	4	8
	(vi) Son Prayag	47	69
	(vii) Gauri Kund	40	72
	(viii) Kedarnath	72	132
Valley of Flowers	(i) Govindghat	4	9
Hemkund	(ii) Ghangharia	38	62
Kauri Pass	(i) Ghat	8	16
	(ii) Ramni	4	12
	(iii) Tapovan	8	14
Rupkund	(i) Tharali	2	6
	(ii) Dewal	4	12
	(iii) Mundoli	12	30
	(iv) Wan	12	28

reach Kumaun, tour round and go satisfied and hardly forget to come next. There are nearly 80 Himalayan peaks in Kumaun exceeding 6,096 m. height snowclad and smiling at the low lands. The perpetual bliss intense emotions, elegance of nature and majestic look of peaks attract every body who seek this fortune. Bracing climate, scenic grandour, lush green forests, serene water bodies, blue-white flowing rivers and the peace makes one to feel that he is in heaven, aspired abode of Gods. Kumaun is known as "West Moreland" of East. Katarmal, Binsar and Shitla Devi temples are the attractions for historians and pilgrims in Kumaun. Jageshwar, Gananath, Baijnath, Bageshwar, are the temples which no pilgrim wants to miss in any circumstance. Untadhura, Pindari, Milam, Nandakot, Kaphini, Gori, Ponting glaciers in Kumaun expose the visitors to the feast of beauty.

Nainital

Settled in the small locality of 11.73 sq. kms. and 30,951 population, there is a cup-like town around the beautiful Naina lake. It is at 1,938 m. height. The Nainital town emerged in 1840-43 under British regime. It was liked by the British for its cold climate and secluded setting amidst the mountains besides its being close to railway station and wider plains. The place has maximum temperature of 26.7°C and minimum of 10.6°C in summer season. During winters the maximum temperature comes to an average of 15.6°C and minimum of 2.8°C. It rains heavily in this locality and the average is 279 cm. every year. It is an ideal place to visit during summer—March end to June end. Again in autumn it becomes exceptionally beautiful and climate keeps very soothing. Nearest airport is Pant Nagar, well linked with Delhi, at a distance of 71 kms. from Nainital by car. Its nearest railway station, Kathgodam, in north-eastern railway. Kathgodam is 34 kms. far from Nainital by road. Very efficient bus service link Nainital with major cities of India. Super delux buses ply affording comfort to the passengers on way. A very large number of travel agencies serve the passengers in Delhi, Agra and Lucknow to rech them Nainital. The city is shaped in a milk-pot design and has a Europen character. The town is known for its fabulous beauty and a highly reputed centre of education of all levels. Its cultural heritage is superb and tourism services are of very high standard. It is the headquarter of Kumaun university, one of the known 'A' grade universities in India. Nainital's maintenance and decoration is of special type. It has a rope-way service for passengers to reach peaks. Tourists choose Nainital as the centre from where they plan their visits to the peripheries in Kumaun. Wildlife sanctuary named after Jim

Corbett is closest to Nainital. Kalagarh and Dhikala are at a distance of 118 kms. and 143 kms. respectively from Nainital. The lake in between the surrounding lush green mountains is a rare beauty specially during nights of autumn season. There are several lakes close-by and everyone of them presents a very picturesque view. Regular organised tourist tours are booked from Nainital and all arrangements are looked after by tour-sponsoring agencies at Nainital. Staying at Nainital tourists go for yatching, boating, skating, dancing, painting, photography, from beautiful hill peaks like Naina-peak, Killburry, Lariakanta, Deopatta, Dorothy Seat, Snow View, Land's end, Hanuman Garhi etc., Bhimtal, Sattal, Naukuchiatal etc., are at 20-25 kms. level-road from Nainital. Bhowali, Mukteshwar, Ramgarh, etc., can be tripped from Nainital by bus or car. The town has a very well developed accommodation for tourists, managed by private hotels, state guest houses, summer holiday homes, youth hostel, Zila Parishad, Tourism Department and Kumaun Division Development Corporation.

Ranikhet

It is also a small township managed by the Cantonment Board. It spreads over 21.76 sq. kms. and feeding 18,190 population at its lap. It is situated at 1,829 m. height, known for its scenic view of Himalayas and cold climate. It also has rare repute for cleanliness. It has a maximum of 32.2°C and 8.4°C minimum temperature during summer and it ranges between 7.2°C and 3.3°C during winters. It has an average of 127 cm. rainfall per year. It is motorable from Kathgodam to Ranikhet by road, at a distance of 84 kms. Ranikhet links Kumaun with Karn Prayag in Garhwal by road at a distance of 134 kms. Ranikhet connects the tourists to Kausani (62 kms.), Badrinath (257 kms.), Ramnagar (95 kms.), Almora (50 kms.) and Pithoragarh (257 kms.). This station is well linked with all major stations of plains by straight motor services. Ranikhet has several hotels and very high quality restaurants. Tourism Department looks after the services. Kumaun Mandal Vikas Nigam has managed good tourist accommodation in Ranikhet. The town has very good sceneries in the periphery. In Chaubattia garden, apples have a nationwide market. Tourists feel highly rewarded having reached such a beautiful site and captivating view of snow-covered Himalayan peaks.

Kausani

It is rather remote from Ranikhet. The height of the town is 6,200 ft. (1,890 m.). The place has its rare value for an extended open view of entire Himalayan snow ranges. Maximum temperature is between 26°C and 15°C during summers and winters respectively. The temperature varies between 10°C and 2°C in summer and winter. Maximum rainfall is 3,048 mm. and minimum is 1,777 mm. September to April the snow ranges are crystal clear. Monsoon months are also enjoyable in Kausani. Accommodation is very well planned and available at cheaper rates. The place is well equipped with transport and the communication facilities.

Almora

Skandh Purana provides a reference to Almora in remote history. It is described as a sacred mountain situation between 2 rivers Kaushika (now known as Kosi) and Shalmali (now named as Suyal). This is perched on a horse saddle shaped ridge extending over 5 kms. It is surrounded by a circle of thickly forested hills. These hills are moderately slopy and their tops are the seats of Goddess or some local deity. The rapturous view of snowclad peaks of Himalaya in the background of green, blue and dark mountains, virgin tranquility, peace and superb climate make Almora an attractive hill station. Almora is the ancient seat of Kumaunese refined culture and great artistic tradition. The inhabitants of Almora are blessed by Goddesses, Banari Devi, Kesar Devi, Shyahi Devi and Katarmal unravaged forests. The area is indeed so beautiful. Almora has extended markets and narrow lanes full of colourful folk from neighbouring areas who make purchases in Almora market. Stone paved streets, stone-built houses, slated hutments spacious wider valleys, fashionable shops on the either side of roads and neat and cleanly conditions allround are very interesting in this town.

Katarmal Temple and Others

Katarmal, at a distance of 17 kms. from Almora is known for the eminent temple of Sun. The temple dates back to the 7th century AD. It is situated at an elevation of 1,554.5 m. The place is the centre of research of environmental protection and ecological balance. Similarly another site in periphery of Almora is Binsar, which is situated at distance of 30 kms. from Almora. It is one of the nature's wonders and presents a hypnoting view. The beauty of the place wins over the heart of the visitor who does not like the idea to leave it. It presents an uninterrupted salitude and natural grandeur so abound far and wide. Few charming cottages are available here for tourists to stay and enjoy. Shyahi Devi near Sitalakhet is also one of such beauty spots at a distance of 36 kms. from Almora city. Jageshwar temple of Almora is situated in a narrow valley surrounded by dense forest of great Deodar trees. The temple represents one of the Jyotirlings built by Katyuri kings of Kumaun in 7th century AD. The place is at 38 kms. from Almora. 200 shrines were built by Katyuri dynasty in this area. Natraj, Lakulisa and Durga temples are more eminently known. Durga temple had been built during the 9th century and its architecture illustrates the craftsmanship of the age. The size of the temple is small. It is around 25 to 30 ft. rectangular with two giant lions squatted and facing the cardinal points. Very massive square rock pillars are at the entrance. Lakulisa and Natraj temples are also 35 ft. high having simple plinth and plan roof. Its art is unique. Chalukyas of Badami had also built a Lakulisa temple in Karnataka in the same period. Gananath temple, 30 kms. from Almora, dedicated to Lord Shiva, is also a very popular site among the tourists.

Baijnath

Baijnath, 71 kms. from Almora is a known tourist site on the bank of Gomti river. The place is on route to Bageshwar via Kausani. From Kausani the distance is only 20 kms. The temples of Baijnath are of great historical significance. There are temples of Lord Shiva, Ganesh, Parvati, Chandika Goddess, Kuber, Surya, Brahma and

Mahisasur Mardini goddess Kali. The temples are date back to 13th century AD. There are life-size statues of Lord Shiva-Parvati and Ganesha. A museum is also there to protect these valuable sculptures. At Kate Ki Mai, 3 kms. from Almora there is a temple known for the finest of Vishnu statue which is the example of the great art of stone-work in the area in the tradition. Bageshwar is also one of the chosen cultural centres of Almora which represent the Katyuri sculptures and is a pilgrimage centre. It has several temples which show the ancient skills in stone-carving. Bageshwar is situated at the confluence of Gomti and Sarju rivers. Its heights is around 975 m. from the mean sea level.

Pindari and Other Glaciers

Almora to Pindari Glacier route is very interesting for trekkers. The route, Almora-Kapkot-Loharkhet-Pindari is most easy and presents vibratingly dramatic scenery of Himalaya all the way. Rhododendrons on way, flowering in red colour, make the view all around very picturesque. Nanda Devi view from immediate close keeps the visitors wonder-struck. The peaks are at 3,656 m. to 4,265 m. elevation. Passing through the glacier at 5,393 m. the trekkers reach Trail's pass, the trekkers have the feeling of Winning over the snows. On way the gurgling hill torrents, roaring water falls, blooming flowers, snow bridges make the journey all the more enjoying. Loharkeht and Dhakuri have the requisite accommodation and facilities for the travellers. Kafni and Phurkia glacier passes afford the best of the views.

The hills of Kumaun are very rich in flora and fauna. The flowering shrubs wild anemone, trefoil, michelmus daisy, butter cups are really so captivating. Jim Corbett's national park, close to Ramnagar-Dhikala, in proximity of Nainital city, is approachable by car or bus. Mammals ranging from obnoxious tigers, panthers, barking deer, marsh crocodiles, python and cobra-snake can be seen there. Elephants of wild growth are seen in Ramnagar jungles. Chirping of birds all around and cool breeze in background of lofty peaks of snowclad mountains, lush-green forest cover make the mission of tourists a grand success. Babblers of a large variety, barbets of golden, blue and green sprinkles on throat, cheeks or breast are common birds. Red, white and black nightingales (bulbul) follow the tourists trekking the hill routes.

Infrastructure and Trends of Tourism in Uttaranchal Himalaya

Electricity

The spread of tourism is a function of beauty resources as well as the capital resource-based infrastructure. Electricity, for example, is basic for promotion of tourism. Uttaranchal Himalaya has developed the electricity yet the area does not have the wider coverage of electricity in remoter areas. The villages of Uttaranchal Himalaya under coverage of electric lights were few till 1985. Table 8.4 shows the number of villages having an electric line nearby. Whether all purpose connections are actually taken or not, these are grouped as electrified.

It is evidenced by the data presented in Table 8.4 that there are only 6,976 light connections and 6,951 all purpose connections in the village sector. In Garhwal sector the connections are fewer. There are 4,491 Harijan villages and localities where

TABLE 8.4: Electrified Villages in Uttaranchal Himalaya

District	No. of electrified villages		Electrified Harijan villages and localities
	Lighting connections	All purpose connections	
1. Nainital	1,519	1,511	900
2. Almora	1,507	1,507	870
3. Pithoragarh	615	615	451
4. Tehri Garhwal	705	705	545
5. Uttarkashi	398	398	337
6. Chamoli	646	640	374
7. Pauri Garhwal	1,054	1,054	590
8. Dehradun	532	521	424
Total	6,976	6,951	4,491

Source: State Electricity Board, U.P., 1985

electricity is provided in this region. The towns of Garhwal have hydel or thermal electricity generating units in remoter areas of north. The supply and servicing of electricity is extremely poor in village sector and northern parts of Himalaya. This primarily is because the UP State Electricity Board operates more as a dullared official department and sense of public service remains to be developed and sense of public service remains to be developed in the personnel at service of these lagging areas.

Accommodation

There are various agencies providing accommodation to tourists of various types. The state are the known traditional parts of accommodation. PWD, irrigation, forest, district board, various banks, universities and other organisation of business and Christian philanthropy are having stay arrangements in Himalaya. Table 8.5 shows number of the accommodation providing guest houses in various districts of Himalaya. The guest houses are invariably small in size and do not have more than 5 to 6 suits. It is used for stay of the visiting administrative heads of capitals of Lucknow or Delhi. These tracts have traditionally been colonies of the richer areas in plains, therefore, the accommodation is not available for the petty local people or ordinary tourist mass.

In the entire Himalayan tract there are 625 guest houses. Forest and PWD have the largest number of guest houses. Since these are the rich departments of the poor country, these guest houses are well equipped and quite luxuriously managed. The development departments and services do not have any of these services. Revenue officials have the major share of gains of this accommodation (Table 8.5).

Communication and Bus Services

Tourism has its base on the development of transport and communications. Since these Himalayan tracts have traditionally been treated as colonies of the ruling headquarters, the attention has never been adequately provided for Uttaranchal Himalaya. Of late some communication and transport services have emerged mainly

TABLE 8.5: Number of State Guest Houses in Uttaranchal Himalaya

District	Guest Houses					Total
	PWD	Irrigation	Forest	District Board	Others	
Nainital	28	15	62	2	24	131
Almora	28	1	41	22	2	94
Pithoragarh	35	–	22	5	1	63
Tehri Garhwal	14	4	33	3	9	63
Pauri Garhwal	18	4	43	2	11	78
Uttarkashi	9	4	52	1	15	81
Chamoli	34	–	19	3	2	58
Dehradun	7	3	30	7	10	57
Total	173	31	302	45	74	625

Source: Annual Administration Reports, 1984.

to the benefit of administration. For most of the time telephone services, postal, telegraph etc., keep out of order. But during summer the administration mends upon them for their own use. Sense of public service as such is largely wanting. Table 8.6 shows the number of district-wise post offices, telegraph offices, telephones, public call centres, bus stops and railway stations located in Uttaranchal Himalaya. In the wider interest of public service and tourism development it is essential that the communication and transport services are improved for this area. The tourism department should try to establish its own networks of communication service in order to protect the interest of the visitors in this area for sporting, trekking and site-seeing.

Road Network

Uttaranchal Himalaya has 9,805 kms. of surfaced roads while the western UP has nearly double of it i.e., 16,137 kms. In spite of the fact that the geographical limitations of hills need greater emphasis on development of transport quick and efficient. Roads in per 1,000 sq. kms. area are 191.78 kms. in Uttaranchal Himalaya, 196.34 kms. in west UP. The southern and eastern UP is still poor in this respect but the topography is not as difficult to prevent

TABLE 8.6: District-wise Telephone Connections and other Infrastructural Facilities in Uttaranchal Himalaya

District	Telegraph office (1997)	Telephone (No.) (1997)	Public call offices (No.) (1988)	Bus stop (No.) (1993)	Railway station (No.) (1993)
Nainital	138	12,242	133	370	19
Almora	131	5,764	122	310	–
Pithoragarh	93	3,876	72	186	–
Tehri Garhwal	75	3,256	38	311	–
Pauri Garhwal	87	5,923	29	426	1
Uttarkashi	15	2,055	28	113	–
Chamoli	72	4,103	11	109	–
Dehradun	81	32,238	124	302	8

Source: Statistical Year Book, 1997, Hill Region.

accessibilities. Population-wise Uttaranchal Himalaya region is quite thinly populated because most of the area is unfit for habitation purpose. Road length per lakh population is around 188.7 kms. in Uttaranchal Himalaya tract.

Postal Services and Communications

The era of post Independence has been a period of growth of postal service development in U.P. Himalaya. There are 2,232 post offices in the tract operating in rural areas. These are very small units and do not provide telegraph and telephone services. In urban centres of Uttaranchal Himalaya there are 148 units adequately developed in most of the cases. The district-wise breakup shown that postal services are area and population-wise distributed over the physical space (Table 8.7).

The flow of tourism is growing and in order to cater to this growing need of tourism development, tremendous improvement in postal and wireless services is needed. The wireless services alone can serve the region in a regular pattern because the telephone lines do not operate owing to wind and rain destruction on lines. Tourism development department may take-up this matter with the government which shall not only help the tourists but shall help administration and public at large in Hill areas.

TABLE 8.7: District-wise Number of Post Offices, 1997

District	Rural	Urban	Total
Nainital	239	25	264
Almora	442	14	456
Pithoragarh	381	11	392
Tehri Garhwal	256	11	267
Pauri Garhwal	416	17	433
Uttarkashi	124	5	129
Chamoli	332	14	346
Dehradun	183	67	250
Total	2,373	164	2,537

Source: Data from PMG, UP Statistical Abstract, March 1997.

Tourist Flows in Uttaranchal Himalaya

There are various accesses to this region. Entrants from Nepal and visitors of north-east part of Uttaranchal Himalaya find access from Tanakpur route. The general category of tourists enter from Rishikesh, Najibabad, Kaladhungi, Kathgodam etc. The passenger and vehicular flow has been counted at these centres for the year 1984-85 and 1994-95 south to north. The vehicles are reclassed as private and UPSRTC/government. Private cars, taxies and other vehicles have been counted separately. Brackets indicate the number of visitors from various routes mentioned in Table 8.8.

Besides the tourist traffic emerging from the outside areas, there is a flow of interregional tourist between Kumaun and Garhwal and the intra-regional flow emerging from sub-regions for pilgrimage and the site-seeing. Sports, school tours, state activities and various other types of traffic flows keep moving which are not included in this estimate. It we take these together, these may make around 20 per cent of the total (i.e. 2,00,877) which means total traffic may be reckoned at 12,05,264.

Variation in Tourist Flows

The tourists visit Himalaya in every month for various interests in small or big numbers but the flow gets intensified in each direction

TABLE 8.8: Tourist Flow in Uttaranchal Himalaya (south to north). 1984-85 and 1994-95

Routes	Vehicles entered					
	1984-85					1994-95
	Private bus	Government bus	Other bus	Taxies	Total	Total
1. Extreme Eastern Tanakpur Route	1,356 (66,960)	96 (5,760)	324 (19,440)	1,872 (9,360)	3,648 (1,01,520)	7,020 (NA)
2. Kumaun Entrance Route (Kathgodam)	1,272 (61,920)	3,126 (1,94,600)	420 (22,052)	6,642 (33,210)	11,460 (3,12,782)	2,040 (NA)
3. Kaladhungi Mid-cross	436 (8,20,208)	18 (1,056)	108 (6,552)	1,866 (10,014)	2,428 (37,830)	4,302 (NA)
4. Najibabad Garhwal Route	1,188 (58,776)	618 (33,680)	204 (11,016)	222 (1,110)	2,232 (11,432)	3,231 (NA)
5. Kailash Gate Rishikesh Route	2,906 (1,56,612)	3,948 (2,21,088)	972 (59,272)	3,606 (18,030)	11,432 (4,55,002)	2,2011 (NA)
6. Other entrances	–	–	456 (26,448)	888 (3,552)	1,344 (30,000)	2,734 (NA)
Total	7,158 (3,64,476)	7,806 (4,57,184)	2,484 (1,44,780)	15,096 (75,276)	32,544 (10,41,716)	59,698 (NA)

The figures have been collected from toll barriers and motor cycles, scooters, trucks and padestrian traffic has been left out to arrive at the tentative figures.
The figures in parentheses are the number of passengers.

after March. Nearly 63,208 and 91,301 tourists had visited the region for a stay in the guest houses and tourist bungalows in April 1988 and April 1998 respectively. The number of such passengers staying in these accommodation jumped to 1,10,659 and 1,91,509 in May 1988 and May 1998 respectively. By June some of these had moved out and fresh had entered. The actual number staying in this accommodation was 1,01,160 and 1,90,600 in June 1988 and June 1998 respectively. With the advent of rains the passengers had fled away and those who occupied the accommodation were 61,881 in 1988 and 83,807 in 1998. July-August is a good season for tourism but roads get damaged and rocks slip on to the roads. The trekkers are not recorded here as they stay in their tents wherever they move during the months. The number of staying tourists grows further in autumn season when all accommodation is engaged in main tourist stations. Table 8.9 shows the month-wise variation in number of staying tourists.

Projections of Visiting Pilgrims

Garhwal Mandal Vikas Nigam has worked with the exercise to estimate the number of pilgrims over the past few years and the year ahead. In 1980, nearly 1,75,000 pilgrims had visited Kedarnath temple and by 1983 the figure rose to 1,80,000 which further grew to 2,40,000 in 1984. The traffic seems to grow every year with gaps in between due to changing weather conditions, peace conditions and general political climate. In 1987 the visitors at Kedarnath has swelled to 2,66,111. The Nigam projects that by 2000, the likely visitors would be 4,12,000 to this station. Visitors to Badrinath are growing every year. These were 2,85,000 in 1980 and 3,62,541 in 1987. These may grow to 6,80,089 by 2000. Similarly Rupkund visitors were 32,000 in 1980 which grew to 47,000 by 1987. These may further grow to 81,200 by 2000. Thus Garhwal region traffic would be above 11,73,289 persons in near future for which management has to be done by the tourism department and the development corporation. Table 8.10 shows the year-wise pilgrim tourst flows to the holy shrines of Garhwal. The trekking expeditions were sponsored by the Kumaon Mandal Vikas Nigam in the last decade.

TABLE 8.9: Monthwise Tourist Arrivals in Tourist Guest Houses of Uttaranchal Himalaya, 1987-88 and 1997-98

Months	Private household guest visitors	Garhwal Mandal Vikas Nigam	Guest houses of others	Kumaun Mandal Vikas Nigam	Private hotels; ashrams and schools	Total Tourists 1987-88	Total Tourists 1997-98
April	4,492	2,769	1,800	3,146	51,001	63,208	91,301
May	5,772	3,480	1,723	4,657	95,027	1,10,659	1,91,509
June	6,169	4,814	2,004	5,391	82,782	1,01,160	1,90,600
July	4,707	3,004	1,711	2,107	50,152	61,881	83,807
August	1,198	2,296	1,208	2,016	32,189	38,907	51,311
September	2,429	1,729	811	1,875	38,311	45,155	62,131
October	3,963	2,205	1,658	3,040	57,600	68,466	84,169
November	1,504	2,711	517	2,404	26,530	33,666	49,712
December	297	3,189	119	3,007	17,058	23,670	31,522
January	488	2,119	172	1,872	18,112	22,763	31,618
February	195	2,072	136	3,048	16,146	21,597	25,200
March	1,211	1,722	152	3,113	18,929	25,127	30,916

Sources: (1) Compiled from quarterly return of Guest Houses of respective Nigams, 1987-88 and 1997-98.
(2) Guest Houses of Forest, P.W.D., Irrigation, District Board and other Corporate bodies in the region.
(3) Private guests are drawn by sample survey data.

TABLE 8.10: Yearwise Tourist Flow Projected by Garhwal Mandal Vikas Nigam in Garhwal

(Projection from bus traffic)

Year	Kedarnath	Badrinath	Rupkund	Total
1980	1,75,000	2,85,000	32,000	4,92,000
1981	1,40,000	2,92,886	41,500	4,74,386
1982	1,50,995	2,95,995	43,000	4,89,990
1983	1,80,000	3,04,087	46,000	5,30,087
1984	2,40,000	3,00,102	20,000	5,60,102
1985	2,19,000	3,25,504	44,000	5,91,504
1986	2,55,129	3,53,450	40,000	6,48,579
1987	2,66,111	3,62,541	47,000	6,75,652
1995	3,00,000	4,57,000	54,000	8,11,000
2000	4,12,000	6,80,089	81,200	11,73,289

Source: Draft Perspective Plan, 1988-91. Tourism in Garhwal, Garhwal Mandal Vikas Nigam Ltd., Dehradun, 1989, 2000.

Goods Traffic to Uttaranchal Himalaya

The passengers do not bring their all requisites except few essential clothes. Rest of the things are to be catered to them locally. The hill areas are not major producers of food and industrial products. These things are brought from outside to meet the needs of the visitors. Vegetables, food items, clothings, construction materials and various equipments are transported by trucks to the remoter hills. A survey of goods-movement during January to December 1991 completed only recently by the author in context of this study tried to estimate the flows from the toll barriers to Uttaranchal Himalayan destinations. The Table 8.12 indicates the itemwise load movement to these stations. These figures show that the number of enthusiast participants is growing over the years. In spite of the sad tragedy of 'malpa' some times ago the enthusiasm for Mansarovar Yatra continues to be high and demand for greater number of tours per year is getting strength (Table 8.11) to the lower side because the trucks not shown as entering or evading are not included. Actual load carried to hills is at least two times greater than obtained by the figures from toll-barriers. Nearly 2,17,956 quintals of load moves annually to hills from plains (Table 8.12).

TABLE 8.11: Tours and Pilgrims to Mansarovar Yatra, 1991-2000

Year	No. of tours	No. of pilgrims
1991	7	227
1992	7	225
1993	12	365
1994	14	348
1995	13	339
1996	14	435
1997	15	516
1998	11	594
1999	15	459
2000	16	492

Source: Record of KMVN, Nainital.

Expenditure per Tourist

A survey of tourist parties from various corners of country and abroad was attempted by the authors to assess per passenger rough amount of expenditure done in Uttaranchal Himalaya. This can enable to guess what gain or sales tourism bring to this demand deficit area. The parties were interviewed at varying locations for reporting their approximate planned expenditure and incurred expenditure on this tour. The amount spent in Himalayan area on all inclusive items excluding asset acquisitions barring craft-goods was separately estimated. Then per passenger average was drawn. It was different for all parties. For example it was Rs.8,000 for parties staying in Rishikesh, Rs.7,500 in groups entering at Kot-dwar station, Rs.4,000 interviewed at Haldwani, Rs.12,000 for passengers staying at Nainital. The amount per passenger was highest in parties which took distant tours to Badrinath, Kedarnath (Rs.17,000). Table 8.13 indicates the details of per passenger average tour expenditure.

The estimates are only approximation of the total expenditure which tourist expected in their entire tour and what they expected to be the expenditure in their visits to the pilgrim centres and other

TABLE 8.12 : Goods Traffic to Hill Area, 1991 (1st January-31st December)

Route	Average vehicles per month		Quintals per month				Total load carried to hills per month	Annual 1991
	No. of trucks laden upward	Other carri-ages	Food-stuffs and grain	Other mate-rials of food	Cons-truction goods	Miscel-laneous goods		
1. Extreme Eastern Route	246 (10.98)	53 (10.88)	600 (10.41)	573 (18.78)	415 (8.52)	170 (9.70)	2,057 (11.33)	24,684
2. Kumaun Entrance Route	815 (36.38)	146 (29.98)	1,918 (33.28)	760 (24.92)	1,100 (22.58)	407 (23.22)	5,146 (28.33)	61,752
3. Kaladhungi Route	18 (0.80)	7 (1.44)	140 (2.43)	800 (26.23)	918 (18.85)	346 (19.74)	2,229 (12.27)	26,748
4. Najibabad Route	213 (9.51)	62 (12.73)	417 (7.24)	210 (6.89)	516 (10.60)	112 (6.39)	1,530 (8.42)	18,360
5. Kailash Gate Route	935 (41.74)	213 (43.74)	2,600 (45.12)	682 (22.36)	1,717 (35.26)	568 (32.40)	6,715 (36.97)	80,580
6. Other passages (estimated)	13 (0.58)	6 (1.23)	88 (1.53)	25 (0.82)	204 (4.19)	150 (8.55)	486 (2.68)	5,832
Total	2,240	487	5,763	3,050	4,870	1,753	18,163	2,17,956

Source: Data compiled from route toll barriers, 1991.
Figures in parenthesis show vertical percentages.

TABLE 8.13: Estimates of Expenditure per Tourist in Uttaranchal Himalaya

(Survey Result – April-Sept. 1998)

Stations	Parties No.	Adults PP* M PP*	Adults PP* F PP*	Non-adults PP* No.	Total tour estimates	Expen-diturc in Hima-layan region
Rishikesh	12	4	3	5	16,000	8,000
Kotdwar	10	5	2	3	11,500	7,500
Haldwani-Kathgodam	15	8	3	4	7,400	4,000
Nainital	28	6	5	5	20,000	12,000
Ranikhet	15	6	5	4	36,000	15,000
Srinagar	20	4	11	7	25,000	18,000
Ramnagar (Tourist Bungalow)	12	6	5	2	1,35,000	8,000
Badrinath	15	5	10	3	32,000	17,000
Average	–	5.5	5.5	4	35,363	11,188

*PP = Average per party of the total parties interviewed.

tourist places in Uttaranchal Himalayas. The per capita expenditure by tourists comes to Rs.746 in the area of Uttaranchal Himalaya. A large part of this expenditure is on the transport and food. Almost two-third of the expenditure is for the stay accommodation. Thus, greater the stay, larger is the expenditure.

Night Halts in Himalayan Paradise

The tourists constitute a moving flow of passengers. Tourist parties had been interviewed at various stations to know their average stay in this area as planned by them. This revealed a very interesting information that these tourist parties had come for pilgrimage or site-seeing and their tours were hurried. Average stay was hardly 4-9 days. In the places like Haridwar, Rishikesh, Dehradun, Mussoorie the average stay was greater than 13 days on average. These were different types of tourists who were old, retired and had come for relaxation or medical treatment. They had no longing for going to trekking, skiing or boating. Those who

TABLE 8.14: Night Halts in Uttaranchal Himalayan Tract

(Survey data)

Place of interview	Parties contacted	Average size of party	Stay nights in Himalaya		
			Already stayed	Likely to stay	Total stay
Rishikesh	12	12	6	1	7
Kotdwar	10	11	4	5	9
Kathgodam	15	14	7	1	8
Nainital	28	10	4	2	6
Ranikhet	15	6	3	5	8
Srinagar	20	8	2	3	5
Ramnagar	12	5	1	4	5
Badrinath	15	11	2	2	4
Total	127	9.7	3.6	2.9	6.5

had come for fun, enjoyment, nature, study, adventure etc., were 127 parties covered by this study in 8 stations. Their stay was only 6.5 days on an average. They felt the arrangements as poor and services costly. Table 8.14 shows the station-wise break-up of parties covered for interview and their average stay in Himalayan resorts.

The average of the interviewed parties indicates that average party size is quite big (9.7 persons) and they had stayed in Himalayan tract for 3.6 nights on an average per party. They were still on tour of Himalayan sites. They intended to make a night halt for 2.9 nights per party in their stay. Thus, if their approximations came true, average stay per party would be 6.5 nights in Himalayan tract.

Development of Way-side Amenities

Since the Uttaranchal Himalayan region is fast growing as tourism resort complex of the country and foreign tourism is growing more rapidly in this region, it is essential that the tourist routes be equipped with better amenities of wireless telephones, postal services, transport, marketing and other supporting services. All trekking route-wise camping facilities, medical care and photography centres be made available to the visitors to make their visits more comfortable. The pilgrims need various facilities for children, old and infirm, specially the medical care. More accommodation, if made available in main tourist resorts, the high charges of private hotels can be controlled. Toilet facilities are lacking every where at stations and cities. Much remains to be done regarding cleanliness in towns, stations and the tourist spots. Dewalgarh (Pauri), Satpuli (Pauri), Thalisain (Pauri), Rudranath (Chamoli), Paner (Chamoli), Baskel (Uttarkashi), Mori (Uttarkashi), Agora (Uttarkashi), Trijugi Narian (Chamoli) need additional space for tourists. Chirwasa (Chamoli), Ghat (Chamoli), Neel Kanth (Pauri), Camptifall area, Davrital area, need more accommodation for tourists. In Kumaun, there is no arrangement of accommodation and essential services in remoter tourist sites. A vast programme of space and amenity development should be formed for filling up the eminent gaps of tourism promotion in Kumaun.

9

Splendour Resource Management and Monitoring in the Himalaya

Stages in Resource Management

Planning and management of resources towards optimisation of human welfare is, both, pragmatic and problematic in nature. The stages through which the process of resource management has to pass are often identified as below:

(a) Resource-definition and assessment of the magnitude and precise scaling of resources point to point;
(b) Identification of the use-alternatives of the scaled resources and deeper analysis of the efficiencies of each alternative from the stand point of return;
(c) Assessment of the disutilities or lost-return in terms of the environmental and ecological costs in diverting the resource to the opted use;
(d) Measurement of the disaster that an opted resource management pattern would invite in the form of land erosion, and endangering the other life-resources which sustain human welfare in the long run. This also brackets the erosion of aesthetic values;
(e) The estimation of precise monetary costs of development of resources and ensured preservation of the resources so that long-run planning could be undertaken basing on these resources;
(f) Choosing the model of development and strategy of

resource-use planning which also includes the winning of mass. Support towards the exercised choice;

(g) Building of the super structure of personnel organisation and development of skill and know-how for the proposed long range and short range plan perspectives;

(h) Preparation and installation of the infrastructure in terms of physical capital and intangible capital for the proposed choice;

(i) Phase-wise division of the work-plan in various dimensions of the plan and inter-linking the inter-phasal growth of the resource-management project;

(j) Building the blue-print of the inter-spatial exchange over the regions which is likely to ensure increased human welfare under the plan with least displacement;

(k) The stage-wise inter-temporal dependence of one sector on the other sector has to be projected quite minutely before the plan is pushed into action.

(l) The regions are dissimilar in terms of resource endowments which paves the ground for the trade and inter-region exchange. This means that a management plan in one region has its linkage with the plan of resource management in the other region.

(m) In the specific context of the splendour resources of the Himalaya, resource management embraces the issues of development of forest resources, water resources, conservation of life resources, preservation of the climatic resources, and above all, the development of an efficient transport network involving the least displacement and interference with the web of nature.

Roles of Transport

'Transport' is one of the basic prerequisites of modern way of life. It had its pivotal role even in traditionally less-developed modes of living yet the present day material prosperity of mankind has a positive correlation with development of transport. It is the basic reason why, we, often take land of development of transport as an indicator of economic and social growth. There is no denying the fact that the countries or regions having a highly grown-up system of transport, whether of men or goods or ideas, such lands have attained far greater material superiority over other regions. In its obvious form, the gains of transport development, are many but the indirect gains are more than numerous. The discussion extending over the first six chapters of this work, has exposed the gains which emerge from transport development in any economy.

It has been derived in the earlier chapters that transport is an inter-linking sector and its development everywhere results in reduction of 'user's cost'. The history of economic progress of human civilisation marks the fact that cost-reduction and quality upgrading of any commodity or service expands the availabilities, consumption, and ultimately raises the living standards of the vast vulnerable groups of human society. The mechanism and the inter-relationships leading to cost reduction are changing input combinations and factor combinations as a result of inter-linked space. Extension of market is impossible without inter-linked space by transport. Division of labour in production process is well nigh impossible without transport.

The spatially diversified and fragmental human habitations are unified in one economic inter-supporting unit by transport. Mastering of space is the function of transport. The gearing up of the production possibilities, expansion of scale of production, generation of surplus, over and above day-to-day consumption, in different human settlements, emergence of exchange as a mode of modern production, and regional specialisation etc. are the direct outcome of the development of transport. Conquering of isolation and promotion of inter-sectoral production co-ordination have taken birth by the development of transport amenities and modes. Isolated human settlements invariably work for fostering autarky and self-sufficiency. As soon as the outside links are formed and outlet emerges, the process of exchange gets established. It is in the interest of the producers and consumers to obtain factor-units and goods from the outside world for the obvious gains of variety, low costs, better quality etc. This process thrives on the transport-base.

Human Fulfilment and Curiosities

Movement of people over space has more than economic gain. Human hunt is for the pleasure, welfare, satiety of curiosities, aesthetic values, participative hunger, social inter-mingling, lust for influencing and bringing others in one's own fold of thoughts. One wants to see with his own eyes beyond the forewalls of own habitation. Thus, 'experience of new' is a natural lust. In fact it is a 'call of life-experience' to tour and travel everywhere as possible within the means. As transport expands, the curiosity increases and mass movement of people, goods and message starts. In this sense modern world is an interwoven threadwork of transport-networks which keeps the world united and co-ordinated. Transport system and its network makes the political entities to exist. Security, peace, justice, economic catering and social integration are fed by transport development. The utilisation of land, labour, enterprize and capital in fact depends on the inter-linked transport over the space.

Growth and large-scale popularity of movement oriented-life style is relatively a new fashion yet the learning by travel, travel for business and trade, travel for new adventures, travel for health reasons, change in climate and environment etc., have been quite a known facts in the annals. The new era has made these styles available and popular among the mass in general due to revolution in the spheres of transport and communication.

Institutionalisation of Travel Experience

Tourism, in modern sense, has taken the institutional garb and now every community is seeking exposure to the external world. Large-scale immigration and migration processes were witnessed even in history but these were by far intended for permanent settlement in the better convenient locations. Now tourism is more for business, learning, experience, fun and frolic, enjoyment, company games, sports, site seeing, changing the climate and getting away from the din and turmoil of over-busy urban life. Pilgrimage as a form of tourism has been the oldest mode of tourism. The development of transport has turned it possible, now, to allow participation of children, young mass adolescents, old and infirm in this activity. The extended discussions in the body of this thesis amply illustrate that wider participation and diversification are the main features of modern outdoor travel.

Tourism has been stimulated by transport facilities. Yet this factor is not decisively the sole factor. The analysis in the foregoing pages has brought us to the conclusion that while geographical unification has been possible by transport, the basic sense of security, conditions of peace and inter-community tolerance and integration of cultures have played significant role in promoting large-scale tourism. The enthusiastic search for new styles of life, modes of living and new combinations has, indeed, promoted enthusiasm for the experimentation in each sphere of life. Now the over-stability and single space confinement has come to be lebelled as stagnation, traditionalism and backwardness. It is well established that unless men get free from the basic livelihood creation worries of day-to-day life, there is no breathing space for any other option. New industrialisation era, its mechanisation and economic organisation has created surplus in terms of output on the one side and surplus in terms of leisure and spare time in human life wherein man is able to think of options and enjoyment. Thus the spare income over and above the day-to-day consumption needs is responsible for the wider popularity of tourism. The facility structure, which has often been promoted by official action, ensures the comfort of the tourists, therefore, the hazards and risks of travel in tourism have been avoided by the new developments along the development of transport network. Social habits are by far a product of suggestions by way of the advertisements and publicity. Men were never so open to suggestions before as they are today. The tourism advertising agencies have played a vital role in promoting tourism in the modern age. Official policies and inter-governmental cooperation has also triggered the growth of tourism in large-scale. The favourable atmosphere for the courtesy and hospitality for tourists is prepared by the atmosphere promoted by the efforts of the state. Along with increased transport network, there is more fostering of amicable relations internationally which promotes tourism now. The transporters, hand-in-hand with tourist authorities, keep a liaison with international tour organisers and see to the network of transport connections these days which was not possible earlier.

A Triggered Mobility of Labour

Transport network removes the imperfections of market in the sense these promote labour mobility and movement of supplies as inputs, finished goods, etc. This is also true in the sphere of the news and message communications which by far help the process of tourism. Millions of tourists are able to undertake outdoor participation in sports, games, conferences, meets, fairs and get-together, due to the transport and the basic infrastructure of tourism developed today round the globe. Tourism of this type is not a valueless loitering and only luxury oriented travel, it is a value in itself and promotes global understanding and cultural ties. It helps coordination of interests and generates closer ties of friendship. Overall impact of growth of tourism on the welfare of humanity has been tremendous. Not only new knowledge and experience emerges in travel process but the reallocation of resources is possible to the optimum uses. At this point a line in caution is also needed to warm the unguarded and unregulated development of tourism. On the name and excuse of tourism some undesired elements also find entry into the land which may work towards endangering the very survival of the country. Similarly, tourism, if promoted without adequate caution, it may spread diseases like "Acquired Immunity Disease Syndrome" or it may spread vulgar habits of drinking wines, liquor, prostitution, conspicuous consumption and a pompous and showy pattern of living. But if the government is alert and due cautions are taken these hurdles are well tackled. There may be diversion of resources from production of essential and socially useful things to luxury-oriented production by excessive emphasis on development of tourism. The spread of incomes generated in the process of tourism may not filter down straight to the down-trodden masses and may be retained mostly by the vested business interests. In such case tourism may not prove to be as beneficial but would be detrimental to the growth of domestic economy.

Resource-Utilisation and Accessibilities

There is ample usefulness of tourism development for the Himalayan hilly tracts which have some typical features. The region of 'Garhkum' has a great historical backgrounds which interests the scholars, anthropologists and historians. Its captivating scenery of foothill based large size mechanised farm greenary, tiny urban localities, hypnotic spell of mountain scenery, water bodies, ravines and fast-flowing Himalayan rivers, identifiably strange cultural traits, isolation and peace and above all the extended view of snow-clad Himalayan peaks are important for tourists. No Sikh, Hindu and others can afford missing a visit to the shrines and holy places in Himalayas. Himalaya has been an attraction for the pilgrims even in the remote history when modes of transport were unknown.

The Himalayan tract has poor accessibilities due to the typical topographical constraints. While the areas at the foothills are relatively well linked by roads and railway, the hilly tracts are still without a good transport network. This is due to the geographical constraints. In the eastern side of Garhkum the slopes are relatively moderate and the transport links are also more comfortable as compared to the difficult topography in the western part. The distances are prohibitive and dreary if the roadways are followed. Better ropeways can come-up to inter-link the hill tops and make the tourism more thrilling and adventurous. The interception by ravines across the mountains makes the road-travel very long and time consuming besides its being more uncomfortable. The network of transport and connectivity depends on the pattern of human settlements and scattering of population. How best the habitational points can be inter-linked and how cost of spatial movement can be reduced in terms of time, money and labour are the challenges faced in transport development in hill areas. Air services and rope-way transport can be enormous help to exploit the beauty resources in these far flung areas to the benefit of humanity. Attempts have been made in the past to study transport-connectivity by Kansky, Taaffe and Abler. Separate studies at length are needed for the hills of India where the general principles, as applied to plain topography, do not apply appropriately.

Himalayan tract offers a typical host of problems in development of transport routes, communication system as well as the management of the tourist traffic across the points. The study of the growth of vehicles on road suggests that the growth of vehicular movement on Himalayan roads links has been very rapid comparing the length of vehicular roads in hill region and the rest of the regions in UP one finds that the road length is greater in hills per

1,000 sq. kms. area. Seen from the angle of served population, one finds that road length per lakh population in Kumaun is greater than in Garhwal. The hill regions seek tourism as a livelihood because the alternate occupations in these regions are quite limited. Whether tourism really helps the process of promoting income and employment of the people there is a major question. Whether the region has developed adequate infrastructure, whether its tourism potentialities are well publicized and whether the management of tourism in these regions is up to the mark to pave a path for further growth are the issues looked into here.

Reaching the Grandeur Resource by Designed Tours

Package tour planning from main nodal centres to Himalayas has been found effective and it does need adequate promotion. This mode of tourism operation has been popular as well as, well managed in the past. The publicity aspect is not yet well attended specially in foreign lands. The facilities and amenities of life essential in day-to-day life of the prosperous westerners are not available even the best accommodation built so far, yet, the pace of growth of infrastructure has been quite assuring due to the efforts of development corporations at work in these regions and the encouragements from transport and tourism ministries of state and the centre.

The policy and strategy of tourism development laid down so far has been quite rewarding in bringing additional tourists specially from the foreign lands. "Tourist-service" offered in STDC accommodation is yet of low quality and attraction as compared to ordinary hotels in private sector. Tourist reception centres have worked with considerable success. The costs are still very prohibitive for middle class tourists. Yatri Niwas are still in making. The organisation of 'youth tourism' is gradually catching attention and is likely to become the principal mode of the new strategy. The strategy evolved in Eighth Plan has looked into the capacity saturation in some tourism concentrates like Nainital. Wider spread of the tourist traffic to the remote Himalaya is likely to emerge in near future. All this depends on the pace of transport and accommodation development.

Intensive Investment on Infrastructure

Accommodation building is costlier in hilly topography specially in public sector which depends on the honesty of the employees. Nearly 90 per cent of the cost of the hotel industry concentrates in fixed assets. The turnover is quite fast and returns are really attractive. Building costs are 52-53 per cent while equipment costs are 40 per cent and the remaining costs are dominated by furniture and labour. Building costs computed in this study come to Rs.30,000-65,000 per two room set at 1990 prices excluding the land costs and cost of sledging and levelling the land site before construction. Such accommodation is of very ordinary type. The better accommodation is more costly. The cost of double room set may be isolated as Rs.1,39,800 to Rs.2,80,000. The room rent rates are fast changing every year and even in every season. The rates are 150 per day in one star to Rs.1,000 per day in the best hotels (in 1990). The actual charges are more than indicated in brochures.

Capacity Use Depends on Occupancy Rate

The space-occupancy rates vary quite extensively over the region from month to month. The average per month is 73.7 per cent in Nainital, 64.16 in Srinagar, 62.9 in Ramnagar, 58.7 in Ranikhet while 27.6 per cent in Sattal and 34 per cent in Gwaldam (Table 6.12). April to June the occupancy rates are highest (76, 88 and 96 per cent) which after a slight fall in July and August, climb to 80 cer cent, 78 and 71 per cent in September, October and November. These are overall averages of the three readings in the tourist places of the different types in different seasons. The overall average occupancy is recorded as 63.5 per cent per month.

Evaluating the excess capacity and utilisation rates on the one hand and revenue realisation on the other, the study found that 72 per cent of the expected income from ready space is realised on an average. While somewhere it is more than the expected rate due to fast turnover. The average of the actually lost revenue due to non-utilisation of ready space and dressed amenities in the sample was Rs.8,40,624 in the year 1989-90. The cost revenue relationships studied in the sample show that average cost (all inclusive) was Rs.246 per room while recovered revenue was Rs.1,449. The per room gain per year was Rs.1,203. Deducting the fixed as well as running costs, the gain per room was Rs.980 only. These are only tentative estimates and depends on the correctly reported data.

The detailed chapter on the morphological dimensions of the tourist centres in Himalaya makes very interesting description of the principal tourist attractions of Uttaranchal Himalayas. It mentions the geographical specialities, locational particulars, historical features and beauty splendour of the places marked for tourist interest. In Garhwal Himalayas the principal religious centres have been the main attractions for the millions of pilgrim flowing into the hills of Garhwal. The great force of inspiration and impetus built a pervasive culture for the entire country in the past. Now the flow of foreign tourists to the temples in Garhwal has rendered these places popular in Europe and South East Asia. Shivism has been the main line of faith promoted by temples here. There are more than 5.5 hundred main temples in Garhwal Himalayas and nearly 350 are related to different forms of Lord Shiva.

Animated Utilisation of Splendour Resource Promotes Economic Activity

The tourist traffic has a significant impact on the economy of local towns. For instance, Dehradun situated in 31° 19' N latitude and 78° 2' E longitude, is one of the important towns in Garhwal. The town is abound by gorgeous ranges from northern and southern sides. To the eastern side of this town holy Ganges flows while to the western side there is Yamuna river. The town is at 640 m. height and extends over 80 sq. kms. area. It is a big and populous town and a capital city of Uttaranchal state. It has temples and Gurudwaras of great religious interest. The town is equipped with most modern civic amenities. The town is an ideal town in respect of its cultural background, natural scenery, climate and the best educational facilities in north India. The wildlife interests, aesthetic interests, religious interests and the climatic advantages of this tourist centre are indeed rare. The accommodation and entertainments available in Dehradun (town place) among the chosen few tourist centres of Garhwal. The lifestyles, cultural fibre, composition of population, the institutions of the town, transport and communication facilities, etc., have been responsible for making Dehradun so popular among the visitors.

Haridwar township, which constitutes the gateway to Himalayan shrines of Badrinath, Kedarnath, Gangotri and Yamunotri is situated on the right side of Ganges in the foothills of Siwaliks. The town has its ancient name "Maya Puri" more popular among the historians. The town has a great past and has the status of Prayag, Ujjain and Nasik for being one of the places where the "nectar" obtained by Samudra Vimanthan had spilled. The town is situated at 292.7 m. height and extends over 42 sq. kms. area. It attracts more visitors per year than any other town in the north India except Delhi. The traffic from all sides of the country visit Haridwar in some or the other religious occasion. Nearly 13 lakh visitors came to Haridwar in the year 1988 while this figure raised upto 24.5 lakh in the year 1999. In 1988, nearly 7.42 lakh of them were visitors coming for some religious purposes. The foreign tourists were counted as 39 thousand of which 5.8 thousand were from Europe, 4.6 thousand were from south east Asia, 1.92 thousand were from middle east, 1.2 thousand from U.S. and Canada. Nearly 4.27 lakh visitors had come from western parts of India, 2.84 lakh from south India and only 1.9 lakh from eastern India. The traffic flow by rail and road constitutes the major part as the air services cater to the needs of only a fraction of the total traffic. Another important feature of Haridwar is that the total stay of the visitors in Haridwar is greater than their total stay in other places. The town has very extensive accommodation facility. It is available in all kinds; very cheap, moderate and dear. Ashrams, Dharamshalas, Holiday Homes, Rest Houses, Dak Bungalows, Stay Homes, Inns and Tourist Houses are available in the town. From Haridwar the visitors plan their tours to the remoter Himalayas. Another notable feature of tourist influx in this town is that it consists of the children, young enthusiasts, old men and women and business tourists. The composition is so because the town offers something to every visitor.

Mussoorie, the queen of hill stations, is very close to Dehradun. It is marked for its rare scenic beauty as well as the typical admixture of Garhwali and British variants of highly pulpitating social life. The town is on a hill top. It is at 30° 27' N latitude and 78° 06' E longitude bearing an elevation of 2,005 m. above sea level. It is only a small town spreading over 68 sq. kms. The town earns its name due to its British styles, salubrious climate, bracing weather, scenic beauty and Elizabethan structure of Hotels. Garhwali population is extremely honest, simple and impressively hard working besides being ungrudging for adequate remuneration. This affords very good atmosphere for the fashion-driven favoured sons of earth to exploit the guideless mass on mountains. The town offers the best avenues to pleasure seekers both indoor and outdoor. The visitors find the types of circle they choose whether hill trekkers, horse-riders, liquor parties, fashion shows, painting, poetry-making and related literary circles, flower shows, or dog shows. Human beings are seen carrying palanquins loaded with beast burden of luxurious rich man and westernised inhuman educated rich. Mussoorie offers less to Garhwal but indeed to big a share of its pleasures to the visitors. It is a living relic of British and feudal luxury. The English touch to every little thing makes a sound of living slavery and imperial impact on the cultural styles. Trolleys of rope-way, moving up and down the cliffs and rocks makes an exciting experience specially the scenery of snowclad mountains from the moving trolley makes the everlasting memory. Though the accommodation in Mussoorie is adequate in view of the size of the town yet the rates and charges are indeed exhorbitant for an average Indian to bear without any exploits of state purse or business hoarding. Clubs, cafeteria and theatres make the impression as if Garhwal has left the economic backwardness miles away which is a false impression made by the atmosphere of excessive boosing drinks, dances and recreations. Except for the parasite feudals and business surplus holders, the tourists usually go for site-seeing and trekking. When the town gets laden with tourists the population of the town swells to 1,00,000 in September-October or even 4 lakh in summer. Still the sanitary standards and supply services keep on working with reasonable pace. The typical twist of tourism is noticeable in recent years. The luxury-oriented visitors are quite few as compared to those who like to visit various sites of the scenic beauty of Garhwal and make visits to the holy shrines.

Rishikesh is the hub of transport links from all sides and offers bus connections as well as rail connection to wider parts of the country. The town is situated at the right bank of Ganges and the town settles itself on a long strip 356 ft. above the mean sea level. Tourists find their way to routes connecting Badrinath, Kedarnath, Yamunotri, Gomukh, Hemkund and valley of flowers from here. Very well organised bus services and tourist-packed tours operate on these lines. Trekking parties are packed, equipped and guided from the centres in this city. Young tourists take themselves to trekking for Panch Kedar, Roopkund, Khatling glaciers, Nanda Devi sanctuary, Nagtibba, Chardham, Tapovan, Kauripass and Dotital. This is indeed the best part of enjoyable tours. Very good arrangements of stay and boarding are made by the organisers.

Badrinath shrine is at 3,122 metres from the sea level. It is situated at 32° 44' N latitude and 79° 30' E longitude. In fact, it is a confluence of Rishi Ganga and Alakhnanda rivers. Though a very few people live permanently in Badrinath, the town is visited by lakhs of devotes pilgrims every year. Badrinath is very close to Indo-Tibetan border. One has to travel on bus along 295 kms. from Rishikesh to Badrinath. The scenery on way and the shrines situated enroute to Badrinath Dham are of great historical interest. Holy shrine of Badrinath is the token of great diversities of India right from sea shore in south to north. Indian unity of culture and geographical identification is marked in the cuplet sung by the devotees while bathing in 'Taptkund'. "Uttaram yet Samundrescher, Himandrescher Dakshinam, Varsham tad Bahara tam Nama, Bharati yet santati". In the north of the ocean and in the south of Himalaya, there is India inhabited by the sons of Bharat king. The striking feature of Badrinath shrine is that its chief priest is always from Namboodiri Brahmin clan of Kerala in the southern-western part of Indian peninsula. The beautiful 122 m. waterfall in Alaknanda stream is really so picturesque. The perpetually snowclad areas of the confluence of river Saraswati and Alaknanda are very captivating specially in its singular background.

The tourist attractions on way to Badrinath are, perhaps, more captivating than a pervasive view of entire Himalayan range of snow covered peaks. Deoprayag the confluence of Alaknanda and Bhagirathi rivers at a distance of 71 kms. from Rishikesh is one of the beautiful tiny hill town. It is at 518 m. from sea level. The temples of Sri Raghunathji and temple of Lord Shiva at Deoprayag attract thousands of pilgrims.

The beautiful townships of Srinagar and Pauri are centres of tourist attraction. From Deoprayag, one travels on the bus 38 kms. long to reach Srinagar. It is enroute to Badrinath. The distance between Rishikesh and Srinagar is 107 kms. It is at 610 m. height. The known temples of Kamaleshwar and Lord Vishnu are visited by every pilgrim. In order to go to Pauri town, one has to change the route here. Srinagar is the seat of learning and a cultural center. At a distance of another 34 kms. one reaches Rudra Prayag, a small township, enroute to Badrinath from Srinagar. This place is at the confluence of rivers Mandakini and Alaknanda. Rudra Prayag has a very captivating natural scenery. It is known for its shrines of Sri Rudranath and Chaumunda temple. Nearly 24 kms. close to Badrinath temple there is Pandukeshwar at a height of 1,920 m. The place has Panchi Badri temples. Yogdhyam Badri is one of them. An interesting meditative posture of Badrinath is shown by an idol. It is known for its historical importance noted in Katyuri copper plate inscriptions here. Narsingh Badri is close to Badrinath and is said to be the winter meditation place of Sri Badrinathji. Similarly Bhavishya Badri at 17 km from Joshimath enroute to Badrinath is very interesting place. It is along the Dhauli Ganga river beyond Tapovan and requires a walk of 3 kms. The stimulating scenic view of the place is unparalleled.

Valley of Flowers has been a centre of attraction for centuries long. To the east of Badrinath at an altitude of 3,658 m., there is a 10 kms. long strip of conical shape, along the bank of Puspavati river. It requires going on foot for 5 to 6 kms. The width of the strip is hardly 2 kms. It is an interesting place to view the variety of flowers, small and beautifully coloured. It is a rare gift of natural described as 'Nandan Kanan' in Sastras. July to September is the appropriate time to see the greatest variety of prettiest of the flowers never to be seen elsewhere. At a distance the strip is seen like a carpet. The height varies from 3,658 m. to 3,862 m. in the strip. The addicts of natural splendour and scenery take to trekking to see dozens of snow-covered peaks like Rataban, Mana, Mukut, Parvat, Kamet, Lampak, Hathi Parvat etc. Lush green meadows of Nanda Devi Sanctuary, chuting white water falls and very rich fauna and flora around attract a great number of tourists from inner parts of the country as well as from the foreign lands.

Socio-Educational Growth by Tourism

Kumaun Himalayan tract is relatively more easily accessible and less rocky. Therefore, the area is well woven with roads and vehicular transport. Tourism is not so much of religious nature here. It is a fancy-tourism meant for site-seeing, business and luxuries in the stylish hill towns of Kumaun. Some towns have the nature of hill resorts of luxurious classes, some are the centres of cultural and educational activities while others are the centres of district administration. Few of them have evolved into their present shape from cantonments and few others have emerged as business and transport centres. Only few places are of great historical relevance and religious importance. Intensified official activities and road building in the recent past has inter-connected the localities paving a very good ground for the spread of tourism in Kumaun.

Nainital known as a city of lakes in Uttaranchal. It is a very small cup-like town on the lofty hill where people settle around a beautiful lake and there is a post office on a bridge. It has a height of 1,938 m. The small locality spreads in 11.73 sq. kms. area and is known for its seclusion and isolation from the din and turmoil of wider plains of Uttar Pradesh. The town is known for its very clod climate, where average temperature in the summer is ranging between 10.6°C and 26.7°C. During winters the temperature ranges between 2.80°C and 15.60°C. The normal rainfall is 279 cm. per year. It invites maximum number of tourists in Kumaun. The tourists are seen in the town in every season and month. Usually the pressure of the tourist traffic grows 30 times greater in summer and 18 times greater in autumn as compared to winter. Its closest air link is Pant Nagar at 71 kms. from Nainital. Its closest metre gauge railway station (NER) is 34 kms. from the town. Nainital town compares well with Mussoorie by its styles, culture and European impact on day-to-day life. The design of the city is like a milk-pot and population settles on the hills surroundings a beautiful lake. It shelters the British style schools and an 'A' grade University of India, which gives to the town its character as an educational centre. Fabulous beauty of nature in its lush green forest, Sky Blue Lake, cold breeze and wide picturesque landscape attracts tourists from all parts of the globe. Foreign tourism has a greater hold in Nainital. Surrounding areas of Nainital are also equally rewarding for the visitors. Transport services are efficient and public amenities are very well arranged. The sanitary standards of the town are fast deteriorating due to over pressure of tourism, congestion and lack of alertness on the part of administration. Rope-ways are a thrilling experience to the tourists as that of yachting, boating, trekking, skating and horse-riding. Every little space has been devoted to hotel building and the lake shrinks to accommodate more buildings all around. The town has a saturation for any further expansion of tourism without potential loss to ecology environment and the cultural base of this tiny cup-like town. Tourism is gradually spreading to the neighbouring areas like Bhowali, Bhimtal, Sattal, Almora, Ranikhet, Kausani, Bageshwar, Baijnath etc. Still the impact of tourism on the economic life and general prosperity and cultural styles is not clearly marked in these neighbouring areas except a few places like Ranikhet, Almora and Kausani. There is over concentration of tourism in Nainital from where the organised tourist buses take rounds of the neighbouring areas but the income from tourism in its large part, is retained in Nainital.

Resource Management Facilitated by Power Development

Develøpment of tourism in Himalaya has been related to the development of transport and electricity. The other infrastructure which has promoted tourism, in its large part, is the policy of the government. The policy package consists of the establishment of regional development corporations, tourism development corporation, loaning policy for construction of hotels, least taxation and heavy subsidies on hotel construction, tourism departmental services at all levels and affording the supporting services for promotion of tourism. The urban townships have good transport links now and the areas have been served with electricity. Thermal plants are also working in urban townships for electric supply. Jal Nigam and Electricity Board have developed the basic facilities. State Hydel Department tries to keep the power feed constant and spread the network of electric lines. Development of transport is mostly to the credit of State Road Transport Corporation and the private bus operators' organisations. The regional banks, scheduled banks and other leading agencies have maintained liberal flow of the loanable funds to this end. The State Government and Central Government, itself constitute a sizeable part of tourist traffic wherein on various excuses the influx of politicians, officers and other official agencies continues to enundate the tourism circles. The communication services have also played a vital role in promoting tourism in the Himalayas. The network of postal and related services have rendered a pivotal role though quite unnoticed and unsung. The pace of expansion of these services in the post-independence period has been quite rapid. Tourist flows, as counted by vehicular movement (1984-85), have evinced that nearly 31,284 vehicles keep on serving the tourist traffic in UP Himalaya. The total traffic handled in these is 10,04,387 in 1984-85. The main routes counted for the estimates are:

(a) Extreme Eastern route
(b) Kumaun Entrance route
(c) Mid-cross Route to Kumaun
(d) Garhwal route
(e) Kailsah Gate Route of Garhwal
(f) Other Entrances.

The actual traffic moving along these is greater than estimated as the vehicles on which the toll rates are not charged and are not included in this count. The traffic may be reckoned at around 12,05,264 per year.

Flows of Tourism on the Routes

The tourist traffic is like a flowing river and the flow increases or decreases by the flow from other stations and the diversions available to the flow. In Garhwal and Kumaun, no systematic records are available to present an account of monthwise variations in the various routes. The monthwise flow date shown in the preceding chapters shows that traffic grows suddenly in April which continues growing till June. It dwindles slightly in July, August and September in gradual manner and tries to pick-up by later August to November again. After November the traffic continues falling consistently before it starts rising up again in March.

The growth of tourism in Garhwal recorded in Garhwal Mandal Vikas Nigam estimates has depicted continues growth after 1982 onwards. The growth prior to this was rather uneven over the years. Flow of tourist traffic is measured as 4,89,990 in 1982 which rises in a regular fashion year after year to 6,75,652 in 1987. The projections show an upward rise till 1995. Himalayas are a supply deficit area. Any diversion of traffic to this area needs an equal flow of goods and services. The routewise load carriage to Himalayan region in 1989-90, as estimated under this study, makes it clear that the goods traffic has grown much faster than the tourist traffic-growth. This is explained by the fact that the needs of day-to-day consumption as well as of the building materials of the inhabitants of the Himalaya have grown over the years. The load carried through the routes, covered by the study, was 2,17,956 quintals in the year 1989-90. If we go to the details of the load, it is found that 5,763 quintals of good stuffs and 3,050 quintals of other food materials were carried per month by trucks and buses. Besides this 4,870 quintals of construction goods and 1,753 quintals of other goods per month were being transported up the hills from the foothill toll bars, the actual load carried may be greater than this. The domestic production of Uttaranchal Himalayan tract has also increased in the last two decades which helps in affording sustenance to the visiting tourists. The distribution system in hilly tracts is not upto the mark insofar as the village supplies are concerned. The urban supplies are relatively better organised but the prices, which are the scarcity prices, are always twice the rates in wider plains.

Tourism Development Activates Sales

Tourism helps in boosting-up the economic activities and investments on the one side and makes a market for the local products specially the cropped vegetables, dairy products and the industrial craft goods. It is highly interesting to note that expenditure by the tourists has been increasing over the years and the duration of the stay has also been growing. Tourists keep on moving from one location to the other for site-seeing and worship in the Shrines of Himalaya. But the total expenditure on touring excluding transport costs per passenger in Himalayan region vary from Rs.4,000 in Kathgodam tourist survey to Rs.18,000 in the tourist survey of passenger expenditure held in Srinagar. The rough estimate of the expected expenditure on tour to Himalayan belt, excluding the spending on transport, was recorded from the tourist parties at eight principal locations. The passengers had come not exclusively for the site-seeing in the Himalaya but had visited several places even before coming to this area. The total tour cost per passenger was Rs.7,400 to 20,000 in Rishikesh, Kotdwara, Haldwani, Nainital and in Kathgodam surveys while the costs of tour was greater in the tourist survey at Srinagar and Badrinath. The reason was related to the greater route coverage. In Nainital, Ranikhet and Rishikesh the per passenger cost of tour estimates ranged between Rs.4,000 to Rs.15,000. The overall average of all the tourist surveys shows the expenditure as Rs.35,363. At Ramnagar the surveyed parties were mostly the foreign tourists from United States, Canada, Sweden and Netherland. Their total tour costs were recorded by conversion of currency values in Indian rupee at current ruling rate. Total tour costs were nearly Rs.35,363 in 1985 and Rs.1,50,000 in 1999 and around one-third of this is spent in Uttaranchal Himalayan tract. Hardly a small fraction of the total visitors stay more than a week in this tract at a stretch in one place. The surveys held in course of the study indicate that the stay was 4 days in Badrinath, 5 days in Srinagar and Ranikhet, 6-9 days in Rishikesh, Kotdwara, Kathgodam and Nainital of passenger parties. The average stay comes to 6.5 days only. Unless the accommodation is enough and cheap and facilities are well arranged in principal cities of the tract, the stay is not likely to extend further. The exorbitant rates in Nainital and the tourist sites in Garhwal foothills are monopoly prices unrelated to costs. Even the rates of tourist agencies in public sector are too much which prohibit the low income tourists from undertaking any tour. This needs policy-makers' intervention in favour of less resourceful tourists.

Exploitation of Potentials Demand Publicity

The 'Visit India Campaign' as proposed in 1991-92 shall work effectively to attract 20 lakh foreign tourists to India. The traditional stereotype image of India built so far has to be replaced with more vibrant image of diversified tourism specially the gift of Himalayan Paradise. Uttaranchal Himalayan tract is likely to receive more tourists from America, South America and Europe in the next decade and shall become the destination of the Nineties. Adventure tourism is getting increasingly popular in Himalayan belt and it needs less infrastructure and pompous decoration. Government of India have identified 18 extension circuits of travel in India so that tourism remains as all weather and all season activity. Uttaranchal Himalayan potential has been exploited for only summers and autumn so far. Open sky policy of aviation sector with regard to charters from abroad and introduction of air taxies are good approaches. Uttaranchal Himalayas need little more to be done regarding air services, rope-ways and comfortable accommodation. Vayudoot charges Rs.10,000 to 16,000 per hour for 19 to 40 seater plane (in 1985) which is quite low as compared to services elsewhere. The transport has the key role in tourism. Motor transport in uphill areas finds difficult to accommodate with the costs specially in the luxury grade buses. The foreign tourism incomes are likely to grow to Rs.5,000 crore by 2000 A.D. in India. India is yet to emerge as a destination for International Conference. National Committee on Tourism (1988) recommended incentives for tourism growth and prime role of central government. An average rate of 7 per cent growth of international tourism in India has been projected for Eighth and Ninth Plans. Snow and water sports can be organised in India at lesser costs.

Motivation and Incentive Lead to Rapidity of Resource-use

Tourism Development Finance Corporation has facilitated the flow of funds to tourism development specially in private sector. 1988-89 Income Tax Act to hotels, tour operators and other tourism activities has helped growth incentives in tourism industry. Fifty per cent of income attributable to foreign exchange earnings of hotels in now allowed for deduction while the rest 50 per cent is also exempted if it is reserved for funds towards investments in tourism industry. Foreign equity investments in tourism industry. Foreign equity investments are needed at present to attract multinationals in tourism industry of India. The luxury hotel accommodation and its management is best handled in such hands and funds are liberally invested. Uttaranchal Himalayan sector does not have good accommodation for foreigners so far. The tariffs changed on very ordinary space are exorbitant in summer. The quality of service is only nominal seen in comparison with that in foreign lands. Better managerial skills are also needed to manage the transport-tourism inter-links. Brighter outlook in 1991 can be expected for tourism the world over yet the flows to India and Indian capacity to manage the flows efficiency depend on the transport, communication, accommodation and such related infrastructural growth. Uttaranchal Himalayas are likely to offer the best potentials for the decade ahead.

Himalayan belt is not yet well served by efficient communications as essential for a brisk tourist activity. Wireless telephone services are needed for this area. The transport system still requires considerable improvement in order to connect the tourist flows to remoter areas.

Bibliography

Alber, R., J.S. Adams and Peter Gould (1971), *Spatial Organisation: A Geographer's View of the World*, Prentice-Hall Inc., Englewood Cliffs, New Jersey.

Anonymous (1985), *Chamoli Charms*, E. and D. Educational Pvt. Ltd., Dehradun.

Archer, B.H. (1973), *The Impact of Domestic Tourism*, University of Wales Press, Bangor.

Armstrong, Lincoln and Bashshur, Rashid (1958), "Ecological Patterns and Value Orientations in Lebanon", *Public Opinion Quarterly*, Vol. XXII, 406-415.

Atkinson, E.T. (1886), *The Himalayan Districts of the North Western Provinces of India*, Vol. II, Allahabad.

Barbier, E.B. (1987), "Concept of Sustainable Development", *Environmental Conservation*, Vol. XIV, No. 2.

Barke, M. and Greg O'Hare (1984), *The Third World: Diversity, Change and Interdependence*, Oliver and Boyd, Edinburgh.

Batten, J.H. (1871), *Report on Tarai*, Government Printing Press, Allahabad.

Beckmann, M.J. (1967), "Principles of Optimum Location for Transportation Network", *Studies in Geography*, 13, N.W. Univ.

Berry, R. (1979), *Story of Doon Valley*, J.K. & Co., Dehradun.

Bhatia, A.K. (1982), *Tourism Development: Principles and Practices*, Sterling Publishers, New Delhi.

Blache, P. Vidal de la (1952), *Principle of Human Geography* (edited by Emmanuel De Martonne, translated from French to English by Millicent Todd Bingham), Constable Publishers, London.

Boesch, H. (1964), *A Geography of World Economy*, D. Van Nostrand Co.

Boo, E. (1990), *Ecotourism: The Potentials and Pitfalls*, Vol. I, Washington WWF.

Bose, S.C. (1976), *Geography of Himalaya*, National Book Trust, Bombay.

Bryden, John M. (1973), *Tourism and Development*, Cambridge University Press.

Bunge, W. (1966), "Theoretical Geography", *Lund Studies in Geogr.*, Ser. C. Gen. & Maths Geogr., 1.

Burckart, A.J. (1975), *The Management of Tourism*, London.

Burton, T.L. (ed.) (1970), *Recreation Research and Planning*, London.

Carrothers, G.A.P. (1956), "The Gravity and Potential Concepts of Human Interaction", *Journal of American Institute of Planners*, Vol. XXII.

Carter, E. (1992), "Profits from Paradise", *Geographical Magazine*, March.

Census of India, U.P. Part II(A), Vol. XV, 1961.

Cole, J.P. and C.A.M. King (1968), *Quantitative Geography*, New York.

Cooper, C. and S. Jackson (1985) "Changing Patterns of Manx Tourism", *Geography* (Journal of Geog. Association), Vol. 70, Part I, No. 306.

Cosgrove, I. and R. Jackson (1972), *The Geography of Recreation and Leisure*, London.

De Kadt, Emamael (1979), *Tourism Passport to Development*, Oxford University Press, London.

Diswell, Roger (1970), *Approach to Hotel Planning*, New University Education, London.

Doswell, R. and P. Gamble (1979), *Marketing and Planning of Hotel and Tourism*, Barrie & Jenkins, London.

Dubey, R.N. (1963), "The Factor Proportions Problem in Under-Developed Areas, *The American Economic Review*, 49, September.

Eisenstadt, S.N. (1963), *Modernisation, Protest and Change*, Englewood Cliffs, New Jersey, Prentice-Hall, New York.

Fisher, J.J. (1964), "The Role of Natural Resources in Economic Development: Principles and Patterns" in Williamson and Buttricks, *Natural Resources and Economic Development*, London.

Garrison, W.L. and D.F. Marble (1961), *The Structure of Transportation Networks*, U.S. Department of Commerce, Office of Technical Services, Washington D.C.

Gauthier, H.L. (1970), "Geography, Transportation and Regional Development", *Economic Geography*, Vol. 46.

Gilbert, A. (1976), *Latin American Development*, Penguin.

Golgan, C.S. (1987), "Sustainable Development and Economic Development Policy: Lessons from Canada", *Economic Development*, Vol. II, No. 2.

Gould, P.R. (1960), *Transportation in Ghana*, Dept. of Geography, Studies in Geography, Series-5, North-Western University Press, Evanston, Illinois.

Govt. of U.P., *Report Tarai and Bhabar Development Committee*, Allahabad, 1947, Appendix-2.

Govt. of India, *Regions, Resources and Development*, New Delhi, 1965.

Govt. of India, *Seventh Five Year Plan*, 1985-90, Vol. II, Planning Commission, New Delhi.

Govt. of India, *The Seventh Five Year Plan*, 1985-90, Draft Outline, Planning Commission, New Delhi.

Govt. of India, *Mid-Year Appraisal*, Planning Commission, New Delhi, 1987-88.

Gray, W.S. and S.C. Liguori (1980), *Hotel and Management Operation*, Prentice-Hall Inc., Chicago.

Gregor, Harward F. (1963) *Environment and Economic Life*, Williamson, New York.

Haggett, P. and R.J. Chorley (1969), *Network Analysis in Geography*, London.

Hinterberger F. and B.F. Schmidt (1997), "Material Flows Versus Natural Capital", *Ecological Economics*, Vol. XXIII, No. 1.

Hirschman, A.Q. (1958), *The Strategy of Economic Development*, Yale University Press, New Haven.

Hodder, B.W. and Roger Lee (1974), *Economic Geography*, Methuen & Co., London.

Hoyle, B.S. (1973), *Transport and Development*, Macmillan & Co., London.

Isard, W. et al. (1960), *Methods of Regional Analysis*, John Wiley & Sons Inc., New York.

James, W.L. (1969), *Demand and Supply of Hotel Rooms in Singapore* (1970-75), Tourist Promotion Board, Singapore.

Kansky, K.J. (1963), *Structure of Transport Networks: Relationship Between Network Geometry and Regional Characteristics*, Chicago University, Dept. of Geogr. Res. Pap., 84.

Kaul, R.N. (1985), *Dynamics of Tourism: A Trilogy*, Vol. I (*The Phenomenon*), Vol. II (*Accommodation*) and Vol. III (*Transportation and Marketing*), Sterling Publishers, New Delhi.

Kaur, Jagdish (1989), "Re-Examining Tourist Capacity of Nainital: A Case for Diffusion of Tourist Activity in the Kumaun Lake Basins of Uttar Pradesh Himalaya" in T.V. Singh and Jagdish Kaur (eds.), *Studies in Himalayan Ecology*, Himalayan Books, New Delhi.

Kayastha, S.L. and S.N. Singh (1983), "Tourism in the U.P. Himalaya" in O.P. Singh et al. (eds.), *The Himalaya: Nature, Man and Culture*, Rajesh Publications, New Delhi.

Kendall, M.G. (1955), *Rank Correlation Methods*, Charles Griffin & Co., London.

Kosinski, L.A. and R.M. Prothero (1974), *People on the Move*, Mathuen & Co. Ltd., London.

Krishnan, M.S. (1949), *Geology of India and Burma*, New Delhi.

Lachene, R. (1965), Networks and the Location of Economic Activities; *Papers and Proceedings of Regional Science Association*, Vol. 14.

Leeming, F.A. (1977), *Street Studies in Hong Kong*, Oxford University Press, London.

Lesure, J.D. and George D Podd (1964), *Planning and Operating Motels and Motor Hotels*, Ahrens Book Co. Inc., Hyden Publishing Co., London.

Lewis, Arthur W. (1954), "Economic Development with Unlimited Supply of Labour", Lecture delivered at Manchester School, May 1954.

Lewis, W.A. (1952), *The Theory of Economic Growth*, Allen and Unwin Publishers, London.

Lloyd, P.E. and Dicken, P. (1972), *Location in Space: A Theoretical Approach to Economic Geography*, London.

Mason, P. and M. Mowforth (1999), "Codes of Conduct in Tourism" in Pande, G.C. and D.C. Pandey (eds.), *Environmental Development and Management: Strategies and Policies*, Anmol Publications, New Delhi, 291-346.

Mathur, R.S. (1980), "Economic Structure and Labour Force Utilisation in Hill Areas, *National Seminar on Development of Backward Areas*, GIDS, Lucknow.

McClelland, John (1885), *Some Enquiries in the Province of Kumaun Relative to Geology*, London.

Meadows, D.H. et al. (1972), *The Limits to Growth*, Universe Books, New York.

Mowforth, M. (1993), *Ecotourism: Terminology and Definitions*, Research Report-1, Deptt. of Geographical Science, University of Plymouth.

Mukerjee, Radha Kamal (1938), *Regional Balance of Man*, Oxford, London.

Nandkarni, M.V. (1996), "Political Economy of Sustainable Development", *Review of Development and Change*, Vol. I, No. 1.

Naylon, J. (1967), "Tourism – Spain's Most Important Industry, *Geography*, Vol. 52, Jan.

Negi, J.M.S. (1964), *Tourism and Hotelliering: A Worldwide Industry*, Geetanjali Publishing House, New Delhi.

Negi, J.M.S. (1984), *Hotels for Tourism Development*, Metropolitan Book Co., New Delhi.

Norval, A.J. (1936), *The Tourism Industry*, Pitman, London.

Ohlin, B.G. (1935), *Inter-Regional and International Trade*, Harvard University Press, Harvard.

Owen, W. (1956), *The Metropolitan Transportation Problem*, Washington D.C., The Brookings' Institution.

Owen, W. (1968), *Distance and Development: Transport and Communications in India*, Brookings Institution.

Pande, G.C. (1968) *Economy of Kumaun: A Field Survey*, Doctoral Dissertation, Deptt. of Economics, Lucknow University, Lucknow.

Pande, G.C. (1989), *Strategies of Rural Development in India*, Anmol Publication, New Delhi.

Pande, G.C. (1989), *Economic Development and Planning*, Vol. I and II, Anmol Publication, New Delhi.

Pande, G.C. and D.C. Pandey (eds.) (1999), *Environmental Development and Management: Strategies and Policies*, Anmol Publications, New Delhi.

Pandey, D.C. (1983), "Transport Network in Nainital Foothill Region", *Himalaya: Man and Nature*, Vol. VII, No. 8.

Pandey, D.C. (1980), "Transport Network Connectivity and Economic Development" in *Dimensions of Development Planning*, ed. D.C. Pandey et al., Criterion Publications, New Delhi.

Pandey, D.C. and P.C. Tiwari (eds.) (1989), *Dimensions of Development Planning*, Vol. I and II, Criterion Publications, New Delhi.

Pandey, D.C. and P.C. Tiwari (1983), "Topological Properties of Transport Net: A Case Study of District Nainital, U.P. Himalaya", in O.P. Singh et al. (eds.), *The Himalaya: Nature, Man and Culture*, Rajesh Publications, New Delhi.

Pandey, P.C. (ed.) (1990), *Current Trends in Development Planning*, Criterion Publications, New Delhi.

Pant, S.D. (1935), *Social Economy of Himalayas*, George Unwin, London.

Papola, T.S. (1980), *Spatial Diversification of Manufacturing Industries: Studies on Development of U.P.*, Giri Instt. of Dev. Studies, Occasional Paper-I, Lucknow.

Prihar, Z. (1956), "Theoretical Properties of Telecommunication Network", *Proceedings of the Institute of Radio Engineers*, 44.

Rao, S.R. Narayana (1958), *Mineral Investigation in U.P.*, Directorate of Geology and Mining, Lucknow.

Ray, S.K. (1983), *Economics of Third World*, Prentice-Hall, New Jersey.

Richmond, Samuel B. (1957), Inter-Spatila Relationships Affecting Air Travel, *Land Economics*, Vol. 33.

Robinson, H. (1976), *A Geography of Tourism*, Macdonald and Evans, London.

Robinson, H. (1976), *Geography and Tourism*, New York.

Robinson, John (1947), *Essays in Theory of Unemployment*, Second Edition, Oxford, London.

Rogers, H.A. and D.K. Phipps (1977), *Economics for the Hotel and Catering Industry*, Barrier & Kenkins, Europe.

Salem, Elie Abib (1973), *Modernisation without Revolution: Lebanon's Experience*, Bloomington, Indiana Univ. Press.

Sample, Ellen Churchill (1932), *Influence of Geographic Environment*, Oxford, London.

Sayer, S. (1973), "Wild Uplands of the South-West", *Geographical Magazine*, Vol. XLV, July.

Seth, P.N. (1978), *Successful Tourism Planning and Management*, New Delhi.

Shastri, R.H. and Prabha Panth (1999), "Global Warming and International Agreements", *Southern Economist*, Vol. 38, No. 7, 3-6.

Siegal, S. (1956), *Non-Parametric Statistics for Behavioural Sciences*, McGraw Hill Book Co., New York.

Singh, A.K. (1981), *Patterns of Regional Development*, Sterling Publishers, New Delhi.

Singh, A.P. (1989), *Himalayan Environment and Tourism*, Chugh Publication, Allahabad.

Singh, Jagdish (1972), "Model for Rural Transport Network" in R.L. Singh et al. (eds.), *Rural Settlement in Monsoon Asia*, NGSI, Varanasi.

Singh, O.P. (1979), *Urban Geography* (in Hindi), Tara Publications, Varanasi.

Singh, O.P. (1983), "U.P. Himalaya: An Overview" in Singh et al. (eds.), *The Himalaya: Nature, Man and Culture*, Rajesh Publication, New Delhi.

Singh, O.P. and D.C. Pandey (1986), *Development Planning: Theory and Practice*, Gyanodaya Prakashan, Nainital.

Singh, R.L. (ed.) (1971), *India: A Regional Geography*, NGSI, Varanasi.

Singh, T.V. (1975), *Tourism and Tourist Industry in U.P. India*, New Heights, Delhi.

Singh, T.V. (1979), "Tourism Takes a Leap into the Himalaya: Planner's Predicament, *Proceedings – Tourism Next Decade Symposium*, Washington.

Singh, T.V. and Jagdish Kaur (eds.) (1989), *Studies in Himalayan Ecology*, Himalayan Books, New Delhi.

Sixth Five Year Plan (1980-85), Government of Uttar Pradesh, Lucknow.

Spicer, E.H. (ed.) (1952), *Human Problems in Technological Change*, Russell Foundation, New York.

Srivastava, S.K. (1951), *The Dynamics of Cultural Change in Nainital Tarai of U.P.*, unpublished dissertation of Ph.D., Deptt. of Sociology, Lucknow University, Lucknow.

Taaffe, E.J., R.L. Morrill and P.R. Gould (1963), "Transport Expansion in Underdeveloped Countries: A Comparative Analysis", *Geographical Review*, Vol. 53.

Tapper, R. (1993), *Tourism: It is a Non-Consumptive Use*, Godalming, WWF, U.K.

Tourist Guide to Garhwal Region (1989), Garhwal Mandal Vikas Nigam.

Ullman, E.L. (1956), "The Role of Transportation and the Bases for Interaction" in *Man's Role in Changing the Face of the Earth*, ed. W.L. Thomas, University of Chicago Press.

United Nations, Economic Commission for Europe, *Six Maps on Transport Network in Europe*, New York.

Valdiya, K.S. (1962), *Geology of a Part of Himalaya*, Ph.D. dissertation, Deptt. of Geology, Lucknow University, Lucknow.

Varley, R.C.G. (1978), "Tourism in Fiji: Some Economic and Social Problems", *Bangor Occasional Papers in Economics*, No. 12.

Viner, Jacob (1954), *International Trade and Economic Development*, Academy Lecture, National University of Brazil, Clarendon Press, Oxford.

Wadia, D.N. (1961), *Geology of India*, MacMillan and Co. Ltd., London.

Walton, H.G. (1910), *District Gazetteer of British Garhwal*, Government Press, Allahabad.

White, J. (1967), *History of Tourism*, London.

Williams, J.E. and W. Zelinsky (1970), "On Some Patterns of International Tourist Flows, *Economic Geography*, October.

Wolfe, R.I. (1966), "Recreational Travel: The New Migration, *Canadian Geographer*, Vol. X, No. 1.

WTTC (1991), *Travel and Tourism in the World Economy*, Brussels, WTTC.

Yeates, Maurice H. (1968), *An Introduction to Qualitative Analysis in Economic Geography*, McGraw Hills, New York.

Yukic, T.S. (1963), *Fundamentals of Recreation*, London.

A view of Devidhura festival, district Nainital.

Kali temple at Kalapani, district Pithoragarh.

Rope way: A source of tourist attraction in Nainital.

A panoramic view of Bhimtal lake.

Parvati Tal at Jolingkong, near Chhota Kailash.

A view of magnificent lake of Nainital.

A view of hot air balloon at Flats in Nainital.

Water rafting at Kali river near Pancheshwar.

Corbett Fall: Located at a distance of 3 km. from Kaladhungri.

A view of paragliding near Naucuchiatal.

Index